Leavenworth Papers

Number 14

Dragon Operations:
Hostage Rescues in the Congo, 1964—1965

by Major Thomas P. Odom

Combat Studies Institute
U.S. Army Command and General Staff College
Fort Leavenworth, Kansas 66027-6900

Library of Congress Cataloging-in-Publication Data

Odom, Thomas P. (Thomas Paul, 1953—
    Dragon operations.

    (Leavenworth papers, ISSN 0195 3451 ; no. 14)
    Bibliography: p.
    1. Zaire—History—Civil War, 1960-1965. 2. Hostages—Zaire—Kisangani.
3. Kisangani, (Zaire)—Massacre, 1964-   . I. Title. II. Series.
DT658.22.036   1988   967.5′103   87-36503

This publication, where noted, contains copyrighted materials reproduced by special permission, and these may not be reproduced, in any manner, without the express permission of the copyright owners.

For sale by the Superintendent of Documents, U.S. Government Printing Office, Washington, D.C. 20402

Going up that river was like traveling back to the earliest beginnings of the world, when vegetation rioted on the earth and the big trees were kings. An empty stream, a great silence, an impenetrable forest. The air was warm, thick, heavy, sluggish. There was no joy in the brilliance of sunshine.

—JOSEPH CONRAD
Heart of Darkness

Contents

Maps vii
Preface ix
Introduction 1
Chapter
   1. The Birth of a Nation 3
   2. An American Crisis 25
   3. A Belgian Crisis 45
   4. Determination and Doubt 61
   5. The Dragon Roars 83
   6. Last Gasp of the Dragon 121
   7. Operational Postmortem 153
Appendix A. Personalities, Code Names and Terms,
   and Acronyms 161
Appendix B. Order of Battle-Command Structure 165
Appendix C. Chronology 173
Appendix D. Results of the Dragon Operations 179
Notes 183
Bibliography 217

Maps

1. Congo situation, 17 July 1964 7
2. Congo situation, 7 August 1964 11
3. Vandewalle plan, 11 September 1964 18
4. Golden Hawk and Stanley Falls 29
5. Air bases and distances 36
6. OPLAN 519 High Beam 39
7. Dragon Rouge air routes 48
8. Vandewalle plan, 18 November 1964 62
9. Colonel Laurent's concept for Dragon Rouge 68
10. Suspected hostage locations, 19 November 1964 70
11. Dragon Rouge, Phases I and II, 0600—0750 95
12. Dragon Rouge, Phase III, search and evacuation, 0750—1400 105
13. L'Ommengang's occupation of Stanleyville, 1100—1815 115
14. Planning map of Paulis 125
15. Dragon Noir assault plan 128
16. Dragon Noir, movement of the 1st Platoon, 11th Company 135
17. Dragon Noir, movement of the 2d and 3d Platoons, 11th Company 138
18. Dragon Noir, the extraction 140

Preface

Leavenworth Paper No. 14, *Dragon Operations: Hostage Rescues in the Congo, 1964—1965* is a useful historical analysis of a cold war crisis, the resolution of which depended upon the planning and execution of joint and combined military operations. It shows how combatants react to the pressures and uncertainties associated with a rapidly changing situation in a highly politicized arena.

Major Thomas P. Odom examines the Congo rescue missions at each level of United States military involvement. As a working group of diplomats, intelligence personnel, and military officers managed the crisis from Washington, their representatives in the field planned and executed the airborne operations. Odom traces the evolution of planning from what was to have been a joint United States Army-Air Force operation to a combined venture in which the major American contribution was to airlift Belgian paratroopers into the Congo and to evacuate the surviving hostages. Based on recently declassified documents and interviews with key American, Belgian, and French participants, *Dragon Operations* combines detailed analysis and a narrative to provide fresh insight into one of the first hostage rescue missions of the cold war. Odom's account shows how the fluidity of an extremely complex situation can defy even the most comprehensive plans. Where planning was defective or the plans proved outdated, the combined team taking part in the mission relied on flexibility and adaptability to see them through.

Dragon Operations, besides chronicling a successful operation, clearly demonstrates the relevance of military history for today's professional soldier. Although the circumstances and considerations of the Congo crisis are unique to that situation, the case study reveals broader interoperability patterns that continually must be addressed in joint and combined operations.

FREDERICK M. FRANKS, Jr.
Major General, U.S. Army
Director, Operational Plans &
 Interoperability Directorate (J-7)
Joint Chiefs of Staff

Author's Preface

The case study that follows grew out of my professional and personal interest in Zaire and evacuation operations. As a second lieutenant in the 82d Airborne in 1978, I was alerted for contingency deployment to Zaire during the Shaba II invasion. Later, in 1984, I visited Zaire, and in the course of conversations with the U.S. defense attaché, who had been assistant attaché in Kinshasa in 1978, I realized that our operational planning in the United States for the invasion was not tailored to the situation in the country. My wife, who had been a Peace Corps volunteer in the area in 1979 to 1980, provided me with additional information on the aftermath of the French and Belgian intervention, information that confirmed my suspicions.

Aside from this brush with planning a rescue or evacuation operation, I have had further experience in planning an evacuation as part of my service as a detachment commander in Turkey and later as a member of the embassy in Sudan, where I became familiar with the problems of evacuation planning. I am convinced that such planning frequently suffers from neglect until a true crisis arises. At this stage, however, it is often too late to improvise effectively.

The United States' record in evacuation or hostage rescue operations is particularly dismal. As such operations are typically joint efforts by the Army, Navy, Marines, or Air Force, interservice rivalry has consistently crept into the picture. The continual realignment of the Unified Command Plan and the establishment of special commands such as U.S. Strike Command, or later, U.S. Central Command, have not eliminated these problems. Unfortunately, the need for evacuation or hostage rescue operations has not decreased. Indeed, in a peacetime environment, such military operations are the most likely contingency facing planners.

Sparked by my interest in Zaire and my concern over evacuation operations, I selected Dragon Rouge as the subject for my study. In reviewing the literature on the operation, I found that several excellent works were available. David Reed's *111 Days in Stanleyville* is a vivid journalistic portrayal of the rescue operation. Fred Wagoner's *DRAGON ROUGE: The Rescue of Hostages in the Congo* delves deeply into political and military decision making behind the rescue. Frederic Vandewalle's *L'Ommengang: Odyseé et Reconquete de Stanleyville* provides the full backdrop to the rescue. However, no author analyzed the operation in military terms.

The Dragon operations posed certain intriguing questions that had so far gone unanswered. Why was Laurent's plan so conservative in the face of what he considered to be an incompetent enemy? Why was the Belgian force so small, when it was to be pitted against 10,000 rebels? Why did the Belgians take so long to get into the city? I sought the answers to these questions.

I owe thanks to many people for their assistance and openness in helping me research the Dragon operations. Fred Wagoner, David Reed, and

James Erdmann opened their papers and willingly shared their research. The Centre de Documentation Historique in Brussels was equally cooperative, as were the archivists at the Lyndon Baines Johnson Library, the State Department, and the U.S. Army Military History Institute. With the material from these archives, I was able to find many of the answers to my questions.

I must, however, extend my special gratitude to the officers who granted me interviews. The American officers, Lieutenant Colonel Erdmann, Major General Rattan, Brigadier General Brashears, and Colonel Poore, all provided me with valuable insights. The major breakthrough came in my interviews with the Belgians. Lieutenant General Janssens, Major General Laurent, and Colonels Vandewalle, Ledant, Mine, Rousseaux, and Raes were all honest and cordial in my interviews with them. I deeply appreciate their help.

I hope that readers will grasp certain fundamentals from this study that they will find applicable to contemporary situations. This work will emphasize the relationship between political decisions and military operations. It will reveal that military planners must work within political constraints, and political leaders must recognize the costs of those constraints to military operations. Further, it will show that the flexible planning of operations is not the same as ad hoc planning. Thus, it is easier to modify existing plans than it is to develop entirely new operations, particularly in complex crisis situations where in-depth knowledge is critical. Also demonstrated in this work is that while joint operations present considerable difficulties in execution, when joint operations are conducted using combined forces, even more considerable problems arise. Such problems of interoperability, when they occur, demand more than ad hoc planning. Finally, mission analysis is paramount, and a firm mission statement is necessary if military operations are not to stray from their intended objectives.

Introduction

On 24 November 1964, dawn broke at its usual time over the central African city of Stanleyville. The routine sunrise, however, did not presage another typical day for the old colonial trade center. As the sun rose over the eastern horizon, the thunder of an approaching armada challenged it from the yet dark western sky. At 0600Z, heralded by an initial pass of two Cuban-exile-piloted B-26s, five C-130s lumbered low across the airfield west of the city. Suddenly, the sky beneath the Hercules transports blossomed with hundreds of parachutes. The Belgian Paracommandos had returned to the Congo.

For the Belgian Paracommando Regiment, the Congo was a familiar, though often hostile, environment. For most of the officers and sergeants of the regiment, the fields, buildings, and river below were as familiar as the Belgian landscape. But for most of the 340 enlisted men drifting in the sky over the airfield, the Congo was an unknown menace outside their military experience. Most of these paras were young draftees to whom the Congo represented a closed chapter in Belgium's colonial history. Yet even with the experience of its senior leadership, the Belgian Paracomandos faced a severe test on this early spring morning.

The young paras and their seasoned leaders were conducting the first international hostage rescue in the post-World War II era. The challenge was enormous, the risks staggering; the Paracommandos were jumping into a perilous den of uncertainty. Stanleyville was at the heart of the Simba Rebellion and the scene of growing desperation. Faced with a government ground assault, the Simba leaders had taken several thousand non-Congolese hostages to guard against what appeared to be imminent defeat.[1]

For the captives inside Stanleyville, the roar of the C-130s was at once a blessing and a nightmare. The appearance of the task force held out hopes for them of their salvation, but it also placed them in grave danger. To the Simbas, the sound overhead was a death knell for their regime and the spark that would ignite their flames of retribution. The Simbas had already slaughtered forty-seven hostages in their conquest of the eastern Congo. By the end of this African morning, some thirty more would lie dead or dying on a street in Stanleyville, victims of another bloody chapter in the Congo's turbulent history.[2]

The Birth of a Nation

The Democratic Republic of the Congo entered the community of independent countries on 30 June 1960. In many respects, its birth was premature, for the Congo was not properly prepared for autonomy. A colonial possession of Belgium since the mid-1870s, the Congo had for too long been a victim of Western exploitation. Originally a private domain of King Leopold II and later a proper Belgian colony, the Congolese people had been subjected to a paternalistic colonial administration that, while it provided improvements for the region, kept the inhabitants subservient through its educational, economic, and ethnic policies. Brutality in the form of the Force Publique—the native military—served as the Belgian tool to enforce their policies. The Belgians' success in controlling the Congo for eighty years made them confident in their abilities to continue that domination. Yet the Congolese people, aroused by the wave of nationalism that swept through Africa in the 1950s, awoke suddenly, late in that decade, and pressed their demands for independence.[1]

But as a new nation, the Congo faced enormous difficulties. With only thirteen university graduates, the Congolese were unprepared to assume the managerial or governmental offices hastily vacated by the Belgians. More important, Congolese tribal rivalries fomented distrust of the centralized governmental authority. Thus, independence ushered in an era of acute instability. Within days, the fledgling government suffered from a mutiny of the Force Publique and a Belgian military intervention that sought to stabilize the situation. During the next three years, continuous conflicts erupted among politicians, local warlords, and tribal leaders.[2]

Following the Belgian intervention, the United Nations sent a peacekeeping force to the Congo. Armed with a flawed mandate, the UN Force in the Congo attempted to preserve law and order without interfering in internal political disputes. By September 1960, the UN faced the problem of maintaining the peace among three rival governments inside the Congo basin. Only by changing its mandate to allow for the use of force and through three years of periodic warfare did the UN succeed in bringing the Congo back under the nominal control of the central government in Leopoldville. By mid-1963, the Congo appeared to be stable. But the appearance was false. The momentary stability was like the eye of a hurricane—only a temporary respite before the violent tempest that would follow.[3]

In 1963, President Joseph Kasavubu and Prime Minister Cyrille Adoula were in power in Leopoldville. Kasavubu, an early militant in the struggle for independence, had been president since 1960. A tribal leader of the Kongo people, he represented only a narrow spectrum of Congolese nationalism. Cyrille Adoula, a member of the Congolese National Movement (MNC) and prime minister since 1961, hoped to install a truly national form of government that would encompass the divergent hopes of the Congolese people.[4]

This calm period in the Congo was short lived. Dissident elements inside and outside the Congo began to coalesce against the Leopoldville government. Inside the country, a revolt broke out in Kwilu province under the leadership of Pierre Muléle, a supposed political associate of Adoula. Adoula's attempts to quell disputes within the Congo had also given birth outside the country to the National Liberation Committee (CNL). Led by Christophe Gbenye and Gaston Soumialot, both members of the MNC, the CNL sought Chinese Communist backing to foment rebellion in the Congo.[5]

To counter this opposition and continue to survive, Adoula's government needed to effect two elusive conditions: a reconciliation among the disparate political leaders that would encompass all their hopes in a single national government; and the creation of an effective military force to maintain security until such a reconciliation government could be formed. These two goals, central to the Congolese dilemma since independence, nonetheless, remained beyond the capabilities of Adoula's government.

The National Congolese Army (ANC), like its predecessor the Force Publique, was Adoula's key to controlling the country. Following the Force Publique's mutiny in 1960, the army had splintered into factions under the control of local warlords. But gradually, under the guidance of Joseph Mobutu, a former clerk in the Force Publique, the ANC achieved at least a superficial reunification. By 1963, General Mobutu, now the ANC commander, had an army of 30,000 men that supposedly owed its allegiance to Leopoldville. An imperfect instrument for maintaining stability, the ANC relied on brutality to control the country. Untrained and poorly led, the ANC was also a disaster in the field. Its cruelty toward unarmed civilians was infamous; its ability to fight a determined foe inconsequential.[6]

Adoula was incapable of creating an effective army or in building a government of national reconciliation. Isolated in Leopoldville and politically stalemated by early 1964, Adoula needed a master stroke to reestablish his credibility. To achieve this coup, he turned, paradoxically, to the man who had thus far been the nemesis of Congolese stability—Moise Tshombe.

Tshombe was to be the object of Adoula's political maneuvers. Tshombe, leader of the separatist CONAKAT party in 1960, had declared the independence of Katanga province within days of the Force Publique's mutiny. Closely allied with Belgian mining interests that were determined to maintain control of Katanga's vast mineral wealth, Tshombe had fought for three years to maintain Katanga's separation from the Congo. Supported by Belgium, Tshombe had recruited white mercenaries to build an indepen-

Moise Tshombe

dent army, the Katanganese gendarmerie. In the Katangan struggle, Tshombe's name became directly associated with the deaths of Patrice Lumumba and Dag Hammarskjöld. Lumumba, the Congo's first prime minister, had captured the hearts of pan-Africanists. His execution had made him into a cult figure within the Congo. Hammarskjöld, secretary-general of the UN prior to his fatal plane crash on 18 September 1961, had restrained the UN force in the Congo from militarily crushing Tshombe. The deaths of Lumumba and Hammarskjöld had turned the UN's peacekeeping mission into open war with Tshombe. After a loss of Belgian support, however, Tshombe surrendered Katanga to Leopoldville and the UN. An African pariah, Tshombe then went into exile.[7]

Adoula's reason for recalling Tshombe was simple: Adoula wanted to build a government of reconciliation, and he needed Tshombe to ensure Katanga's continued loyalty. Moreover, Tshombe was in contact with the CNL and Adoula's rivals inside the Leopoldville government and still had a private army waiting across the border in Angola. To neutralize his enemies, Adoula thought he needed Tshombe inside his government. But recalling the exiled leader was a mistake. When Tshombe answered Adoula's call, within days of his return, he had outmaneuvered Adoula and supplanted him as prime minister.[8]

Tshombe now had become the key figure through which the United States hoped to attain its objectives in the Congo. The United States' strategic aims from the time of John F. Kennedy's inauguration in 1961 were to reconcile the political factions in the Congo and rebuild the ANC to stabilize the situation. American policy makers preferred to work for these goals through a third party in order to avoid Soviet interference. From 1960 to 1963, the United States had supported the UN in pursuit of these aims. Since the realignment of the Belgian government against the Katangan secession in 1962 and the UN withdrawal beginning in 1963, the United

States pursued the same policy in a coalition with Belgium. Now with Tshombe in Leopoldville, the United States hoped to continue that policy by supporting a white man's puppet through the offices of his colonial master.[9]

Indeed, by the time of Tshombe's return, the Belgian-American coalition was already hard at work. Both countries had opened military assistance missions in the country in 1963. CAMAC, the Belgian mission under Colonel Guillame Logiest, was providing advisers and training for the ANC. COMISH, the American mission under Colonel Frank Williams, concentrated on technical assistance to improve Congolese logistical capabilities. The intent of the Belgian-American assistance team was to reduce the size of the ANC and improve its quality.[10]

T-6s of the 21st Squadron at Bunia

Courtesy of Maj. Gen. D. V. Rattan, USA, Ret.

New turmoil in the Congolese countryside, however, overtook the effort to retrain the ANC. Pierre Mulélé's continuing revolt had Kwilu province in flames by early 1964 (see map 1). The ANC's incompetence in handling Mulélé's followers, and disturbances in other provinces, resulted in a spreading wave of rebellion. To contain the rebellion, the Central Intelligence Agency (CIA) created an instant air force of mercenary Cuban pilots. Using T-6s, the Cubans provided desperately needed air support against Mulélé's rebels. The success of the CIA operation stimulated an expansion of the air force to include six T-28 fighters, six H-21 helicopters, and ten C-47 transports. Even with the escalation in American and Belgian assistance efforts, however, the Congolese situation continued to deteriorate, until by July 1964, Tshombe faced disaster. Local uprisings among the tribes in the eastern Congo, fanned by ANC reprisals, had turned into full rebellion. During May, the ANC almost lost Bukavu to Bafulero tribesmen marching north from Uvira. Concurrent with this uprising, the ANC took heavy reprisals against dissidents in Albertville. The army's actions so angered

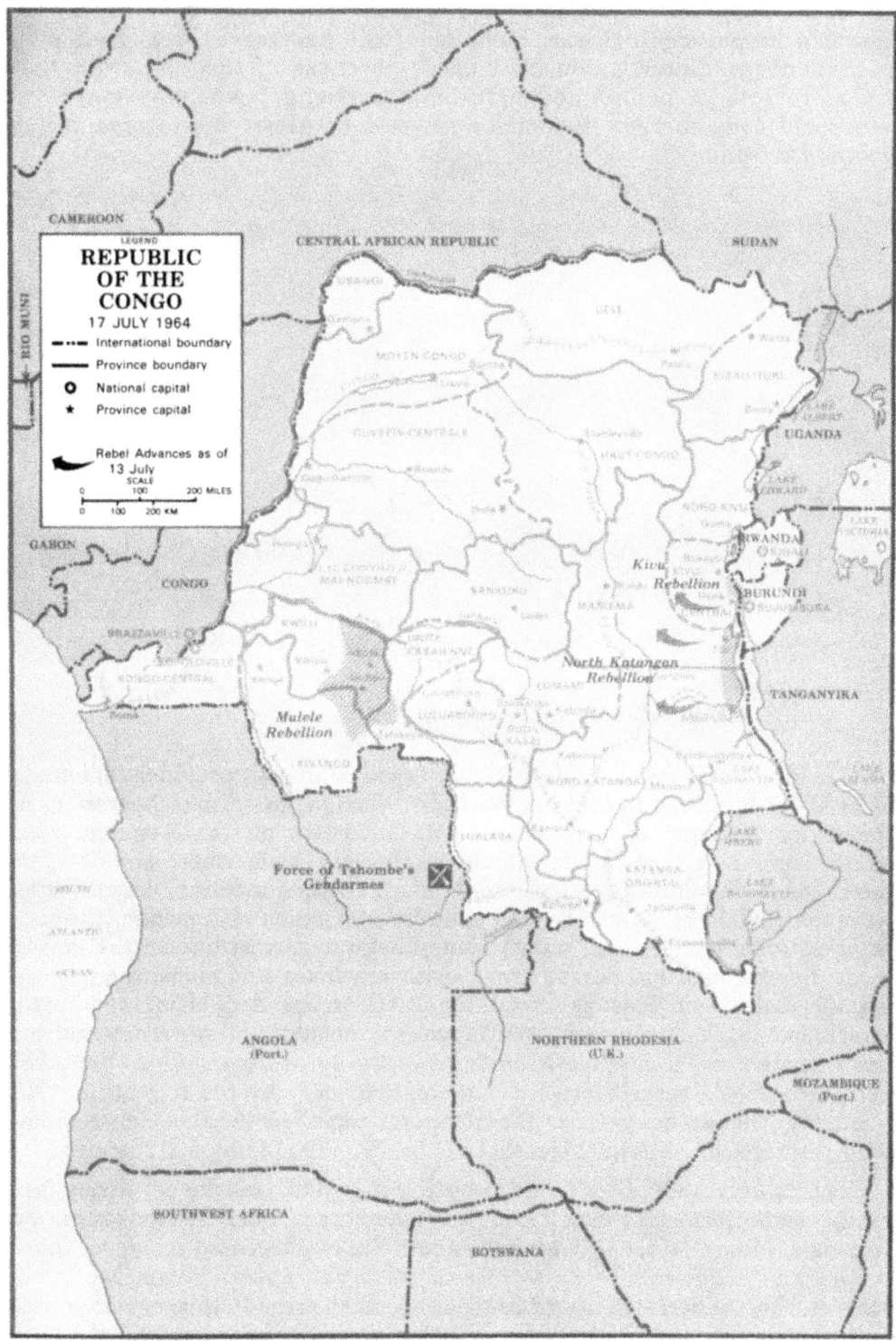

Map 1. Congo situation, 17 July 1964

the local population that it overturned the provincial government and executed its president. Gaston Soumialot, who had moved from Brazzaville to Bujumbura, Burundi, quickly linked the cause of the CNL with these tribal revolts. Accompanied by Nicholas Olenga, who had staged an attempted coup in 1963, Soumialot traveled to Albertville to organize the growing rebellion.[11]

T-28s near Bukavu

Looking north in early July 1964 toward Maniema province, Soumialot ordered his military lieutenant, Nicholas Olenga, to initiate operations in the region. Olenga, at the head of one band, set off for Kasongo, while another group paralleled his march on the city. Somewhere en route, the image of a popular army took hold, along with a nominal identification with the Mulélé rebellion. By the time Olenga reached Kasongo, the local *jeunesse* (disaffected youth gangs sympathetic to any attack on the government) had swollen his ranks. Armed with machetes and clubs, the *jeunesse* led the assault on Kasongo, and the ANC troops fled before the ragtag attack, leaving behind nearly 200 Congolese, including all governmental and tribal leaders, to be massacred in front of the town's population. From this point, the rebels surged forward, outdistanced only by the retreating ANC. Suddenly, Olenga emerged as the dominant figure in the rebellion complete with the rank of lieutenant general in the "Popular Army of Liberation."[12]

By 22 July 1964, Olenga had control of Kindu, and he set about fashioning some form of control over his following. Under his guidance, two fetishists, Mama Maria Onema and Mama Fumu, dispensed magic, or *dawa*, to Olenga's followers. Those so blessed were guaranteed invulnerability as long as they adhered to a puritanical code that forbade thievery or contact with the uninitiated. So transformed, they were now Simbas and the backbone of Olenga's army. By late July, General Olenga was ready to march on Stanleyville with an army numbering in the thousands that was convinced of its invulnerability. The ANC, however, was equally convinced of its impregnability.[13]

An H-21 helicopter ferrying supplies to the mercenaries

A city of more than 300,000, Stanleyville had an ANC garrison of 1,500 troops under a highly effective leader, Colonel Leonard Mulamba. Well armed with heavy machine guns, armored cars, mortars, and automatic weapons, the normally well-led ANC force had one fatal weakness: Colonel Mulamba was not present. At Mobutu's direction, he was busy saving Bukavu. On 5 August, after staving off an assault by around forty poorly armed *jeunesse*, ANC defenders fled the city. Stanleyville was now under rebel control.[14]

If Western observers were unprepared for the sudden loss of Stanleyville, so the rebel leadership was ill prepared to maintain power in the city. Olenga had chased the ANC for 500 miles from Albertville to Stanleyville in under a month, achieving a stunning military success that lent an air of legitimacy to his heretofore disorganized rabble. But at the same time, the city became a magnet for Western intervention; sometime later, Olenga was to mutter, "We should never have taken Stanleyville."[15]

For the American consular staff in Stanleyville, 5 August 1964 was not a good day. Neither were the next 111 days. At 1315, Simbas attacked the consulate in Stanleyville, forcing the remaining Americans to take refuge inside the communications vault (see map 2).[16] Inside the vault, praying that the door would hold, were Michael Hoyt, the American consul; David Grinwis, the CIA's representative under the cover of vice-consul;[17] and two communications personnel, James Stauffer and Donald Parkes. Another American official, Ernest Houle, was downtown in Stanleyville hastily packing his bags and waiting for a lift to the airport. Houle was to wait nearly three months for that ride.

At the time of the Simba conquest, more than 1,600 foreigners lived in Stanleyville. The largest national contingent was around 500 Belgians. Some 165 Belgians—160 women and children and 5 military advisers—had evacuated immediately before the city fell. The remaining Belgians, under the consular care of Baron Patrick Nothomb, were mostly businessmen, technicians, and planters. The next broad category consisted of 700 other Western nationals, consisting of businessmen, planters, and missionaries, some of whom were Americans. Finally, the remaining 400 were primarily Indians and Pakistanis, who provided the same marketing skills in Stanleyville as they did in the rest of Africa.[18]

Why did these people stay in the eastern Congo, when some, if not most, could have fled? Guy Humphreys, an American missionary turned plantation owner, resolved to stay because Africa was the source of his identity. He had been in the Congo for seventeen years, the last eleven continuously. Humphreys had stayed when his family had returned to the United States years before, and like the old colonists of the past, he could not give up Africa, which had become a part of him. Others, like Hoyt, Nothomb, or Dr. Alexander Barlovatz, resolved to stay out of professional considerations. Of Hungarian birth and almost seventy years old, Dr. Barlovatz was a frontier doctor who had first set foot in the Congo in 1923. Along with his wife, the doctor never considered leaving his home and practice on Stanley Falls. For the missionaries, their perception of their duty in Africa made the thought of leaving collectively abhorrent; the last plane out of Stanleyville had twenty-nine empty seats, all reserved for missionaries.[19] For most foreigners who stayed, however, the reason was economic: their fortunes were tied to the Congo.

The history of the Congo also played a role in the foreigners' determinations to remain. First, those Westerners who had experienced the troubles of the early 1960s felt that any trouble in 1964 would be equally manageable. Some, particularly the missionaries, felt guilty over their flight in 1960 and resolved to remain. Second, intertribal violence was the norm for the Congo, and so far, the violence in the Simba Rebellion had been largely directed against other Congolese. Those Westerners who had been killed had been isolated cases in distant locations. It seemed unlikely that the violence would turn against a large number of Westerners in a systematic massacre. The statements of the Simbas supported this belief. Soumialot, Gbenye, and Olenga had reassured the foreign population of its safety, and

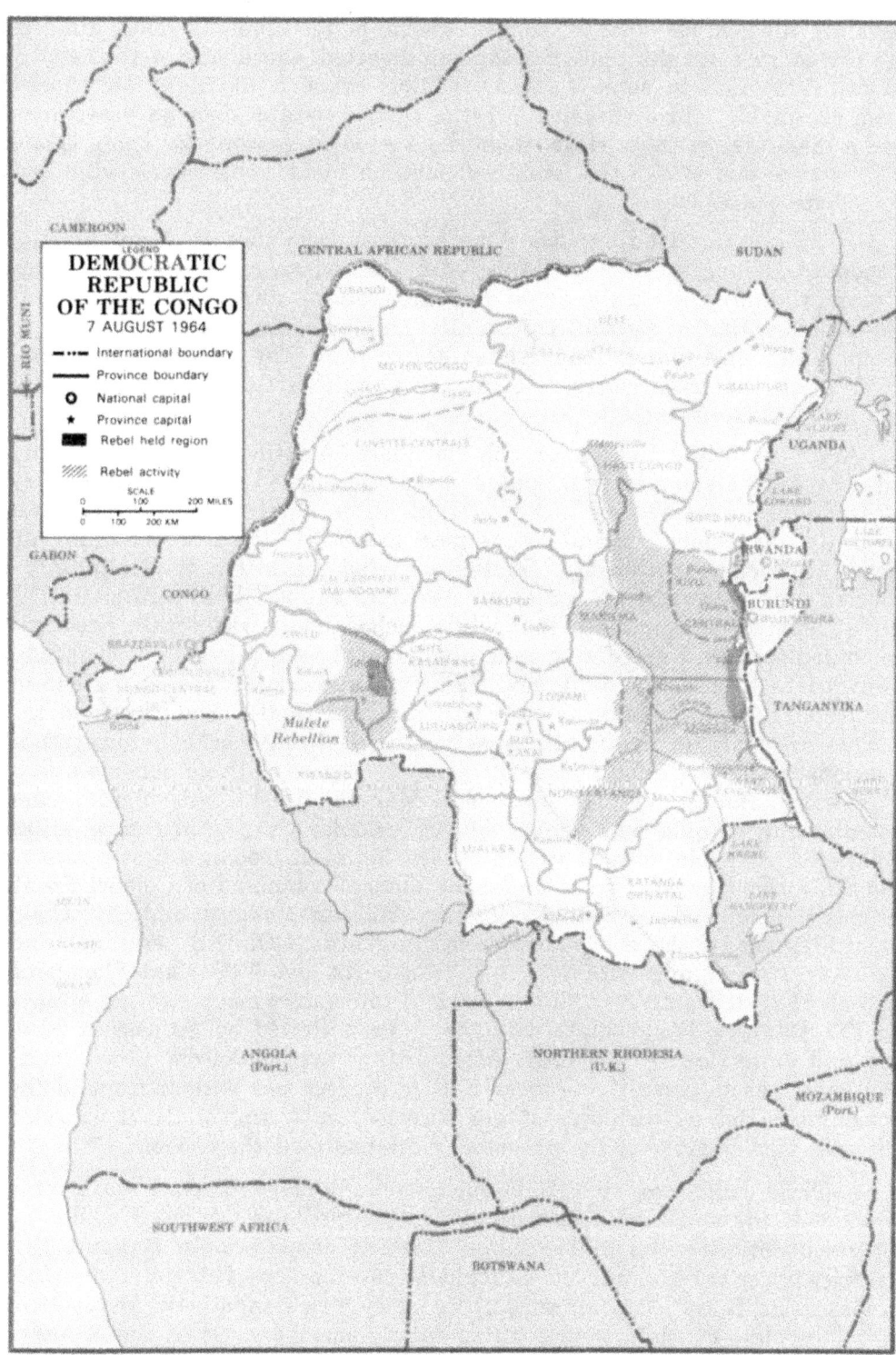

Map 2. Congo situation, 7 August 1964

certainly the Simbas were, in some respects, better than the ANC. Finally, the Congo was not the place for the fainthearted; those who were there in August 1964 had in some form or fashion weighed the risks and found them acceptable. The expression *"c'est le Congo"* was at once an acceptance and a dismissal of those risks. Regardless of their reasons for being there, the presence and size of the foreign population inside rebel Stanleyville had immediate consequences.

G. McMurtrie Godley, the American ambassador in Leopoldville, responded first to the fall of Stanleyville. Godley, an ex-Marine and career diplomat, had previously acted as ambassador during the Katangan secession. A man of forceful personality, Godley tended to dominate those around him and to challenge those above him. The military personnel involved in the crisis referred to him as CINCCONGO, a nickname fully justified by his actions.[20]

After the initial assault on the consulate, American consul Hoyt and his companions emerged from hiding and reestablished contact with Godley at Leopoldville. Based on this communication, Godley and his staff sat down and developed a small rescue plan to liberate the five remaining official Americans in the city. Godley signaled his intent to Washington, coupled with a request for naval air assets to support his operation.[21] The State Department responded that while such support was within one-day's combined steaming and flying time, the helicopters required that jet fuel be provided between Leopoldville and Stanleyville. Tucked away at the end of the response was a query as to whether or not Godley had discussed the rescue or possible negotiations with the Belgians or other national missions.[22] Godley, giving little attention to either of these considerations except for contacts with Tshombe and Mobutu, finished his plan.[23] After coordinating signals with Hoyt, the ambassador's task force, now called Operation Flagpole, formed within fifteen hours of Godley's first notice to the State Department. Placed under the tactical command of Colonel Frank Williams, chief of United States Military Mission, Congo (COMISH), Operation Flagpole consisted of Marine security guards, COMISH personnel, and embassy staff—along with two C-47 transports, two T-28 fighter-bombers, and an H-21 helicopter.[24] Williams planned to conduct mock strafing attacks on the Stanleyville consulate with the T-28s, followed by an assault landing and extraction by the H-21. After getting approval from Leopoldville, Williams was to commit the force if Hoyt's green car was in front of the consulate.[25] But as the force staged forward on 7 August, Hoyt canceled the operation because of the presence of Simbas near the consulate.[26]

Godley's willingness to attempt such a hastily planned rescue was symptomatic of the sense of desperation that gripped the Congo. The Simba seizure of Stanleyville had stunned Western observers. In Bukavu, the American consul considered evacuation and in the interim requested increased airlift and close air support.[27] Godley was sympathetic; he reported that Congolese officials were sending family members out of the country. The ambassador asked for two C-130s and ten B-26s to reinforce the faltering government's army in the field and a "non-African" battalion to reinforce Leopoldville. Until such aid reached the besieged city, Godley wanted a carrier task force to put on a "nice bellicose" demonstration.[28]

In Washington, the fall of Stanleyville overcame the State Department's hostility to Tshombe. Ambassador W. Averell Harriman traveled to Brussels to meet with Foreign Minister Paul-Henri Spaak, whom he knew well from the post-World War II reconstruction period. Harriman, with direct access to President Lyndon B. Johnson, would serve as the administration's front man in the crisis. As events progressed, Harriman's charter would allow him to bypass his ordinary superiors and communicate directly with the White House. Harriman had three items to discuss: increased Belgian advisory support, Tshombe's Katanganese gendarmerie, and the issue of mercenaries. On each point, the United States wanted Belgium to take the lead.[29]

Spaak was not in the most cooperative mood on the issue of Belgian support for the Congo. His country had just endured three years of scorn for its actions in 1960 and in the Katangan secession. On assuming office in 1961, Spaak had been able to repair some of the damage to his country's prestige by ending Belgium's controversial support of Tshombe. But other difficult decisions concerning the Stanleyville crisis would have to be made. The lack of domestic support in Belgium for increased involvement in the Congo would hamper Spaak's efforts to resolve problems there. Moreover, should he decide to take military action, he would not only have to consider the Belgian response but also the Simba's reaction against the thousands of Belgians in rebel territory.[30]

A C-130 of JTF Leo lands at Bukavu

Courtesy of Maj. Gen. D. V. Rattan, USA, Ret.

To overcome Belgium's reluctance to act, Harriman went to Brussels with a plan that already had President Johnson's approval. Harriman wanted the United States and Belgium to support Tshombe by creating a 4,000-man force commanded by "two hundred white officers." The first element of this proposed organization, some 500 men, was to be in action within weeks, led by Belgian mercenaries.[31]

Harriman hoped that the Belgians, bolstered by U.S. political support, would replicate the Katangan model throughout the Congo. In hopes of stimulating such Belgian support, Harriman portrayed the Simba Rebellion as a concerted Communist effort to wrest the mineral wealth of the Congo from the West.

Amazingly, Harriman's mission was a success. While Spaak refuted the idea of Communist control of the Simbas and opposed using Belgian mercenaries, he agreed to the formation of a mercenary-led organization to stabilize the situation. Belgium would provide logistical advisers to a special strike force and give increased training support to the ANC. These agreements were the principal military features of the Harriman-Spaak consultations.

The other side of Harriman's mission dealt with the international aspects of the Congo crisis. Neither Harriman nor Spaak believed that the Simba Rebellion or the larger question of Congolese political legitimacy could be resolved through the use of white mercenaries, the Katanganese gendarmerie, and a Congolese prime minister viewed as a white man's puppet. Spaak and Harriman, therefore, agreed once again to internationalize the crisis. They saw two possible paths: one was to Africanize the crisis through the offices of the Organization of African Unity (OAU), perhaps even militarily with African troops; the second was to create a European model of the UN force out of disinterested Western European powers.[32] Only by placing the crisis in such a context could the United States and Belgium hope to disassociate their direct support for Leopoldville from the threat to the thousands of people who remained deep inside Simba territory.

The dual strategy for the Congo—military intervention to provide stability and internationalization to disguise direct United States-Belgium participation—seemed appropriate at the beginning of August 1964. The immediate security demand was to contain the Simba Rebellion and assure the continued survival of a central government. The Belgian-American agreement to support a mercenary-led strike force would achieve this military goal. The use of an international agency to negotiate the long-standing issues might achieve some form of Congolese reconciliation and might distance the United States and Belgium from their military support of Leopoldville. As long as that distance existed in the eyes of the rebel leaders, the Westerners in their hands might remain safe. Certainly, rebel assurances that the Westerners were in no danger and that the rebellion was against Leopoldville supported the assumption that such a distance could be maintained.

However, such a two-handed strategy contained defects. While the Simba rebels, heady from their smashing victories over the ANC, could afford to be magnanimous toward their Western guests, how would the rebels react to military defeat at the hands of Belgian troops or mercenaries and American supplied aircraft? The assumption that the Simbas would continue to treat their Western captives as civilian detainees or prisoners of war was questionable.

Tshombe, on his part, was also unlikely to accept the implementation of Western strategy. The Congolese leader had just lost nearly one-half of his country to the Simbas. That he would accept a measured military campaign of containment without attempting to destroy the Simbas at the first opportunity was a poor Western assessment of possibilities. That Tshombe would accept an international solution for what he viewed as a Congolese problem was even less likely considering his record in dealing with the UN in Katanga.

The fall of Stanleyville represented a turning point in the Congolese crisis of 1964. While it handed the Simbas control of the eastern Congo, it led to the strategy, faulty though it might be, that would destroy them. This strategy depended on a cast of reluctant, often rebellious, actors. As long as the strategy seemed to be working, serious considerations of direct action to rescue the Westerners inside Simba territory remained a subordinate concern. In the future, however, when events and actors disrupted the pursuit of Belgian-American goals, the idea of direct military intervention would again surface.

By 8 August, Harriman was back in Washington where an informal task force was now operating inside the State Department. The members of the group were all department members drawn from the African Bureau. Officially under Assistant Secretary for Africa G. Mennen "Soapy" Williams, they soon realized that Harriman was in control. On 10 August, Harriman asked the Joint Chiefs of Staff (JCS) to deploy a task force to the Congo.[33]

The JCS tasking went to MacDill Air Force Base, Headquarters, U.S. Strike Command (USSTRICOM), where it received the personal attention of General Paul DeWitt Adams. General Adams, an old soldier and general officer for more than ten years, had been the executive officer of the 1st Special Service Force during World War II. Known for his dominant personality, Adams could be ruthless in dealing with those who disagreed with him, no matter what position they held.[34]

As commander in chief of USSTRICOM (CINCSTRIKE), General Adams held regional military responsibility for the Congo under the Unified Command Plan (UCP). Intended to clarify the command responsibilities of each of the unified commands, the UCP served as a focal point for inter- and intra-service rivalries. Though most of the unified commands had specific regional responsibilities, USSTRICOM was created to serve as the controlling headquarters for forces deployed into areas not specified by the UCP or to augment the forces of other unified commands. Even when unified commands had a specific region to control, the boundaries between them and other commands were not drawn according to military deployment considerations. Consequently, shifting of operational control from one command to another often produced friction. During the early years of the Congo crisis, United States European Command (USEUCOM) had operational control of the airlift supporting the UN, though most of the squadrons involved were deployed out of the United States. To facilitate operations, the UCP had been revised in 1963, assigning USSTRICOM a specific regional responsibility for the Middle East, Africa, and South Asia. Since the title CINCSTRIKE was likely to offend some of the newly independent countries in the region, Adams received the additional title of commander in chief Middle East, Africa, and South Asia (CINCMEAFSA), though CINCSTRIKE was more appropriate to his personality. Under his CINCMEAFSA title, Adams was responsible for the military assistance programs in those areas. In addition to COMISH, Adams had his own independent observer in the Congo, Colonel William A. Dodds. With Dodds as his senior representative in Leopoldville (SENREPLEO), Adams was familiar with the situation.[35]

Adams had already prepared one operations plan, OPLAN (operation plan) 515 Ready Move, back in January, when Mulélé's revolt exploded. Now that a new demand had arisen, he resurrected and restructured OPLAN 515 under the title OPLAN 515/1 Ready Move II. After surveying the conditions in the Congo, Adams recommended a joint task force be assembled. The task force, ultimately named JTF LEO (Joint Task Force Leopoldville), was to contain a small joint staff, an airborne infantry platoon for aircraft security, two UH-1B helicopters, and two C-130s. After reviewing Adams' proposal, the JCS modified it by replacing the two UH-1Bs with H-34 helicopters from Europe and adding two more C-130s. JTF LEO launched from MacDill Air Force Base on 11 August 1964. Under the command of Colonel Robert W. Teller, USMC, the joint task force was drawn from USSTRICOM headquarters, the 464th Troop Carrier Wing at Pope Air Force Base, the 11th Transportation Company (Light Helicopter) at Nelligen, Germany, and the 82d Airborne Division. Teller arrived in Leopoldville with two passengers, G. Mennen Williams and William E. Lang, the deputy assistant secretary for Africa in the Office of the Assistant Secretary of Defense for International Security Affairs.[36]

Williams went to Leopoldville to present the strategy agreed on in Brussels. Shortly before his departure, he had learned that Tshombe had requested military aid from South Africa. With Lang, Williams assured Tshombe that immediate aid was on the way in the form of B-26 light attack bombers to reinforce the CIA's air force. Williams, however, did not meet all the Congolese demands: Tshombe wanted three American airborne battalions, and Mobutu wanted 200 special forces troops. After refusing these demands, Williams raised the issue of Tshombe's contacts with South Africa. If exposed to the public, such relations would destroy any attempt to develop pan-African support for Leopoldville. Tshombe dismissed Williams' comments on the matter, demonstrating that the Harriman-Spaak strategy was already in trouble.[37]

The Belgian response to the fall of Stanleyville came in the form of the Vandewalle mission. On 5 August, in Brussels, Spaak met with Defense

Minister Paul W. Segers; the Belgian military attaché to the Congo, Colonel Emile Monmaert; and Colonel Logiest of CAMAC. Tshombe had requested a Belgian military adviser. Spaak told those present he had someone in mind to fulfill the request. The next day, an old Congo hand, Colonel BEM Frédéric Vandewalle, received a telephone call from Davignon, Spaak's assistant. Davignon said, "You know certainly, why I'm calling you. Mr. Spaak wants to see you." With a real sense of déjà vu, Vandewalle was on a plane to the Congo the next evening.[38]

Vandewalle had served as the Belgian consul in Katanga during Tshombe's secession. On that trip to Katanga, Vandewalle had coordinated a confused military assistance program intended to restructure the local ANC garrison into an army. His solution then was a blend of Belgian advisers, African troops, and a liberal sprinkling of mercenaries. After completing that task, he sat in on Tshombe's inner council. Now in 1964, he was going back into the Congo to do it again. This time, he faced the problem of reconquering an area roughly the size of France. He knew, however, that if he concentrated on controlling the existing transportation network of rivers, railways, and roads, he could, in fact, control the area. His campaign would depend on using airfields both as logistic bases and for close air support.[39]

As the hub of the eastern Congo transportation network, Stanleyville represented the key to the puzzle. To take it by direct attack, however, would only push the rebels out the opposite side. Vandewalle saw that he would have to converge on Stanleyville from all sides,[40] block the rebel retreat, and thrust into the city with his main column (see map 3). But his plan to reconquer the eastern Congo with Stanleyville as the ultimate objective had one catch. Designed to force the Simbas back on Stanleyville, the plan risked concentrating an explosive mixture of desperate and unstable rebels and the largest number of Westerners in the region, particularly if the separate columns moved too quickly. If Vandewalle lost control over his support operations and they precipitated an early rebel retreat, the safety of this foreign population would be jeopardized. In any case, the non-Congolese might become the Simbas' hostages—a final barricade against Vandewalle's advance. Thus, while Vandewalle's plan might succeed in achieving the military goal of the Harriman-Spaak strategy, any failure in his timing might force the United States and Belgium to abandon their international efforts in favor of intervention.

In Stanleyville, Olenga and his army, the native Congolese, and the foreign population were all trying to sort out the consequences of the city's capture. For Olenga, the experience was exciting and more than a little confusing. A tribal leader with little or no education, he was now the conqueror of a modern city. To aid him in its administration, Olenga turned to Stanleyville's *jeunesse*. As the new provincial president, he selected Alphonse Kinghis, a raving maniac who had been arrested once and imprisoned for two years for attempted crucifixion. Olenga's political and economic judgment was also inept: he removed all persons holding positions

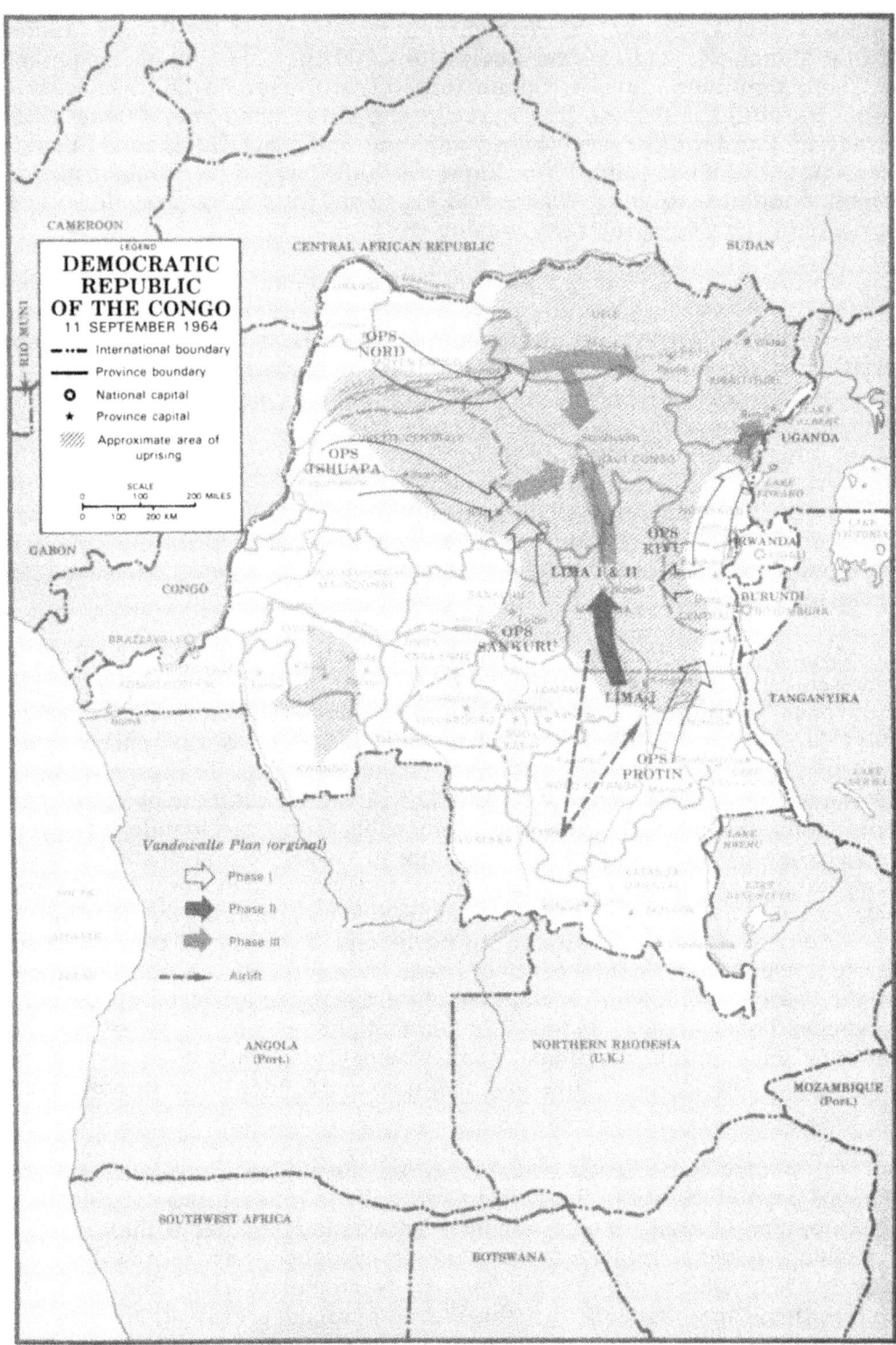

Map 3. Vandewalle plan, 11 September 1964

of power, arbitrarily cut prices, and ordered the beer parlors to stay open twenty-four hours a day. Olenga remained puritanical concerning his injunction against looting. Killing was tolerable, but stealing was not, and Olenga enforced the prohibition with death. This conflict between Simba dogma and *jeunesse* greed led to tension between the two groups. Nevertheless, Olenga soon felt he had things well enough in control to continue his campaign. After summoning Soumialot from Albertville, Olenga marched his Popular Army of Liberation toward Bukavu. His absence was soon felt by the Congolese in Stanleyville.[41]

Cannibalism—the aftermath of an attack

The real victims in the Simba Rebellion were the native Congolese, and those in Stanleyville were merely representative of the larger massacre. Before Olenga left on 13 August, the slaughter of the city's elite, while widespread and merciless, was spontaneous. With Olenga's departure, the nature of the bloodletting turned into ritualistic madness under the direction of Kinghis. The favorite location for these murders was the Lumumba Monument, where on 16 August, Kinghis ritually slaughtered a dozen men while a mob cheered. For the next five days, the killing went on until complaints from a women's delegation convinced Kinghis to stop the public rituals. But the killings continued at night on the Tshopo Bridge, where victims were thrown alive, dead, or dying into the cataract below, the crocodiles taking care of the remains. When it was all over in November, some 1,000 to 2,000 Congolese had been murdered in Stanleyville. Massacres elsewhere were worse; for example, Paulis was the scene of 2,000 to 4,000 deaths. When Olenga returned to Stanleyville, he threw Kinghis and his mob into jail for misuse of public funds, extortion-motivated killings, and the deaths of several Simbas.[42]

Lieutenant Colonels Mulamba and Rattan

The Simbas' mindless violence against fellow Congolese did not extend at first to the foreign population, which, although threatened and harassed, was generally left alone. Olenga sought to reassure the foreigners on 10 August when he met with a delegation led by José Romnée, a former Belgian SAS trooper who pressed Olenga for reassurances on safety, property, and freedom. Olenga granted most of the demands and assured the group that his regime needed their help. However, the same did not apply to the American officials under his control.[43]

For the Americans in the consulate, the first few days after the city's fall were reasonably safe. Several times, Hoyt managed to establish communications with Leopoldville (as when the rescue by Operation Flagpole was under consideration). All that changed the day after Olenga had reassured the foreigners of their safety. On 11 August, the rebels took all five of the American officials to Camp Ketele, where they were beaten and forced to chew on American flags. Olenga followed this action on 13 August by having them thrown in prison shortly before he set off for Bukavu. Still, the Americans' status was not clear. On 16 August, writing on scraps of paper from which they later assembled their journal, Hoyt and Grinwis mused: "In general, the attitude of the new authorities toward the American Consulate staff and by extension Belgians and other foreigners is not yet clearly defined. It is possible we are regarded simply as hostages who must be ransomed, although the ransom price or its character cannot yet be determined."[44]

Ensuing events in Bukavu, which sits on the eastern frontier adjacent to Rwanda, answered Hoyt's question. Under periodic threat from the rebellion since June, Bukavu sat athwart the fragile rebel lines of communication with neighboring Bujumbura, Burundi. Olenga attacked Bukavu on 19 August with a column of 1,000 rebels. Mounted on trucks, the rebels barreled headlong into the city, but the ANC, led personally by Colonel Mulamba, fought back bravely in house-to-house actions that drove back the attackers. To support Mulamba, the C-130s of JTF LEO flew in a battalion of Katanganese gendarmerie, and the CIA's T-28s flew close air support.

Bukavu was a watershed battle, because it ruined the effort to distance the United States from the fighting. At the outbreak of the battle, three Americans, Colonel Dodds, Lieutenant Colonel Donald V. Rattan, and Lewis R. Macfarlane were cut off by the rebel advance and narrowly escaped capture. Rattan had just arrived in the Congo to provide logistics advice to

Rattan and Richard Matheron, consul in Bukavu, in Congo operation

the ANC. Macfarlane was a member of the Bukavu consulate. They spent the next few days hiding but eventually returned unharmed. Their disappearance, nonetheless, brought the question of American use of force of arms to the forefront. General Adams and Ambassador Godley wanted to use all means necessary, including force, to save the missing party. Dean Rusk, the secretary of state, overruled any use of force, fearing retaliation by the Simbas against Westerners in their territory. But Rusk's prohibition against the overt use of force, while in accordance with the overall Congo strategy, was too late. Even without the Dodds episode, Olenga's forces had suffered heavily from American close air support, and he attributed this directly to the United States.[45]

Rattan on operations with Mulamba's men

On 21 August in Stanleyville, the Belgian consul, Baron Nothomb, and others came to the American consulate to ask the members, "Do you have any last messages for your family?" Following his defeat in Bukavu, Olenga had sent a cable to Stanleyville ordering the arrest and trial of all Americans. They were to be "judged without mercy." Since this order amounted to a death sentence, Hoyt and Grinwis proposed sending a diplomatic delegation to the American government to "reconsider" its aid to the Tshombe administration.[46] The message contained the following key phrase: "The continuation of American military aid puts, without doubt, in immediate repeat immediate danger the lives of Americans living in the territory controlled by the Popular Liberation Army."[47]

The rebel's defeat at Bukavu disrupted the Harriman-Spaak strategy. The American strategy, based on the assumption that U.S. and Belgian military support of Tshombe could be distanced from the plight of the hostages through international negotiations, began to disintegrate. Tshombe had already demonstrated his reluctance to pursue international support for his actions. Olenga, after his defeat in Bukavu (which he attributed to American aircraft), openly brandished the American officials as a weapon to be used to stave off United States support for Leopoldville. While the Belgians were as yet unthreatened, Vandewalle's campaign might turn the rebels against them; it remained to be seen how long Spaak could remain comfortable with the dual strategy. In any case, the Americans recognized the threat: on 22 August, the State Department cabled Godley to say: "We need counter hostages."[48]

An American Crisis

The troubles in the Congo had become an American crisis. Secretary of State Dean Rusk officially recognized the crisis on 29 August, when he circulated a memorandum announcing the establishment of an interagency task force to coordinate all actions dealing with the Congo. What had been a small-action staff within the African Bureau officially became the Congo Working Group (CWG). Headed by Ambassador Joseph Palmer II, the CWG included members of the Department of Defense, the United States Agency for International Development (USAID), the CIA, the United States Information Agency (USIA), and the White House.[1]

Nevertheless, Harriman remained the dominant figure within the CWG due to his intimate personal relationship with Spaak. Working closely with McGeorge Bundy, President Johnson's chief of staff, Harriman continued to push the strategy agreed on in Brussels, especially for international alternatives to a direct American involvement in the Congo. President Johnson, in contrast to his predecessor, did not consider the Congo a high-priority situation in comparison with the Gulf of Tonkin incident and a new crisis between Turkey and Greece. In any case, the president did not need another foreign policy issue to complicate his upcoming November bid for election.[2]

The greatest problem facing the CWG was a complete lack of intelligence on the situation inside rebel territory. Analysts struggled to identify the Simba Rebellion's true character and leadership. While estimates generally agreed that Communist influence among the Simbas was at this stage minimal, the chaotic and fluid nature of the rebel leadership frustrated efforts to determine who actually was in charge in Stanleyville. Furthermore, no information existed on the location of American officials inside the city. Consequently, the CWG's intelligence concentrated necessarily on the broad international and political aspects of the crisis.[3]

After an initial study of the situation, the CWG paid the JCS a visit on 4 September. Expecting to find a contingency plan to save the American officials, the CWG was disappointed. Other than a USSTRICOM plan to augment the United States Atlantic Command for conventional operations in the Congo, the JCS had nothing ready. At the request of the CWG, Assistant Secretary of Defense Cyrus Vance directed that the JCS evaluate possible military requirements for a rescue of the five American officials or for a rescue of the entire American population in Stanleyville.[4] The JCS passed the order on to General Adams and directed that he respond by 8 September. Pulling in Colonel Edward E. Mayer, commanding officer of the 7th Special Forces Group from Fort Bragg, Adams briefed him on the situation and told him to prepare a covert plan to rescue the American officials.[5] While Mayer worked out his draft, Adams ordered JTF LEO to provide current intelligence on Stanleyville.[6] Both Mayer and the intelligence report came back the next day, the former arriving first.

Mayer's concept was simple to state and difficult to accomplish (see map 1). He planned to "parachute several Special Forces A Teams at night several miles upriver [east] from Stanleyville, float and infiltrate the teams downstream on rubber rafts to the city, land, and rescue the Americans in a dawn raid, and withdraw several hundred yards to a recovery area near the Congo River for a helicopter pickup." Evidently Adams approved the concept, and Mayer went off to put it in writing.[7]

But the JTF LEO intelligence summary doomed Mayer's plan. While intelligence indicated some 300 Westerners were in Stanleyville, their exact locations were unavailable. JTF LEO believed Hoyt and his companions were under guard, but the composition of the guard force was unknown. Faced with inadequate intelligence to support a covert rescue, Adams developed two overt courses of actions. In his message to the JCS on 7 September, Adams recommended that if they wished to hold an American-only rescue, then Mayer's covert plan, backed by an overt contingency force, was best. Adams, however, pointed out that the best option was to take Stanleyville and evacuate the entire foreign population.[8]

Following Adams' recommendations, the JCS sent their response, JCSM-788-64, to the secretary of defense on 12 September. Their first course of action, with an objective of rescuing all the Americans, recommended that two airborne rifle companies be dropped on multiple drop zones to search the city, seize the airfield, and evacuate the Americans. Such an operation, supported by eight fighters, KC-135 tankers, and seventeen C-130E transports, could be executed within three days. The second course of action recommended that Mayer's covert rescue be implemented using 100 U.S. Army Special Forces and U.S. Air Force Special Air Warfare personnel. This option, supported by two C-46 transports, three UH-1B helicopters, and three H-34 helicopters, would require eleven days' preparation. Either option could succeed *if* (1) precise locations of the Americans were known beforehand; (2) the operation achieved surprise; and (3) the commander was authorized to use force.[9]

The JCS weighed the advantages and disadvantages of each option. Under the overt option, their considerations were

> (1) The operation would show, in an area where turmoil will probably exist for many years to come, that the United States does not intend to permit its citizens legitimately in a country to be harassed, imprisoned, or otherwise molested.

(2) There are various numbers of non-Congolese reported to be in Stanleyville with one figure being as high as four to five hundred. The rescue of U.S. personnel alone, assuming there are other non-Congolese who would like to get out, could well react unfavorably to the general interests of the United States and her relationships with countries of western Europe and Africa.

(3) The overt operation has every promise of recapturing the city and making it feasible to secure it and return it to Congolese governmental control. This would, however, constitute U.S. military involvement in Congolese internal affairs versus a rescue operation.

(4) Since Stanleyville has apparently become the capital of the rebellious Communist movement, its reduction and pacification would constitute a serious setback to the general movement and, in net effect, would probably be more useful at this time than the capture of the town of Uvira [near the Burundi border] which is the rebel-Communist supply base.[10]

The advantages of the covert option were then cataloged:

(1) It involves fewer complications than does the overt operation.

(2) Casualties should be minimized and the possibility exists that the mission could be accomplished without any casualties.

(3) Explanations to other countries as to why their people were not also liberated would be unnecessary.

(4) The covert operation would appear to have a greater chance of successfully accomplishing the mission in view of the rebels' announced intention of taking reprisal action against U.S. personnel if the "U.S. imperialists" continued to intervene in Congolese affairs.[11]

The JCS formally recommended that, if ordered, the covert option be selected for execution, backed by the overt force in a "pre-positioned and ready for contingency employment" role.[12]

However, the memorandum contained other messages. The first, probably based on Adams' recommendation, was written thusly:

Both of the courses of action ... might prove to be infeasible because locations of US personnel may not be known, because of the opposition of the Belgian Government due to anticipated reprisals against foreigners in the Stanleyville area, or because the element of surprise may be lost. Accordingly, a third course of action might be required which would provide for the capture of Stanleyville and its control long enough to transfer control to Congolese security forces and/or evacuate all foreign personnel. This course of action would probably require additional force.[13]

The meaning of JCSM-788-64 seems clear: conditions unfavorable to the two courses of action rendered them futile considerations. Adams and the JCS both knew that the precise locations of Americans were not available, nor likely to be revealed.[14] Moreover, to rescue only the official Americans—even if their locations could be determined—after Olenga had threatened all Americans would be seriously damaging on the American political level. On the other hand, to evacuate all Americans and abandon the other non-

Congolese would cause an international furor. The potential third course of action, that of taking the city and holding it until the government could secure it, was the most valid course of action. Furthermore, the JCS was careful to point out the value of taking Stanleyville as a means of breaking the back of the rebellion. The JCS argued that hostile observers would consider anything greater than the covert operation as an intervention rather than a rescue. So, if a price had to be paid in hostile reaction to the operation, why risk antagonistic Western reaction to an American-only rescue? To redirect the CWG's thinking, the JCS emphasized that the United States should show resolve to protect its citizens.[15] That was the meaning of JCSM-788-64: to get the CWG to face the issues and to accept the costs. If the memorandum failed, it at least prepared the CWG for later events. In the words of one analyst, Adams' "suggestion was the forerunner of the ultimate DRAGON ROUGE operation."[16]

While the CWG considered JCSM-788-64, the JCS had Adams alert Mayer's team. Under the code name Golden Hawk, Mayer began rehearsing the operation. Incredibly, the team practiced for an airborne operation that would occur east of the city; they would float downriver into the city from there. This would have been a very rough ride; fortunately, someone recalled that Stanleyville was located on Stanley Falls. Determining the location of the falls and the flow rate over them soon became a priority intelligence requirement. For some strange reason, however, Mayer did not turn to the numerous terrain studies available on the Congo. Instead, his information came from Mrs. John W. Bowen, the wife of the commander, U.S. XVIII Airborne Corps. Raised in Stanleyville, she informed Mayer that the falls were upriver, or east of the city, and were impassable in September. Mayer altered the plan to reflect a drop zone west of the city, and those practicing Golden Hawk began to exercise with motorized boats.[17] The plan's alteration put it back in accordance with JCSM-788-64, which stated that the covert force would be dropped west of the city. The planning gaff concerning the falls indicates a serious lack of professionalism in the initial planning, since basic information is essential for a covert rescue. Had Mayer initiated his plan, his men would have met disaster by drowning or by impalement on the fish traps that were permanently constructed across the falls east of Stanleyville (see map 4).

In any case, the CWG was not ready to commit itself to any of the options postulated in JCSM-788-64. Instead, it adhered to the tenets of the Harriman-Spaak consultations. Thus, while Vandewalle prepared his campaign to defeat the rebels militarily, the CWG intensified its efforts to internationalize the crisis.

The military campaign to contain and eventually roll back the Simba Rebellion began with Colonel Vandewalle's return to the Congo. Vandewalle was very much on his own. Though his mission was to advise Tshombe, and though his Belgian officers were to provide "non-operational logistic support," Vandewalle knew that ultimately the officers would be engaged in combat. Spaak knew it too, but he and Vandewalle arrived at an unwritten understanding. Spaak would adhere to the logistic support story,

Map 4. Golden Hawk and Stanley Falls

and Vandewalle would maintain a low profile. They reached a similar agreement on the issue of mercenaries. Vandewalle's mission was to support the Congolese military, and his association with mercenary elements was to be at the direction of the Tshombe government. In fact, Vandewalle's plan depended on having a solid strike force of non-Congolese troops as the fer-de-lance of each column. Since Belgium could not provide combat troops, Vandewalle knew that he would be working with mercenaries. Vandewalle had an enormous latitude of action in his mission, and once he began, he would be difficult to control. On the other hand, his mission could seriously backfire on him since the Belgian government could state that he had exceeded his orders.[18]

In early August, while Vandewalle was negotiating and forming the broad outlines of his plan, other actors were arriving on the scene. In the words of Ambassador Godley, "all kinds of adventurers and confidence men" were arriving in the Congo.[19] Some of these adventurers, namely Jeremiah Puren and Michael Hoare, had arrived in late July at the behest of Tshombe. In anticipation of new work in the Congo, Puren, onetime head of Tshombe's Katangan air force, had contacted Hoare, himself an old Katangan hand, and had him fly up from South Africa. Both were, in circumspect terms, colorful men. Puren, then in his forties, had stayed with Tshombe until the very end of the Katangan secession. Now, he arrived in Leopoldville in the company of his Belgian spouse Julia and booked into the Hotel Memling. Hoare, a former British officer, had been expelled from Katanga by the UN in April 1961 after he had been captured by Ethiopian troops. He joined Puren a few days later, and they settled down to wait for a summons from Tshombe; their arrival in the Congo did not go unnoticed.[20]

Prime Minister Tshombe summoned Hoare immediately after G. Mennen Williams departed for the United States. In an effort to show his personal independence from American control, he handed Hoare a charter to raise the initial 500 troops agreed on by Harriman and Spaak and ordered Hoare to begin immediate operations in the Albertville area. Since some 120 Belgians were threatened in Albertville, Hoare decided to assault the city with thirty men, followed by a coordinated attack by the ANC. Hoare began his attack, Operation Watch Chain, on 24 August. By 28 August, his part of the operation had ended in disaster when his force escaped with two dead and seven wounded after failing to reach its target. Fortunately, the ANC took the city on 30 August and saved the lives of 135 Europeans.[21]

Operation Watch Chain had lasting effects. One of Hoare's men was a Belgian. Soon the presence of Belgian mercenaries in the Congo was world news, and Vandewalle had to deal with the backlash. Following this incident, Vandewalle was determined to bring Hoare under control and began immediate consultations with Tshombe and Mobutu. Vandewalle secured a charter giving him operational control of all military operations against the rebels. Using this charter, he spent the next several weeks building his force, which he named L'Ommengang after an annual Mardi Gras-type parade in Brussels. By 1 October, Vandewalle had a growing brigade that reflected its carnival nickname. With six Belgian logistic teams, some 250 mercenaries, and several thousand Katanganese, L'Ommengang began preparations for its march through Simba territory.[22]

In Stanleyville, serious changes occurred that would drastically alter the Belgian-American approach to the crisis. By mid-September, all of the leaders of the rebellion were present in Stanleyville and eyeing one another uneasily. Fresh from a European and African tour as head of the CNL, Gbenye was the titular head of the Popular Revolutionary Government. But his government was a sham, and he had little control over his defense minister, Soumialot, and even less over Olenga and his Popular Army. The Popular Army and its *jeunesse* were a self-directed mob. The internal tension inside Stanleyville was developing into a ticking bomb as the rebels' military situation deteriorated.[23]

By early September, the rebel advances to the east, west, and south had been contained by a combination of ANC forces, mercenary strike teams, and air strikes. In contrast, the rebel advance to the north and northwest proceeded unchecked into a vacuum created by the retreating ANC. Only the emergency deployment of two mercenary platoons prevented the rebellion from expanding past Coquilhatville, 400 miles east of Leopoldville.[24]

The confusing military situation had serious implications within Stanleyville. Battered on three fronts but victorious on another, Olenga vacillated between antagonism and friendship toward his political masters. He regarded the Americans as hostages to be executed in retribution for his military setbacks and pressured his masters to enforce this threat. Gbenye and Soumialot wavered between using an evacuation of all foreigners as a gesture of their international goodwill or retaining the Western population as hostages against the growing military threat.[25]

Maintaining the Harriman-Spaak strategy was proving difficult for Ambassador Godley. Godley had to convince Tshombe that an international forum would benefit his government. After expelling all the citizens of Congo-Brazzaville, Mali, and Burundi for subversion, Tshombe was suspicious of his pan-African brothers. His open association with the South African government in the hiring of mercenaries made pan-African leaders equally suspicious of him.

Tshombe's actions against the Simbas made the situation even more difficult. After the disaster of Operation Watch Chain, he and Mobutu wanted to demonstrate their ability to strike back at the rebel leadership. They decided to order an air strike against Radio Stanleyville. Only after some heavy arm twisting at the behest of the CWG did Ambassador Godley prevent the air strike.[26] Forcing Tshombe into a rapprochement with the Organization of African Unity (OAU) required equal pressure. After Nigeria expressed a willingness to participate in an African peacekeeping operation in the Congo under the auspices of the OAU, that organization opened an extraordinary session on 5 September, which Tshombe attended.

The Western belief that the meeting would disassociate their military support of Leopoldville from the overall context of the African political scene was in error. The session agreed that Jomo Kenyatta, president of Kenya, should head a special conciliatory commission on the Congo. American observers predicted Kenyatta would minimize OAU meddling in the Congo; they were wrong. Kenyatta seated a CNL delegation on the committee and called for a cease-fire coupled with a halt to American and Belgian military support to Leopoldville. When President Johnson refused to meet with a delegation from Kenyatta's commission, the diplomatic rebuke put Kenyatta in support of the CNL. After this unexpected turn in the OAU discussions, the status of American officials and other Westerners in the Congo would be tied to American and Belgian military support of Tshombe.[27]

Although the OAU's efforts proved futile in establishing calm, another international body provided a breakthrough. On 25 September, Jean-Maurice Rubli and another Red Cross official flew into Stanleyville to discuss the possible evacuation of all foreigners. After a day of talks with Gbenye and Soumialot, they departed without reaching any agreement on the non-Congolese population. Although this mission failed to negotiate an end to the crisis, it did provide the first reliable reports on the city.[28] American officials who debriefed the negotiators in Bangui reported: "Rubli emphasized he greatly feared for lives of 'all foreigners and suspects' in Stanleyville in event of any bombings or even overflights of city. Any military action to take city would have to be so sudden and massive that key points could be secured in quarter of hour, or run risk of general massacre...."[29] The Red Cross report, along with another from Khartoum, Sudan,[30] demonstrated the validity of JCSM-788-64 and provided the minimum tactical requirements for Operation Golden Hawk, but the danger to the other non-Congolese who would be left at the mercy of the Simbas made an American-only rescue unthinkable. Clearly, Adams' suggestion that Stanleyville be seized and all the non-Congolese evacuated warranted serious study. The CWG, however, remained reluctant to abandon the Harriman-Spaak strategy in favor of direct intervention.

As with the initial apparent success of the international prong of the Harriman-Spaak strategy, so with the military prong: apparent success degenerated into failure and defeat. By 1 October, Tshombe's mercenaries were in action, rolling back the rebels from their easy gains of September. The campaign was a confusing and often comic affair of sporadic advances and temporary retreats. Success by the government forces resulted through their use of mercenary troops to spearhead the assaults and their use of close air support to terrify the Simbas.

Vandewalle designed his plan to reconquer the Congo on the premise that converging columns, Ops Nord, Tshuapa, and Bukavu, would exert simultaneous pressure on the rebels, gradually and inexorably reducing their territory. At the final moment, Vandewalle envisioned a lightning thrust from the south into Stanleyville to topple the Simba leadership and save the non-Congolese. Such a plan rested on his ability to control each column, and Vandewalle thought he had received that charter from Tshombe and Mobutu after Hoare's abortive Operation Watch Chain. Unfortunately, Vandewalle experienced difficulties controlling the columns. Tshombe and

Mobutu reacted to the rebel gains in the northwest Congo by stripping Hoare of most of his newly recruited mercenaries and flinging them into action outside of Vandewalle's control. Out of 390 mercenaries in the Congo by mid-October, 156 were already in combat providing the assault elements for Ops Nord, Tshuapa, and Bukavu. Once organized under proper leadership—usually Belgian—each of these columns fought its own private war without regard to the Vandewalle plan.[31]

Ops Tshuapa was typical of the separate operations going on in the Congo. In mid-September, Hoare had sent Captain Siegfried Mueller, a holder of the German Iron Cross from World War II, along with a platoon of mercenaries, to Coquilhatville to halt the Simba advance. Mueller's men succeeded and soon were on the advance to Boende, where they made an unsuccessful attack on 19 September. After this abortive effort, Major Pierre Lemercier, a Belgian army officer, joined the column as its logistic adviser along with a second mercenary platoon. Using two ANC companies, the two mercenary platoons, and close air support, Lemercier took Boende on 24 October and by 6 November had seized Ikela.[32]

Ops Tshuapa, along with Ops Nord and Ops Bukavu, which made similar advances, owed their progress to the close air support provided by the CIA controlled T-28s and B-26s. CIA aircraft terrified the Simbas, who learned that their magic did not protect them from .50-caliber machine guns or rockets. Both Tshombe and Mobutu grasped the importance of the close air support in their campaign against the rebels. As evidenced by their attempt in September to bomb Stanleyville, Tshombe and Mobutu considered any rebel-held location to be a legitimate target for the air strikes.

Yet the air strikes were not without a cost. On 1 October, after an air strike on Bumba, a ham operator in Leopoldville intercepted a request by Colonel Opepe, Olenga's lieutenant in Stanleyville, to kill all the Americans. Olenga heightened the tension when on 7 October, he ordered Gbenye to kill one foreigner for each Congolese death caused by air strikes.[33] The threat to the foreigners was real: when he took Boende on 24 October, Lermercier found three victims who had been executed after an air strike on 15 October. He further discovered that the Simbas were taking their foreign prisoners with them as protection against more air strikes.[34]

This increased danger to Americans and other foreigners caused an immediate reaction in Washington. The CWG now saw that it had to restrain Tshombe and Mobutu to avoid an immediate massacre in Stanleyville. The CWG also realized that the United States might have to take military action to rescue the hostages if Tshombe continued with his arbitrary air attacks.

Restraining Tshombe's use of the tactical air force, however, proved difficult. Back in July, Godley had warned that the prime minister might create an independent air arm, particularly if the United States tried to use the CIA's T-28s as political leverage. After the pressure applied by Washington in September over the planned air strike on Radio Stanleyville, Godley repeated his warning—a warning that was all too valid.[35]

Tshombe had begun building his own air force in late July. Jeremiah Puren, his former Katangan air force chief, was a natural choice to form his new private air force. Puren put this force in action as early as August. Naming his unit *Aile Chaka*, after the terrible Zulu warlord, Puren's early results were as disastrous as Hoare's Watch Chain. During these initial operations, the pilots crashed two of Puren's aircraft, both T-6s donated by Italy at the behest of the United States. Puren recruited another Katangan alumni, Captain Bracco. A Belgian, Bracco, became his operational chief, and together they began a serious training effort at the end of September. On 3 October, Leopoldville activated the 21st Squadron and placed it under the Tactical Air Force at Kamina.

Predictably, the CWG reacted strongly to the activation order. Godley received orders to inform Tshombe that continued operations by the 21st Squadron would result in a complete stand down and possible withdrawal of the CIA's air force. Though he had strong reservations concerning the wisdom of the CWG's orders, Godley passed on the sternly worded complaint.[36]

In passing the message to Tshombe, Godley had several problems. On 3 October, as a part of an effort to reduce American visibility, the CWG had directed Godley to inform Tshombe that one C-130 of JTF LEO was being withdrawn and a second would follow at a later date. He was to assure Tshombe that the planned withdrawal would be phased in accordance with the development of the Congolese's own C-47 transport capability. Though the CWG emphasized on 7 October that the United States was not "pulling [the] rug out from under" Tshombe, the program to provide C-47s was seriously behind schedule, as the Belgians had not as yet supplied the required pilots. Furthermore, the C-47s could not lift the tonnage or equipment that Vandewalle needed at Kamina. Even the tactical air support program was in trouble: only eight of the twelve T-28s and three of the seven B-26s were operational. So any reassurances that Godley might have presented to Tshombe within the context of the 21st Squadron demarche appeared shallow.[37]

Despite the warning, Tshombe went ahead with the activation of the 21st Squadron, and predictably, Secretary of State Dean Rusk ordered a seventy-two-hour suspension of American air support on 15 October. Rather than lasting three days, however, the suspension order remained in effect until 23 October. After an American threat of complete withdrawal of the aircraft, Tshombe agreed to disband the mercenary squadron. To ensure that further incidents of unrestricted air strikes did not occur, the CWG imposed severe limitations on overflights of rebel-held territory, including a prohibition of any flight within twenty-five miles of Stanleyville.[38] While the CWG worked to prevent a massacre of the Westerners, due to Tshombe's use of air strikes, General Adams was again coming up with a plan to rescue the foreigners.

Even as the CWG suspended air operations to prevent a massacre of the hostages, General Adams put the finishing touches on a new plan to save them. On 9 October, after Gbenye threatened to kill the hostages,

Lieutenant Colonel James E. Dunn had phoned USSTRICOM. Dunn, the JCS action officer on the CWG, notified General Adams to develop a plan to seize and hold Stanleyville.[39] When on 14 October Gbenye again threatened the American officials, the JCS ordered Adams to alert his forces. The JCS gave Adams two contingency missions: either the Golden Hawk force backed by two companies or an outright intervention to take the city. In passing on the options, the JCS ordered Adams to report when he was prepared to execute and to consider Ascension Island, Wheelus Air Base, or Monrovia (Roberts Field in Liberia) as staging areas. The JCS cautioned Adams not to dispatch liaison teams to the Congo or consult any "non-U.S. personnel" during his planning.[40]

With the advance warning of 9 October, Adams had OPLAN 514 Ready Move III finished and its forces on alert at 142310Z October, less than two hours after the JCS order. In a major escalation over earlier plans, OPLAN 514 Ready Move III called for the use of one airborne battalion and one Composite Air Strike Force (CASF) backed by a second airborne battalion.[41]

Adams considered the three staging areas as directed. The ability of the second battalion to reach Stanleyville depended on the staging area selected. The use of Wheelus Air Base meant that forces could be over the objective within fifty-five hours and fifty-five minutes of the decision to execute. If Ascension Island was used, the operation could not be executed until 20 October, assuming that an immediate decision was taken to forward stock fuel. Once fuel was in place, the operation could be executed within fifty-nine hours and fifty minutes, but the CASF would be required to utilize Roberts Field, Monrovia, in order to rendezvous over the Congo. Adams also planned for the use of Roberts Field only, but this option required sixty-five hours and twenty minutes between decision time and its execution (see map 5).[42]

Aside from simple time delays, the provision to utilize different staging bases would have complicated the operation. In addition to the two airborne infantry battalions, Ready Move III required sixteen F-4C Phantom fighter-bombers, sixty C-130 Hercules transports, and twenty KC-135 fuel-tanker aircraft. Just providing for command and control from a single staging base would have been a challenge. To coordinate and control the departure of the airborne assault force from Ascension and that of the CASF from Roberts Field in order to rendezvous over Stanleyville would have been extremely difficult. At a minimum, such an operation would have doubled the communications support required and multiplied fuel consumption several times over.

Consequently, Adams followed his initial message with a second message within an hour, apparently to establish firmly two points: first, that the option for a covert operation was unrealistic without a minimum of two weeks' planning and coordination; and second, that Wheelus was the best staging area, and the Ascension-Roberts Field route should be approved only as a last resort. He also requested immediate aerial photography of the area using T-29s inside the Congo and U-2s from Europe. Adams was wrong about the covert operation, but he did not know that on 15 October.[43]

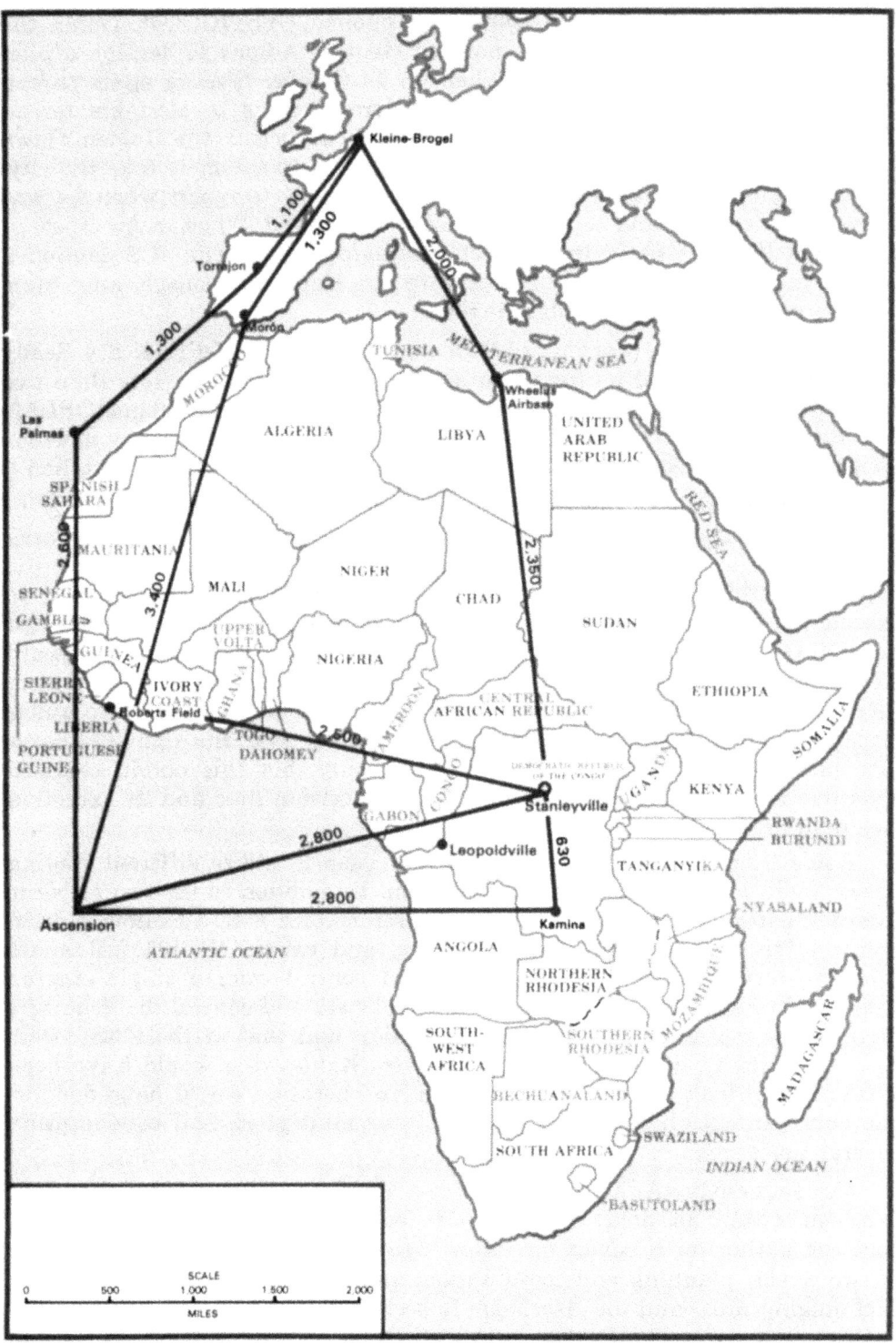

Map 5. Air bases and distances

The JCS supported Wheelus as the proposed staging base but was having difficulty securing the State Department's approval for its use. Consequently, Adams was to plan using both routes until the debate over staging areas was settled. Though a White House memo on 14 October indicated Harriman's tentative approval, the CWG denied Adams' request for photographic coverage because of the overflight restrictions with respect to Stanleyville. Then, the chairman of the JCS directed Adams to strengthen his plan. General Earl Wheeler wanted the second battalion into the target area right behind the initial assault battalion, with a third battalion on call in the United States. To coordinate the brigade's deployment, Adams was to send up to four planners to the Congo.[44]

During Adams' planning, General Wheeler had continued jousting with the State Department over the issue of staging areas. On 14 October, Wheeler sent Secretary of Defense Robert McNamara a formal memorandum urging him to support the Wheelus option. Wheeler felt that State Department fears over possible political reactions to the use of Wheelus were being given priority over military considerations. The chairman pointed out that the use of Ascension "added 1,600 nautical miles to the flight and cost $2,400 more per aircraft," and "that it was doubtful that the State Department was fully aware of the military implications created by such rerouting." When Wheeler received OPLAN 514 on 15 October, he again picked up his cudgel and pressed the issue with McNamara and his deputy, Cyrus Vance, by pointing out that lengthy refueling and cycle times for Ascension and Roberts Field would delay any follow-up force by as much as twenty-four hours after the initial assault.[45]

The issue that weakened Wheeler's and Adams' case for Wheelus Air Base was that of secrecy. The State Department considered Ascension Island preferable since it offered greater security. To buttress his argument, Wheeler had directed Adams to get the second battalion in over the objective area behind the assault unit and to plan for an additional backup force. By adding this option, Wheeler attempted to give preeminence to the logistical complications inherent in using Ascension and Roberts Field, thereby forcing the State Department to acquiesce to his demands. It did not work, as became evident later in the planning for Dragon Rouge. Meanwhile, Adams was reviewing the Congo situation and formulating his plan under the chairman's new requirements.[46]

Adams felt strongly about the Congo situation. Through his "eyes" (JTF LEO, SENREPLEO, and COMISH), he had a fairly good picture of the situation in the country, at least of what was known. Intelligence remained scanty, however, about the situation inside Stanleyville. Another break came on 13 October, when embassy officials in Leopoldville received a report of the Sureté Militaire, passed by an Israeli officer working in the intelligence office of the ANC, concerning the debriefing of Narcisse Alhadeff. The Sureté had interrogated Alhadeff after his departure from Stanleyville on 2 October.[47] The report confirmed much of the earlier information developed from the Red Cross. The report's biggest impact was in its description of the rebels' harsh treatment of the American officials after Olenga's defeat in Bukavu. The source reported that Hoyt and party had spent time in the Central Prison at Olenga's direction but were now in the Sabena Guest House, a salutary effect of the Red Cross visit.

Of military interest, the report indicated that rebels had blocked the airport with a few oil drums but that they had no antiaircraft weapons. The report speculated that a "sudden drop of 50 paratroops" could take the field.[48] The report also gave the current military organization of the Popular Army of Liberation inside the city, along with the residences of the principal military and political leaders. Finally, it provided an estimate of enemy strength in the city: rebel strength was 1,500 to 2,700 men, of which only 10 percent were considered effective, though all were armed in some fashion with semiautomatic and Mauser rifles. The rebels had 1,500 men on the south bank and the rest around Camp Ketele, on the north bank just east of Stanleyville.[49] According to Vandewalle, who received a copy from a fellow Belgian officer, the report ended with the following:

> The European population requires an airborne/airland attack on Stanleyville airfield with a simultaneous neutralization of Camp Ketele and its approaches. Accordingly, all ideas to bomb Stanleyville without thinking of immediate occupation would cost the lives of a large number of people who would be killed as hostages.[50]

General Adams was thinking along the same lines. Furthermore, he recognized that the rebels seemed more competent in defensive operations and that to attack and hold Stanleyville until government forces arrived would require a substantially stronger force than earlier conceived. Adams' proposed plan, OPLAN 519 High Beam—renumbered and renamed due to a security compromise—went to the JCS on 19 October at 0725Z.[51]

High Beam was both a rescue and a knockout punch against the rebellion. It would open, after ten minutes of aerial preparation by four F-4 fighter-bombers, with a multiple-drop-zone airborne assault by one battalion. As in the earlier planning for a two-company assault, Adams still did not know the exact locations of the Westerners. Consequently, he intended to invest the city from all axes as quickly as possible. With continuous air cover, Adams planned to place two companies north and east of the city, while the remainder of the battalion seized the airfield. If required, he planned to bring the second battalion in thirty-five minutes after the first. The assault companies would evacuate all Americans and any other non-Congolese who wished to leave (see map 6).[52]

High Beam was more than just an evacuation operation. Adams hoped to end the rebellion with it. One assault company was ordered to capture Olenga, Soumialot, and any other key leaders; another was to raise the flag on the American consulate. Meanwhile, American troops, equipped with tapes in Lingala and French, were to seize Radio Stanleyville and broadcast appeals to end the rebellion.[53]

The CWG and Ambassador Godley were hostile to High Beam. Though the JCS ultimately approved the plan on 12 November, the CWG rejected it as military overkill; some members began calling Adams "the Big Hawk."

Map 6. OPLAN 519 High Beam

Godley also argued against such a large operation; he remained in favor of a two-company assault.[54] The diplomats were not ready to face the military realities of an operation in Stanleyville.

As if to confirm the reluctance of the CWG to consider military action, Ambassador Palmer flew to Belgium to reaffirm the Harriman-Spaak strategy. Palmer and Spaak agreed to maintain firm control on Tshombe's military campaign. They hoped that this control would allow the United States and Belgium to resurrect the international effort to mediate an end to the crisis.[55] They were too late.

Inside Stanleyville, the defeat of rebels by Tshombe's mercenaries had changed the situation. Tension among the rebels over the use of the hostages led to continual discontent among the ruling triumvirate of Gbenye, Soumialot, and Olenga. Olenga pressed his superiors to use the foreigners as a bargaining ploy, and they gave into his demands. Soumialot turned the hostage weapon against Belgium on 19 October by making veiled threats against thirty Belgian children in the city. Known to be out of the city in the middle of the month, Gbenye returned to Stanleyville on 24 October with a "captured US Major," Dr. Paul Carlson, as his latest bargaining chip. Carlson, an American doctor, had been taken by the Simbas in Ubangi province and now became a symbol of hatred for the rebels. The major change came on 28 October, when the Simbas arrested all Belgians and Americans. Gbenye publicly announced the arrests the next day, and on 31 October, Olenga issued an order that "all Americans and Belgians should be guarded in a secure place. In case the region is bombarded, exterminate them all without explanation."[56]

The Belgian response to the 28 October decree from Stanleyville and the subsequent arrests was slow in building. On the day after the announcement, Lieutenant Colonel Bouzin, the Belgian adviser to the Congolese air force, approached the American air attaché with a proposal to use two Belgian paratroop battalions, airlifted in American C-130s, to seize Stanleyville. Bouzin's activist proposal was atypical; the reaction among the Belgian press and business community was muted. A rebel announcement on 5 November that the Westerners were prisoners of war cooled fears that the hostages would be slaughtered out of hand and raised hopes that the Red Cross or the UN might intervene to avert a massacre.[57]

The American response to the arrest order was similar to that of the Belgians. The CWG recognized that the Belgians were now directly involved in the hostage crisis. With their standing order to keep Belgium out front in dealing with the Congo, the arrest of Belgians in Stanleyville made CWG policy more achievable. Like the Belgians, the CWG analysts and diplomats seized on the prisoners of war announcement as an indication of the rebels' willingness to negotiate.[58]

If the rebels were actually interested in negotiations, the march of L'Ommengang on 1 November ended that doubtful possibility. After a month of frustrating delays, Vandewalle unleashed his drive on Stanleyville. From Kongolo, Lima I, the lead column under Lieutenant Colonel Albert

Liegeois, drove north against scattered resistance through Kibombo to seize Kindu on 5 November.

With his interpreter, Sergeant Sam Wiesel, Lieutenant Colonel Rattan accompained Liegeois and witnessed the assault. Liegeois' attack, while a brilliant victory for L'Ommengang, demonstrated that rebel promises to adhere to the Geneva Convention were worthless; as Liegeois pushed the rebels back, they began to kill their hostages. In Kibombo, the men of L'Ommengang found two dead Europeans and another dying. Based on the last words of the mortally wounded individual, Liegeois ordered a night march to reach Kindu to prevent a similar slaughter of 100 Westerners. Liegeois succeeded and the hostages were saved, but the reports out of Kindu ended the complacent mood in Washington and Brussels.[59]

Ferret driver, Wiesel, and Frenchy

Following the seizure of Kindu, analysts from the State Department flew in to debrief the rescued Europeans, whose reports were harrowing. In the days preceding Lima I's attack, the rebels had collected over seventy Europeans in Kindu, some from as far away as Punia. As the government column drew closer, the rebels became increasingly unstable and their threats against the hostages correspondingly more bloodthirsty. By the morning of 5 November, the rebels were ready to systematically kill the Westerners. That morning, the rebels took all the male hostages out into the street, stripped them to their underwear, and prepared to execute them.

L'Ommengang's assault saved the hostages. Liegeois used his close air support to disrupt the rebels' defense of the city. A B-26 conducted strafing runs on identifiable targets and buzzed the city while the ground column launched its attack. Terrified of air attacks, the rebels broke and ran for cover, abandoning their hostages. In the lull between the air attack and ground assault, the Westerners were able to hide from their hysterical captors.[60] The reports issuing from Kindu emphasized the need for close air support, followed by rapid ground action, and the continued use of close air support as a psychological weapon to disrupt the rebels.

Young mercenary recruit at Kindu (with Simba bodies in a canoe in the background)

Until the 5 November incident, deaths of Europeans at the hands of the Simbas could be attributed to spontaneous acts of revenge. But in Kindu, the attempted massacre had been planned, organized, and almost executed in the face of the ground attack. One report warned: "Europeans in Stanleyville are in for very hard times unless attack can be pressed with maximum speed, preferably with paratroopers. They all convinced that Europeans would be massacred if Stanleyville bombed. They kept repeating need for speed, since real danger is *jeunesse* who are violent in their hatred of whites."[61]

Urgently responding to the Kindu reports, Paul-Henri Spaak met with Averell Harriman in Washington on 8 November. Spaak proposed a combined operation to rescue the non-Congolese in Stanleyville, suggesting that the United States provide the airlift for a Belgian paratroop force that would conduct the intervention. Spaak's proposal probably came after some American prompting, as a week later, Ambassador MacArthur cabled from Brussels that Spaak "has come a long way since last weekend when we pressed him hard to assume the heavy political responsibility of using Belgian paratroops to free Americans, Belgians, and others."[62]

Harriman and Spaak's agreement to plan a combined operation did not represent an American-Belgian consensus on an overall approach to the Congo. Nonetheless, Spaak now became the driving force behind a combined operation to save the Belgian citizens who were directly threatened. Spaak cynically considered any rebel offers to negotiate to be mere stall tactics as they waited in hopes of receiving radical or Communist aid against Leopoldville. Moreover, further U.S. contacts with the rebels—in particular through their negotiator in Nairobi, Thomas Kanza—would be viewed with Belgian disfavor.[63]

For Spaak, the idea of open intervention in the Congo was a political bombshell. Memories of the 1960 intervention and its resultant uproar still troubled Belgian relations with Africa. Moreover, Spaak had to consider the possible effects of any such operation on those Belgians outside the Stanleyville area. Still, he carried through with the idea of a combined operation upon his return to Brussels, where, supported by his deputy Davignon, he met with Prime Minister Théo Lefevre. Next, Spaak met with Defense Minister Segers, and lastly, King Baudouin; all accepted Spaak's proposal after a review of the events at Kindu. At last, Belgium was ready to accept the risks entailed in protecting its citizens in the Congo.[64]

The American viewpoint was much more complex. While activists such as Adams and Godley advocated increased support for military action against the rebels, the CWG grasped at any opportunity to negotiate an end to the crisis. At the same time, the CWG wanted to keep American visibility in the planned military operation at a minimum. Thus, the CWG's attention remained riveted on its international peacekeeping efforts rather than on the military implications of planning a rescue in Stanleyville.[65]

After Spaak's return to Belgium, McGeorge Bundy, Dean Rusk, Robert McNamara, and Cyrus Vance made a trip to President Johnson's ranch. There, the president gave them permission to go through with planning an operation. Johnson, however, retained control over the decision to execute; that decision would be reluctantly given.[66]

Like its predecessor in August, the second Harriman-Spaak meeting marked a change in the American and Belgian approach to the Congo. Where their earlier talks created a greater unity between the two allies, the second talks represented a divergence in the two countries' policies—a divergence that would effect the planning and execution of Dragon Rouge.

A Belgian Crisis 3

On 10 November, at President Johnson's bidding, the JCS sent orders to United States European Command (USEUCOM) to assemble a planning team from the United States Air Force Europe (USAFE) and the 8th Infantry Division. By 11 November, this American team was in Brussels to meet with their Belgian counterparts. Brigadier General Russell E. Dougherty, USAF, from USEUCOM operations, headed the team. Lieutenant Colonel James L. Gray, from USAFE's Directorate of Operations and Training, and Captain Bobby F. Brashears, 8th Infantry Division, were Dougherty's subordinates. Lieutenant Colonel James E. Dunn, the JCS action officer on the CWG, completed the team.[1]

Significantly, USSTRICOM was not represented. When Bouzin proposed a combined operation, General Adams had demanded that his command be involved. When the JCS sent orders out for the Brussels conference, Adams had been an information addressee. But his immediate request to send planners to Brussels was denied on the grounds that the operation was to be Belgian, with the United States only providing airlift.[2]

General Dougherty's operational guidance from the JCS was to keep the operation small. At least at this stage, the CWG did not want a Belgian version of Adams' High Beam. Furthermore, the American planning team was forbidden to discuss any American unilateral plans; the guidance prohibited giving any indication that the United States would consider committing troops to the Congo. Instead, Dougherty's instructions specified that the operation should be planned around a one-company, non-American force.[3]

The American military planners in Brussels began the conference with several handicaps. First, their charter placed greater emphasis on what they could not do, rather than on what they could. Second, only one member of the team, Dunn, had any in-depth knowledge of the Congo crisis. Dunn had seen Adams' plans, and he had been exposed to the voluminous reporting on Stanleyville. However, Dunn was in Brussels as a member of the CWG; his job was to enforce its wishes. Therefore, Dougherty's team would have to rely heavily on the experience of their Belgian counterparts to plan a rescue of the Westerners.

Fortunately, the Belgian planning team represented a great deal of experience in the Congo. Colonel Robert Louvigny, head of the team and designated chief coordinator for all Belgian activities concerning the intervention, was the current chief of staff for the Belgian Joint Staff. Louvigny had commanded the air base at Kamina and was intimately familiar with its support capabilities. Colonel Charles Laurent, commander of the Belgian Paracommando Regiment, accompanied Louvigny. Laurent, a prisoner of war in World War II, was an experienced soldier who had led the 1st Parachute Battalion into the Congo during the 1960 intervention and had jumped on Stanleyville's airport during routine training exercises. Other Belgian planners participated at various times during the conference: Colonel Vivario, secretary to the ministry of defense; Colonel Monmaert, defense attaché to Leopoldville; Lieutenant Colonel Matteys, attaché to the ministry of defense; Lieutenant Colonel Dargent, joint staff operations; Lieutenant Colonel Janssens, second in command of the Paracommando Regiment; and Adjutant Ernest Dumont, the regimental sergeant major.[4] As in the case of Louvigny and Laurent, most, if not all, were old Congo hands. Regrettably, only Monmaert had any experience in the post-1960 Congo.

Both the Americans and the Belgians came into the planning session with certain parameters already established. Planners on both sides understood that each country would retain command of its own forces in the operation. Futhermore, the brunt of U.S. involvement would be to support a one-company Belgian force, with any mention of American unilaterial plans forbidden. Underlying these operational assumptions was the firm belief that the Belgians, on the basis of their experience, understood more about the Congo and would be able to do more with less. Hence the idea of using one Belgian company.[5]

Both parties planned while unaware of conditions in the Congo. The Americans were hampered by their inexperience and ignorance of the realities of the Congo. Much worse, however, the Belgians came into the conference with the paternalistic confidence of 1960, exemplified by Laurent, who, upon hearing of the proposed operation, exclaimed, "I say we should just jump on Stan and take them [the hostages] out!"[6] Isolated from events in the Congo, nothing could challenge Belgian overconfidence.

Even as the conference began, another government suggested a plan similar to Adams' High Beam. On 12 November, emissaries of the United Kingdom made simultaneous approaches to the American and Belgian governments in Washington, Brussels, and Leopoldville. The most specific proposal came in Brussels, where the British chargé d'affaires offered his government's participation in any combined planning concerning Stanleyville. More pointedly, he stated that his government, with the sanction of the Belgian and American governments, was prepared to intervene unilaterally. The British had a force of two airborne battalions supported by thirty-six aircraft "prepared to go at any time." The next day, the British, after learning of the Belgian-American plans, withdrew their offer. Though they remained supportive of the operation, the British—like Adams, Wheeler, and Bouzin—viewed two battalions as the minimum force necessary to complete the operation.[7]

The next two days of planning were long ones for all the participants. Discussions first centered on the ways and means of the operation. Laurent recognized that the size of his force depended on the available aircraft, but he was surprised when the Americans expected him to be satisfied with only one company. Fortunately, Ambassador MacArthur agreed with Colonel Laurent and indicated that the Belgians would, indeed, need a larger force. The State Department questioned this but allowed the decision to stand, and when the Americans indicated that one squadron of sixteen C-130Es was available, Laurent was able to plan for a battalion-size operation. With an operational rate of 75 percent, the sixteen available C-130Es would just meet the Belgian requirement for twelve aircraft.[8]

Next, discussions centered on staging the force into the area of operations. In spite of known State Department opposition, the Americans and the Belgians favored Wheelus Air Base in Libya as the immediate point of departure for the operation. Ascension Island, the alternative, was not American territory, nor did it have the facilities for handling a large air movement. Again, the State Department intervened and, as in the case of High Beam, succeeded in overruling the use of Wheelus (see map 7).[9]

The choice of Ascension Island seriously affected the question of staging bases inside the Congo. While the debate had raged over High Beam's staging routes, General Lyman Lemnitzer, the commander in chief of USEUCOM (CINCEUR), pointed out the danger of staging directly from Ascension Island without refueling. So now that Ascension had been selected, the planners needed a base inside the Congo, something the Belgians had wished to avoid. The planners' choices were either Leopoldville or Kamina. Kamina was selected because of its better security position inside the Congo. But since the planners expected to execute the operation from a standing start in Belgium, the additional flight time required to stage through Ascension *and* Kamina would add critical hours to the forces' reaction time.[10]

Another area of concern addressed by the planners was the lack of operational intelligence on Stanleyville. The officers, evidently based on the State Department's estimate, expected around 800 non-Congolese in the city. To gain further intelligence, the planners requested very early that aerial reconnaissance be conducted over the city, as available photography dated back to 1958. While the Americans expected the Belgians to have an adequate collection of maps, they were surprised at the poor quality of maps the Belgians used; better maps would be provided by the United States. Neither did the planning team have an accurate idea of the location of the hostages; they only knew where the hostages might be located. Both parties in the planning assumed that the Belgians' familiarity with Stanleyville would offset these intelligence deficiencies.[11]

One of the major operational issues to be resolved was the selection of the drop zone. The Belgians favored using the golf course between the air-

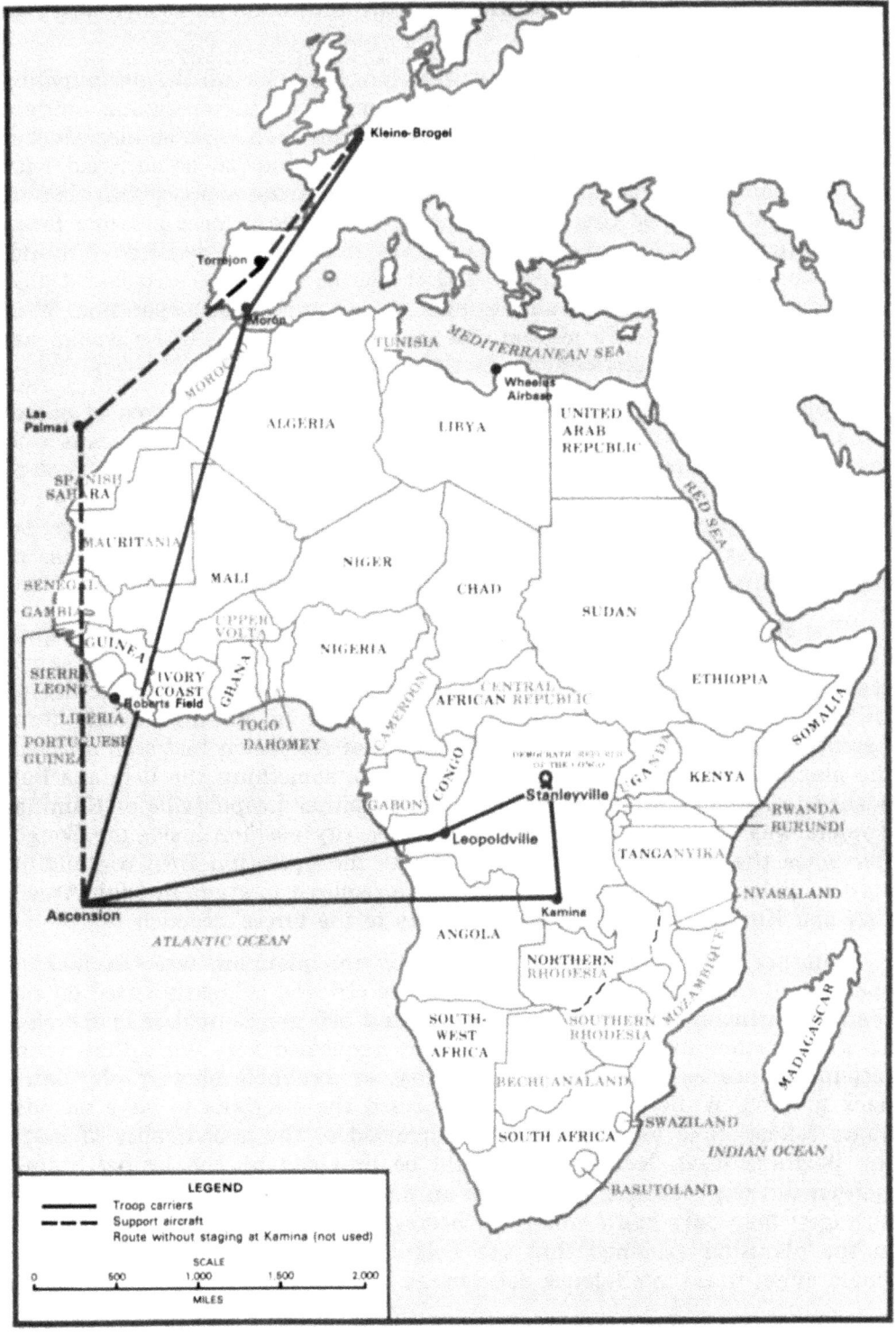

Map 7. Dragon Rouge air routes

field and the city, avoiding enemy resistance believed present around the airport. In using the golf course, the Belgians planned to drop in sixteen-man sticks* at the direction of a Belgian jumpmaster on the flight deck of each aircraft. The Americans, specifically Dunn, Gray, and Brashears, all favored the airfield as the drop zone. The paras could jump on the easily recognizable airstrip in one pass and assemble to clear and control the airport. The Belgians remained unconvinced, and the issue was not resolved until the combined task force was en route to Africa.[12]

The CIA, under the coordinating guidance of Lieutenant Colonel Bouzin, would provide close air support for the operation using T-28s and B-26s already in the Congo. However, the Americans and Belgians wanted only defensive close air support; there would be no offensive preparation of the drop zone.[13] The specific details of the close air support, like those of the airborne procedure, were resolved later.

The planners also had to consider certain special requirements for the operation. Intelligence indicated that the airstrip might be blocked by fuel drums, wrecked cars, or worse. They feared the strip might be blockaded by "dog collars," long metal strips with foot-long spikes used to control vehicular movement, which would play havoc with landing aircraft. To help clear the runway, the planners added stable brooms to the packing list, and they also added bullhorns to facilitate gathering and controlling the hostages.[14]

Further concern arose over the Paracommando's lack of mobility and medical support. Laurent had planned to take four Minerva armored jeeps and four communications jeeps. The planners added an additional twelve AS-24 motorized tricycles, which could be used for reconnaissance and light transport duty. More medical support was another obvious requirement, and the Americans agreed to supply an emergency medical team along with medical supplies. The Belgians also planned to reinforce their organic medical staff from within the Paracommando Regiment and the military hospital at D'Anvers.[15]

So the Belgians could communicate with the American aircraft, they asked the American planners to provide radios suitable for ground-to-air communications and personnel to train the Belgian operators in their use. Additional communications support in the form of a "Talking Bird" C-130 from USAFE would be attached to the task force. Finally, the Belgian Navy was to supply additional communications support for the intervention.[16]

Like all operations, the intervention in Stanleyville demanded logistical support. USAFE was to airlift the bulk of the required supplies, including additional air items, rations, and ammunition. JTF LEO was also to support the operation. Moreover, to facilitate refueling at Kamina, C-124s would airlift an F-6 refueling truck into the base ahead of the task force. The Belgians also recognized the need for improving the forward support at Kamina, and they planned to dispatch an advance team of jumpmasters to the base.[17]

---

*Sticks are men dropped for each pass of an aircraft.

Since the operation was a combined operation by a force controlled by two national authorities, the planners had to develop some scheme of command and control palatable to both countries. It was decided that en route to Stanleyville, operational control would remain with the American airlift commander. Over the drop zone, that control would pass to Colonel Laurent, while in each aircraft, the Belgian jumpmasters would decide on when to execute. The command and control arrangements provided for a cooperative, rather than a combined, operation. However, decisions made on the American side complicated the command and control. Even though USSTRICOM had been prohibited from participating in the conference, Dougherty recommended that CINCSTRIKE (i.e., Adams, commander of USSTRICOM) be responsible for the operation, a recommendation that Adams would find particularly irritating. Ultimately, General Dougherty and Colonel Louvigny signed the planning agreements for the combined operation, and the planning conference broke up on 13 November, with each side beginning active preparations.[18]

On 14 November, USEUCOM published Special OPLAN 319/64 under the title Dragon Rouge, a code name selected by Colonel Laurent. Laurent picked the name with the vision of a dragon whose flaming breath would be represented by the red berets of the Paracommandos and whose sinuous body would be made up of an airstream of C-130s, an appropriate choice as it reflected the very style of the operation: a Belgian show with American support.[19]

OPLAN 319/64 called for Dragon Rouge's execution in three broad phases. In the first (en route) phase, the United States would employ twelve C-130E aircraft to transport a Belgian paratroop battalion of around 545 men, 8 jeeps, and 12 AS-24 tricycles from Kleine-Brogel Air Base in Belgium through Spain, Ascension Island, Kamina, and then on to Stanleyville. Largely an American responsibility, this phase rested on detailed planning for staged movement.[20] One of the major difficulties in planning the phase was to balance the question of timing with that of security.

As in the planning conference, the operation plan stressed security throughout. Based on the assumption that an execution order would be issued while the Dragon force was in Belgium, the Belgians would not be able to muster their force without attracting attention. They dismissed the use of an active deception plan because it might attract attention to the operation rather than diffuse it. Consequently, the American planners accepted a Belgian deception plan that rested simply on the story that, if a compromise occurred, the force represented a "Joint US/Belgian Long Range Airborne Training Exercise." Since neither military had been participants in such an exercise prior to this operation, the story was weak. In any case, the Belgians needed at least twelve hours after notification to begin the air movement. At this time, however, they did not envision the execution signal being given before 17 November, two days before Vandewalle would resume L'Ommengang.[21]

The Americans felt that the secrecy of the operation could be best maintained by night movement through critical areas such as Belgium, Spain, and the Congo. On the other hand, the American aircrews required daylight to land at Ascension Island. Accounting for these factors and for refueling in Spain, Ascension, and Kamina, planners calculated that it would take twenty-eight hours from the time the first aircraft landed at Kleine-Brogel until the last aircraft delivered its cargo at Stanleyville.[22]

The Belgian requirement for twelve hours' notification increased that time to forty hours. Security requirements, mentioned earlier, mandated that the first launch from Kleine-Brogel be completed by 1840Z. Coupled with the twelve-hour notification, this launch time made it clear that the decision to launch would have to be made before 0640Z, of any given day, to avoid a further eighteen-hour delay. In other words, if the United States and Belgium decided to intervene and issued the order at 0740Z, the force could not be over Stanleyville until sixty-three hours later,[23] a lag that soon disturbed those concerned with issuing the execution order.

The assault phase was the second major phase under OPLAN 319/64. Once the paras were over their target, Colonel Laurent, as the airborne force commander, was the responsible officer. Laurent had approached the problem of taking Stanleyville in a systematic manner and in doing so developed a priority of tasks that served as the principles for Dragon Rouge and subsequent planning. These principles were

- parachute on the airfield.
- take the airport.
- clear the runway.
- land vehicles and reinforcements.
- block routes from the city.
- liberate and protect the hostages.
- evacuate the hostages by air.[24]

Using these principles, Laurent outlined his concept for taking Stanleyville. He planned to assault the airfield in an airborne operation using 320 men from 5 C-130s, followed by the airlanding of his vehicles and then his remaining troops. OPLAN 319/64 gave his concept:

> Belgian paratroop commander presently plans for air assault element to form into three groups to accomplish initial task as follows:
>
> A. Block and control road leading to airport
> B. Clear and occupy tower and Sabena Guest House
> C. Clear airfield
>
> ... Immediately following airstrip clearing and arrival of radio and armored jeeps, paratroopers will proceed into city proper to other known areas of hostage imprisonment. As additional personnel and motorized equipment are available, he plans to broaden his penetration into city and consolidate his initial probing action.[25]

In planning for the third phase, that of airlanding and redeployment, OPLAN 319/64 covered several additional details. Planners believed that the Stanleyville Airport could accommodate no more than three C-130s at any given time. Consequently, aircraft numbers eight, nine, and eleven were to plan for quick off-loads, while six, seven, ten, and twelve would have more time to off-load equipment. Aircraft number twelve was designated as the medical evacuation aircraft, while six, seven, and ten would remain on the ground for up to an hour and one-half with their engines running for loading refugees. JTF LEO would conduct further refugee evacuation as the Dragon aircraft recovered and refueled at Leopoldville to return to Europe via Wheelus.[26]

OPLAN 319/64 also addressed the American command and control issues. CINCEUR would pass operational control of the assault airlift force to CINCSTRIKE upon its closure into Kamina. CINCSTRIKE would maintain that control through the assault phase and through redeployment from Leopoldville. At that time, operational control would return to CINCEUR. The operational control discussed in the plan dealt strictly with the American assault airlift force and not with the combined task force. This difference would lead to friction during the operation.[27]

Even as USEUCOM published OPLAN 319/64, the plan came under fire from different sides. In fact, even before the plan was complete, the CWG had questioned some of its content in a way that reflected the CWG's preoccupation with political affairs. When the question arose over staging areas, the CWG wanted the force to stage from three locations within the Congo as the method least politically objectionable. The same line of thought gave rise to the idea of using a one-company force to rescue an estimated 800 Westerners, an estimate that seems to have been deliberately numbered too small. Though the CWG succeeded in forcing the use of Ascension for both prepositioning and withdrawal, the Belgians held fast to the use of one battalion. The CWG's preoccupation with the use of minimum force, however, prevented that group from asking if one battalion was in fact sufficient.[28]

Military leaders also questioned OPLAN 319/64. Confused by the cooperative nature of the mission, General Lemnitzer wanted to know who would actually make the operational decision to execute once a political commitment had been made. The answer that Colonel Laurent would shoulder that responsibility satisfied General Lemnitzer, but the atmosphere at MacDill Air Force Base was less enthusiastic about OPLAN 319/64.[29]

General Adams, sitting at USSTRICOM headquarters and irritated by his exclusion from the planning conference, did not like any part of OPLAN 319/64—in particular its command and control. On 16 November, he sent the JCS a cable detailing his concerns. As the executive officer of the 1st Special Service Force during World War II, Adams understood airborne assault operations, and he did not like the plan for this one.

Adams pointed out that delivering Laurent's force in twelve-man sticks would waste precious time in getting the assault force on the ground and argued for a mass assault. The American experience in World War II had shown that successful assembly of an airborne force was dependent on its delivery en masse, which increased its striking power. Adams feared that using an independent execution signal for each aircraft would scatter the assault force. Laurent's force was small enough without having a third of it up in the air waiting to land behind the C-130s carrying the armored jeeps. The Big Hawk's next thrust hit at the heart of OPLAN 319/64: "The plan insofar as we can read it provides for the first probes to be in Stanleyville, H Plus One and One Half hours. Thus the interval of time between assault and contact with hostages is more than ample for execution, or spiriting away the hostages."[30] Adams' timing of an hour and one-half was only ten minutes too generous as events later proved.

Even the USEUCOM plan for the airlift assault force drew criticism from Adams. Commenting that the C-130s would make excellent targets for the two antiaircraft weapons believed located at the airfield, he called for an airstrike on the field to prevent the loss of any of the C-130s, each of which were loaded with sixty-four paras. Neither did Adams care for the routing described in the plan, especially the use of Kamina. He disagreed with Lemnitzer's contention that staging directly from Ascension, without stopping in the Congo, was infeasible.[31] Overall, Adams spelled out his frustration with the situation thusly:

> Since this command has not been permitted to participate in the planning for DRAGON ROUGE in spite of our offer to do so, and in view of planning arrangements which did obtain for all deployment and employing [employment] planning for Operation DRAGON ROUGE and the importance of an understanding in detail with the Belgians as regards respective US and Belgian responsibilities and authorities... recommend that USCINCEUR retain operational command of US airlift forces throughout entire operation, including the airborne assault. Regardless of final command arrangements, this command will provide the support enumerated in [OPLAN 319/64].[32]

Generals do not lay down responsibilities easily, particularly generals with Adams' long experience. He attempted once more to impress his viewpoint upon the JCS:

> In view of the considerable planning experience gained in [this] command concerning the problem of liberation of U.S. nationals and the security of all non-Congolese in Stanleyville, it is my belief that the best chance of success now lies in the continued vigorous execution of the Van Der Valle [Vandewalle] operation, and the coordinated execution of OPLAN LOW BEAM repeat LOW BEAM. In the event that these actions should fail to achieve objectives, OPLAN HIGH BEAM should be immediately implemented.[33]

Neither the JCS nor the CWG heeded Adams. In a note written on the White House copy of Adams' message, an unidentified staffer scribbled, "Gen. McPherson [the JCS, J-5 and] Harriman talked re [in reference to] this, military will work out with CINCSTRIKE. No substance of importance involved."[34]

General Lemnitzer, however, sought to ease the strained relations between USSTRICOM, the JCS, and USEUCOM. He recommended that Adams assume operational control of the assault airlift force at Ascension or Kamina. Adams and the JCS agreed, and Adams dispatched a liaison officer to

Ascension Island. More importantly, Adams pulled the communications annex out of OPLAN High Beam to use in support of Dragon Rouge.[35]

As the concept for Dragon Rouge evolved into a planning document, the commanders involved prepared for its execution. Both Belgians and Americans faced difficulties in shifting from peacetime to operational duties. Belgian preparations naturally centered on the Paracommando Regiment, a unit with a short but proud military history. The Paracommandos, or paras as they referred to themselves, became a single regiment in 1952. The *1er Bataillon Parachutiste SAS,* which evolved from the 1st Belgian SAS Squadron of World War II, and the *1er Bataillon Commando,* formerly a troop of the 10th Interallied Commando, were unified and redesignated as the Belgian Paracommando Regiment. Many of its members had served with the Belgian contingent in Korea. During the next eight years, the regiment served both as a NATO unit and as the Belgian Army's principal shock force in the Congo. In 1964, the regiment consisted of three battalions: the 1st Parachute Battalion, the 2d Commando Battalion, and the 3d Parachute Battalion. In addition, the regiment contained a regimental headquarters, the Commando Training Center, and the Parachute Training Center. Despite the different unit designations, each battalion received the same training and missions.[36]

Training in the Paracommando Regiment was based on the Belgian system of national service. As young Belgian draftees entered the service, they had the opportunity of volunteering for the elite regiment, subject to their passing a screening and selection process. Once in their unit, they received two months' training, after which they earned the right to wear their unit berets, red for the Paracommandos and green for the Commandos. Following this initial unit training, the trainees split into two groups and alternated between the Parachute Training Center and the Commando Training Center. After their completion of both training courses, the volunteers achieved the status of Paracommandos and served another full year on active duty.[37]

Since the soldiers entered the regiment at different levels, each battalion was at a different level of training when OPLAN 319/64 was published. Only the 1st Parachute Battalion was fully qualified with ten and one-half months of service. The 2d Commando Battalion had four months' training but had not completed its equipment jumps at the Parachute Training Center, and the 3d Parachute Battalion had only two weeks' training as a unit. Therefore, the 1st Parachute Battalion was to provide the bulk of the forces for Dragon Rouge.[38]

As their regimental commander, Colonel Laurent realized that the 1st Parachute Battalion would provide most of his task force, but there were other considerations. Each battalion had only two active rifle companies, with a third reserve company. Laurent could not activate the reserve company without parliamentary approval, and such an action would certainly draw unwelcome attention to the regiment. In fact, he considered mobilizing the recent veterans of the 3d Parachute Battalion, who had been released from active service in mid-October. Again, however, legal and security requirements made such a step inadvisable. Consequently, Laurent turned to the 2d Commando Battalion to provide his third rifle company. The 12th Company, under Captain Luc Raes, had completed all its training with the exception of equipment jumps. Laurent decided to airland it to back up his main airborne assault, but it would jump only if needed. Therefore, the majority of Laurent's force would be inexperienced draftees.[39]

From the beginning of the planning for Dragon Rouge, Laurent recognized the mission's political implications. When first notified, he never expected to execute the operation: there were just too many complications, too many political traps inherent in a return to the Congo. Based on his 1960 experience in seizing Ndjili Airport at Leopoldville, Laurent could not believe that Belgium would again intervene. While the planning conference convinced the doughty colonel that the intervention would occur, it also drove home to him the significance of political factors associated with the operation. This it effected through its negotiations over the size of the force and the question of staging. By the time Laurent was prepared to mobilize his own unit, he recognized that the paras would not be going to Stanleyville "to make war but rather to conduct a humanitarian rescue."[40]

Laurent's meetings with Foreign Minister Spaak and Defense Minister Segers reinforced this conclusion. On 15 November, Spaak told Laurent, "Colonel, you realize how delicate your mission is. There can be no mistakes, world opinion will not stand for a large-scale slaughter of blacks in the Congo." Thus counseled by Spaak to avoid native casualties, Laurent met with Segers on 17 November, who cautioned him not to lose any men, since Belgium was not at war and public opinion would not countenance the loss of young draftees in another Congo venture. Segers also reminded him to avoid killing too many natives, but, "if possible, to save the hostages."[41]

Laurent, faced with the nature of his mission, had to make certain concessions regarding its style and the use of his troops. As his mission was to seize Stanleyville and rescue the hostages, independent of Vandewalle's ground column, Laurent needed to get a large body of troops on the ground and into the city as rapidly as possible. In Adams' view, this mission required the use of multiple drop zones and forces converging from all axes to cordon and penetrate the city. Instead, Laurent had developed a conservative plan to seize the city in stages. He could not risk losing his young volunteers to a concerted Simba attack. Nor could he use air strikes to suppress Simba defenses, for that would entail heavy Congolese casualties and possibly casualties among any hostages near the airport. What Laurent planned for was a reliance on his career soldiers, who could be risked more easily than the regimental draftees.[42]

Laurent used his regiment's professional soldiers to ready it for Dragon Rouge. He established a special regimental staff to direct the operation. Major BEM Jacques Rousseaux, currently the commanding officer of the 2d Commando Battalion, became his chief of staff. A veteran of Korea, Rousseaux got the job as chief of staff to facilitate his assumption of command of the 2d Commando Battalion, if the Belgian Joint Staff reinforced the strike force. Major BEM Roger Hardenne was Laurent's operations officer. Commandant Jacques Holvoet also secured a place on the rolls for Dragon Rouge, as the force's civil affairs officer. Laurent's men with real operational experience, however, came from the Parachute Training Center.[43]

Major Georges Ledant of the Parachute Training Center provided an elite element to the Dragon Rouge assault force. All of the jumpmasters assigned to Ledant's command were experienced soldiers, most of whom had soldiered in the Congo. Though each battalion had its own jumpmasters, Laurent tasked Ledant to provide a cadre of sixteen officers and sergeants to handle the jumpmaster responsibilities on the C-130s. The regiment normally utilized Belgian Air Force C-119s and had never jumped from C-130s, and Laurent felt that the thousands of jumps represented in the instructor cadre would ease the transition. He further tasked the Parachute Training Center to provide the advance support element at Kamina. While all these responsibilities were normal for Ledant's men, Colonel Laurent had other ideas for their operational employment. He intended to use them as mobile elements to seek out the hostages independent of the main force operation.[44]

Once his troop list was complete, Laurent's next task was to muster his forces. The 1st Parachute Battalion had peacetime commitments. The 13th Company, along with the battalion's 4.2-inch mortar platoon, was on guard duty at the Royal Palace, where a parade was scheduled for Sunday, 15 November. The remainder of the 1st Parachute Battalion, along with the 2d Commando Battalion, were due to go on normal weekend pass. Laurent directed that the 14th Company, 2d Commando Battalion, assume the palace guard duty, and at 1300 local time, on 15 November, the 1st Parachute Battalion went on alert.[45]

A large strapping individual, Major Jean Mine commanded the 1st Parachute Battalion. Like his regimental commander, Mine had been a prisoner of war during World War II, but unlike Laurent, Mine had escaped and had fought with the Belgian infantry as the Allies retook Europe. After conferring with Laurent on 13 November, Mine returned to his unit with a brief outline of the proposed operation. He immediately convened an orders group to study Laurent's concept of the operation.[46]

Certain conditions made Mine's task in preparing for Dragon Rouge relatively simple. The existence of OPLAN 319/64 reduced operational planning requirements to a minimum. In fact, Mine published his order after the unit's arrival at Ascension Island. His principal task now was to ensure that the unit would be ready to board the aircraft on twelve hours' notice. Since the 1st Parachute Battalion was currently on standby alert as part of NATO's Allied Mobile Force (AMF), preparations, such as medical screening, were complete. The majority of the unit's ammunition and arms was in the garrison, and special requisitions were not necessary. The nature of the regiment's contingency missions also made it easier to conceal the purpose of the alert. As part of the AMF, the regiment had contingency missions for employment in Norway or Turkey, and its issue of hot-weather clothing, quinine, and other items fit the parameters of the Turkish mission. Moreover, inside Belgium, the regiment had a defensive mission to provide security against sabotage around Kleine-Brogel, so a large-scale movement to the air base could be concealed under that contingency.

To increase his combat strength on the ground, Mine made a number of adjustments. He reorganized his headquarters support company into rifle platoons. Furthermore, he stripped both his heavy mortar platoon and transport platoon of their organic equipment. He also reduced his fire support to a single 81-mm mortar and light 60-mm mortars. However, he maintained the full complement of his antiarmor weapons to counter any Simba use of captured ANC armored cars. To take advantage of any vehicles that might be seized in Stanleyville, Mine issued stocks of yellow paint to mark them and set up teams from his transport platoon to hot-wire the vehicles as necessary. Finally, Mine limited the issue of fragmentation grenades to officers and sergeants. In keeping with Laurent's instructions, Mine did not intend to allow indiscriminate killing.[47]

While Mine prepared his reinforced battalion, other Belgian contingents joined the task force. The Belgian armed forces reinforced Laurent's headquarters with the special contingents called for under OPLAN 319/64. Members of an air-ground liaison team consisting of Lieutenant Colonel Steve Cailleau and Lieutenant Jean Dedoncker, Belgian Air Force, joined Laurent's staff to fulfill the Belgian responsibility for controlling the expected close air support. An Air Force photo interpreter, Captain Defreyne, joined the force in expectation of receiving new imagery from American reconnaissance aircraft in the Congo. The last special contingent to report was a three-man surgical detachment commanded by Commandant Herman Moons, from the Belgian military hospital at D'Anvers. This team would deploy to Stanleyville after the assault. Laurent had already taken steps to reinforce Mine's medical assets from the regiment's organic complement. By 16 November, Laurent's regiment was ready.[48]

American preparations for the operation concentrated on providing the necessary airlift. The greatest part of this responsibility went to the 322d Air Division at Evreux, France. Since the mission's parameters dictated long flight legs, C-130Es were the only aircraft capable of meeting these demands. Detachment One of the 322d Air Division had on hand sixteen C-130Es from the Tactical Air Command. The C-130E squadron, currently in Europe as part of the normal rotation of units, was a composite squadron drawn from the 776th and 777th Troop Carrier Squadrons of the 464th Troop Carrier Wing based at Pope Air Force Base, which was also providing the C-130s for JTF LEO.[49] General Robert Foreman, the 322d commander, decided that Colonel Burgess Gradwell, the commander of Detachment One, would command the airlift for Dragon Rouge.

Gradwell, who had just returned from an exercise, received instructions on the evening of 14 November to report the next day to Headquarters, 322d Air Division. When Gradwell walked in the following morning, the operations staff handed him OPLAN 319/64, which he had time to read in detail only once. But as he was an old Congo hand, Gradwell was not surprised at its content. During the UN operations in the Congo, he had flown Irish troops in to help suppress Tshombe's secession, and now he was to fly Belgian troops in to help out the former Katangan leader.[50]

On 15 November, Gradwell met with General Foreman to discuss the operation. Major James E. Poore, USAF air liaison officer to the 8th Infantry and friend of Captain Brashears, accompanied Foreman. A former company commander in the 82d Airborne Division, Poore would serve as a special operations officer for Gradwell's force. The next day, Foreman, Gradwell, and Poore traveled to USAFE headquarters at Wiesbaden for further consultations. At Wiesbaden, Gradwell further clarified his staff's composition. Lieutenant Colonel Eugene Adams, the Tactical Air Command (TAC) representative at Evreux, along with Poore, would serve as operations officers. Lieutenant Colonel Robert Lindsay, commander of the C-130E squadron, would be the mission commander. Captain Donald Strobaugh and Sergeant Robert Dias, members of the Combat Control Team of the 5th Aerial Port Squadron, in addition to helping Poore teach airborne operations procedures in C-130s, were to provide instructions to the Belgians on the use of the American-supplied ground-to-air radios.

Gradwell and his staff worked until midnight on Monday, 16 November. Their biggest problem was in assembling the necessary aircraft. They had decided on twelve primary aircraft, one maintenance aircraft, one spare aircraft, and a "Talking Bird" communications aircraft. In addition to a normal crew, they needed twenty-eight maintenance personnel with spare-part flyaway kits and a spare engine and prop. Many of the needed aircraft were out on missions, one as far away as Libya, and Gradwell's staff had to recall, service, and ready them within twenty-four hours, for by now Gradwell knew that he would be launching for Belgium the next day.[51]

The American commander received additional staff support, one element of which was a three-man public-affairs team under Major John Robinson. For medical support, Lieutenant Colonel George Banning and a medical team readied an emergency medical kit and joined the airlift force at Evreux. They flew to France in the company of Lieutenant Colonel James M. Erdmann.[52]

A member of USAFE's J-2 section, Erdmann was to serve as Gradwell's principal intelligence officer and as the rear detachment commander. Notified of his mission early on 17 November, Erdmann had the next four hours to study the Congo situation. While he crammed on the Simba Rebellion, his assistant, Master Sergeant Walton, prepared an intelligence fly-away kit that included enough tactical commander's terrain analysis maps (TACTA) to supply the assault force down to platoon level. After his hurried study of the situation, Erdmann gathered up Banning's medical team and flew to Evreux. Erdmann arrived in time to attend the mission briefing before the squadron launched for Kleine-Brogel at 1840Z.[53]

The last aircraft flew into Kleine-Brogel by 1955 local, but if Gradwell was anticipating a reception party, he was disappointed. Finally, Erdmann flagged down a passing jeep and hitched a ride to the Base Operations Center. There, a rather short but determined-looking Belgian officer approached him. Offering his hand, the Belgian introduced himself to Erdmann by addressing him as his "new colleague, the USAF Commander." It was a natural mistake, as Colonel Laurent had never met Gradwell or Erdmann. Erdmann quickly introduced the two principals, and a lasting partnership was formed.[54]

While Gradwell and Laurent had prepared their forces and moved them to Kleine-Brogel, a debate over deception planning erupted between the State Department and USEUCOM. In accordance with OPLAN 319/64, the Dragon force was counting on secrecy to cover its movement. While the cover story was thin, the JCS agreed that it was the best available. However, the CWG disagreed, and after devising a complex deception plan, it forced its use on the Dragon force. The new plan called for British aircraft to fly dummy runs into Kleine-Brogel to indicate that the Belgians were engaged in an Anglo-Belgian training exercise. Meanwhile, the American airlift force, using fake flight plans, would slip into Kleine-Brogel and pick up Laurent's force.[55]

The State Department's otherwise commendable plan had several flaws. During peacetime, for safety's sake, air traffic density over Europe made flight plans critical. Consequently, while the pilots could file false plans, they had to file accurate ones simultaneously. The timing of the decision to utilize the new deception plan caused further problems, for by the time the JCS notified CINCEUR, Gradwell's men had already filed true plans. Moreover, diplomatic clearances for the overflights had not been secured from France or Spain. At the direction of CINCEUR, Gradwell launched from Evreux without proper clearance in order to maintain the timing necessary for landing at Ascension. While at Kleine-Brogel, the pilots had to refile false plans according to the JCS directive, and this slowed and confused the deployment.[56]

Ironically, whereas the task force launched from Kleine-Brogel without overflight clearances due to the State Department's last-minute stab at cover planning, the American embassies in Niger and Nigeria nearly destroyed any security the next day. These missions almost asked their host governments for overflight clearances for the task force's return. Fortunately, Ambassador Godley, as an information addressee, recognized the potential security blunder and stopped the requests from going forward. In any case, the deception plan failed, for on the morning of the operation, several European newspapers, sparked by a Belgian Defense Ministry communiqué, reported the troop movement and speculated that it was headed for Africa.[57]

Determination and Doubt   4

While Laurent and Gradwell had worked feverishly to prepare for Dragon Rouge, the CWG and Belgian Foreign Minister Paul-Henri Spaak engaged in a serious debate. After receiving OPLAN 319/64, Spaak reviewed the plan with an eye to events in the Congo. He realized that rebel diplomatic maneuvers in Nairobi were intended to stall matters until military aid reached the rebels. He also recognized that the CWG still cultivated hopes for a diplomatic settlement, which Spaak believed would never occur. Furthermore, Spaak felt that the time requirements for Dragon Rouge's execution from Belgium made a successful operation unlikely. In addition, he knew that no one could anticipate the rebel reactions in Stanleyville for forty hours. With Vandewalle scheduled to begin his final advance on the city on 19 November, Spaak was aware that the following four to five days would become increasingly dangerous for the hostages. He made his fears known to Washington on 14 November, and he recommended that the force be staged forward to either Ascension or Kamina on 17 November.[1]

The CWG was not prepared for Spaak's activist approach. It wanted to witness a "demonstrated imminent peril" to the hostages before initiating Dragon Rouge. But after a two-day debate with Ambassadors MacArthur and Godley—both of whom supported Spaak's proposal—the CWG agreed to move the force to Ascension (see map 8).[2]

The debate over the move to Ascension had far-reaching effects. On the American side, it influenced the CWG not to look on the movement of the Dragon force as a commitment to act. In fact, the CWG returned to its international strategy as the best solution to the crisis. The CWG's adherence to an international strategy had its roots in several related issues. For one thing, rebel leaders in Stanleyville and Nairobi continued to hold out an offer of negotiated settlement to the crisis. Furthermore, Dr. Paul Carlson's plight—that of an American sentenced to die as a spy—encouraged movement toward further negotiations that would render Dragon Rouge unnecessary.[3] Moreover, the CWG agonized over many serious questions provoked by Dragon Rouge. Was the operation's purpose a rescue or an intervention? As indicated in JCSM-788-64, should Dragon Rouge be tied to Vandewalle's assault on the city? Or should it occur in advance of the attack, to preserve its humanitarian nature? Would such a white man's rescue be humanitarian

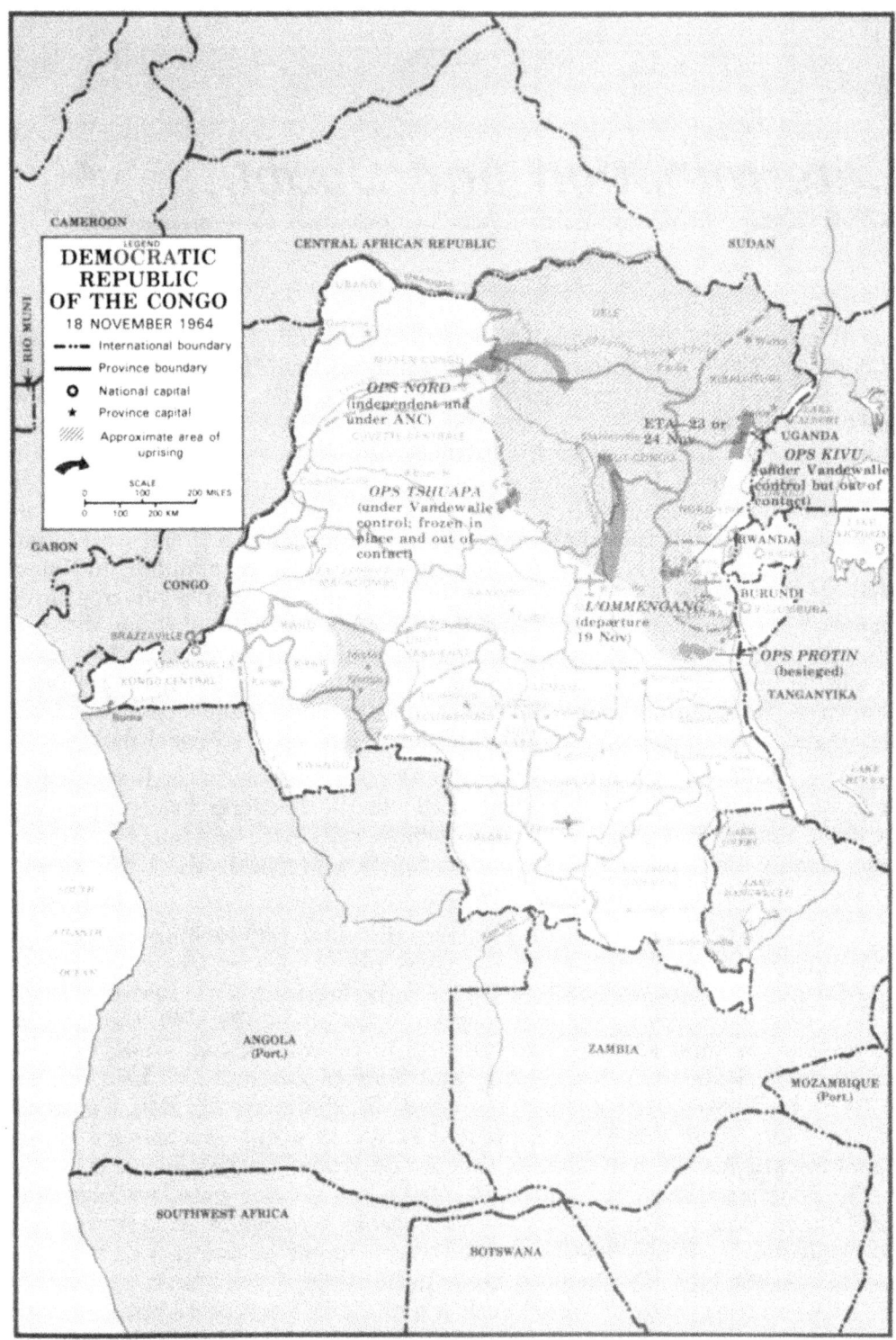

Map 8. Vandewalle plan, 18 November 1964

to the Congolese left behind? How could success be defined in relation to Dragon Rouge?[4] What steps were necessary to build a diplomatic justification for the operation?[5] If Dragon Rouge was executed, what would happen to the remaining foreigners in other areas of the Congo?[6]

The CWG's anguish over the above issues, in some respects, had a positive impact on the ultimate execution of Dragon Rouge. For instance, the indecisiveness of the CWG allowed Spaak to push for deployment to the Ascension Island. In ordering the move to Ascension, the CWG was forced to develop a command and control procedure suitable for initiating the intervention. The procedure—using the code words Big Punch to specify the concurrence of both the United States and Belgium—thus added a delay to the Dragon force's reaction time. This delay would compel the force to deploy to Kamina. Hence, more time had to be allotted for further planning to coordinate a team effort. Furthermore, the delay in decision making made the linkage with Vandewalle inevitable, as it became apparent that his assault on Stanleyville was beyond Washington's or Brussels' control. In addition, the issue of a rescue in Stanleyville forced Belgium and the United States to consider the need for other similar operations. Finally, the CWG's insistence on attempting to negotiate a solution to the crisis also distracted the rebel leaders and forestalled Carlson's execution.[7]

The CWG's struggle with the political implications of Dragon Rouge also had a negative side. From 14 November to 22 November, the CWG became increasingly absorbed in international efforts to resolve the crisis. The last-minute change to the deception plan reflected this trend. The CWG's intrusive political efforts, however, alarmed and angered the Belgians and Congolese involved in the crisis. The CWG's preoccupation with political considerations also caused it to be dilatory in studying the plan for Dragon Rouge.

As the Dragon force assembled and deployed to Ascension Island, other events unfolded. After consultations with Vandewalle on 14 November on the necessity of Dragon Rouge and follow-on operations, the United States and Belgium agreed to hold a second planning conference to consider operations in Bunia, Paulis, and Watsa. The CWG, concerned over Belgian intentions, dispatched John Clingerman, the former consul in Stanleyville, to Brussels to ensure that the rescue of the American officials remained the priority mission of Dragon Rouge.[8] After a brief stay in Brussels, Clingerman flew to Ascension Island to join the force. At the same time, the CWG, after discussions with the White House, decided to pursue negotiations with the rebels in Nairobi. As the CWG hesitated over Dragon Rouge, the CIA pulled the plan for Golden Hawk off the shelf and began to plan its own covert rescue.

Back in September, when General Adams tasked Colonel Mayer to plan for a covert rescue in Stanleyville, Mayer had planned for a military show with some CIA backing. With the shelving of Operation Golden Hawk, the Low Beam option, under the auspices of the CIA, took on new life. According to Thomas Powers, in *The Man Who Kept the Secrets*, the CIA was very concerned over their people in Stanleyville, and a meeting consisting of Director John McCone; Richard Helms, deputy director for plans; Ray Cline, deputy director for intelligence; and two junior officers convened at the CIA headquarters in late October or early November. Cline reportedly supported direct action to extract the American officials, but Powers states that Helms' cautious counsel successfully persuaded McCone that such an operation was impracticable.[9] In fact, Helms' effort was only partially successful. Low Beam was resurrected in official traffic soon afterward.

Like Golden Hawk, Low Beam, as it was discussed in early November, was a covert plan to extract only the official Americans from Stanleyville. Originally designed as a nighttime operation, its target was the Americans supposedly in the Sabena Guest House. Planners evidently decided that such an operation should be a daylight boat assault by the Low Beam force, coordinated with Vandewalle's attack from the southeast. To further distract the rebels, they planned to drop simulators on the airfield while the Low Beam force located the Americans, presumably aided by intelligence gained from a clandestine seizure and interrogation of a guard.[10]

The CWG members were not overly impressed with this concept, but due to their reservations over Dragon Rouge, they agreed that a covert operation might become necessary. Nonetheless, they pointed out the difficulty of successfully coordinating such an operation and the danger if such coordination failed—particularly if movement of the Low Beam team was picked up and transmitted via "jungle drums" to Stanleyville. Instead, the CWG proposed a much simpler plan for accomplishing Low Beam.[11]

Recognizing that Vandewalle might be the first to reach Stanleyville, the CWG felt that the Low Beam team, "led by two foreign documented Americans," should be attached to L'Ommengang during Vandewalle's advance. Their mission was to be the "speediest possible release and protection of five official Americans and subsequently release and roundup of non-official Americans," since in the CWG's view, the "official Americans will be in the greatest danger." The team was to interrogate prisoners for the required intelligence. The CWG directed the embassy to coordinate this plan with Vandewalle while making every effort to keep the Low Beam team invisible to any news correspondents.[12]

In the company of the Belgian defense attaché, Colonel Monmaert, Colonel Williams traveled to Kamina on 14 November to apprise Vandewalle on Dragon Rouge and Low Beam planning. Vandewalle welcomed the Low Beam concept, but he required that any such force be self-sustaining in transport, weapons, and supplies. Vandewalle did not object to the independent mission of the proposed force, but he recommended that it concentrate its intelligence-gathering efforts on debriefing Europeans rather than on interrogating African prisoners. Following this positive response, Godley recommended that the Low Beam planner, referred to as Farnsworth, proceed to Kindu to coordinate the operation. Godley expected that the team could be flown into Punia, where they would join the column.[13] Thus, the idea for Low Beam was firmly laid.

While the CWG agonized over the political aspects of Dragon Rouge and the CIA planned Low Beam, Gradwell and Laurent seized on the delay to coordinate their operation. The tactical planning for Dragon Rouge actually began as the lead aircraft climbed off the runway at Kleine-Brogel and turned southward toward Africa. Sitting in the back of that aircraft, an informal orders group met to discuss the existing operations plan. The composition of that group and its chemistry facilitated cooperation between each individual and each national element. Colonels Gradwell and Laurent, assisted by Lieutenant Colonel Erdmann and Major Poore, sat down and discussed the plan for Dragon Rouge.[14]

The initial discussion centered on the use of the airport as the drop zone. Stanleyville Airport was located two miles to the west of the city. An international airport, it had an asphalt strip 7,086 feet long and could handle up to three C-130s at a time. A grass strip some 9,050 feet in length paralleled the main runway. The airport complex, consisting of the control tower, parking area, hangars, terminal, and Sabena Guest House, was located on the southeastern end of the strip. To the north of the airport was a partially wooded, large, open area. To its east was the golf course and to the west a wooded area. South of the airport, across the road to Yakusu, was the European hospital and the governor's residence. USSTRICOM, in an area analysis completed in 1963, considered this airport complex and the area north of it to be the primary drop zone in Stanleyville.[15]

Like General Adams, Gradwell and Poore did not like the jump procedures or the drop zone as specified in OPLAN 319/64. The use of a Belgian officer to control the drop from the cockpit of each aircraft violated an American airborne operations procedure and might confuse the operation. Moreover, while the golf course might be free of heavy weapons, the C-130s would have to make four passes over the drop zone to get all the Belgians out. That amount of time would add to the danger of the hostages by slowing assembly and the seizure of the airfield.[16]

Instead, Gradwell and Poore pushed to use the new, operationally untested, Close Look Doctrine; flying in line astern formation at twenty-second intervals, the C-130s would approach the drop zone at an altitude under 500 feet. A mile out from the target, they would pop up to the jump altitude for their run on the drop zone. Instead of using the golf course as the drop zone, Poore pushed for jumping on the airfield, which, with its greater length, could accommodate all the paras in one pass. Furthermore, Poore was convinced that jumping on the airfield was safer than jumping onto the golf course. The 8th Infantry Division viewed airfields as preferred drop zones and jumped on them quite regularly, so Poore was speaking from experience.[17]

To execute the operation in this fashion, the Americans insisted that they control the drop and give the execute signal based on the navigator's computed airborne release point (CARP). Allowing a Belgian jumpmaster to attempt to visually compute the release point could result in confusion. Impressed with these arguments, Colonel Laurent agreed to the changes, since they would simplify his tactical planning while allowing the Americans to use their own standard procedures. He promised to alter his plan once they arrived at Ascension Island.[18]

A British possession, Ascension Island served as a down-range tracking station for the American space agency, NASA. The British had willingly supported the American request to utilize the island as a staging base and agreed to a communications blackout on the volcanic slag heap. A somewhat surprised U.S. Air Force officer, Captain Roy Dixon, greeted the first aircraft as it landed at 1425Z on 18 November. Alerted by the British on the island that American aircraft would soon arrive, Captain Dixon was surprised when fourteen C-130s and close to 700 personnel, including almost 600 armed Belgian paras, arrived on his doorstep. Nevertheless, the officer turned over all his available facilities to the task force for their support. Pending the next day's arrival of a tent city complete with dining hall, showers, exchange, and movie theater, the Dragon task force was to spend one uncomfortable night.[19]

The task force at Ascension Island

While Colonel Gradwell and his operations staff established a parking plan, Lieutenant Colonel Erdmann hustled off to set up the command post, or Baldwin CP as it was code named, using the Talking Bird C-130 that had arrived four hours earlier. Erdmann's task proved difficult, particularly with his limited manpower. He needed at least two other officers to man the communications facility, to plot out tactical information, and to keep his commanders—both Gradwell and Laurent—fully informed. Once he had the circuits open for encrypted top-secret messages, the world began to speak to Baldwin CP. With only two stations for such high-level traffic, Erdmann found the system hopelessly backlogged for the next two days.[20]

In desperation, at midnight on 20 November, he sent a message that listed all important traffic that had gotten through and asked for retransmission of any "other traffic of great importance." Still, the communications continued to snarl up, and Baldwin CP relied more and more on open-voice communications via USAFE's single-sideband "Twilight Net." Confusion plagued the Twilight Net, since the basic OPLAN 319/64 had no communications annex, and two different code-word systems were soon in use. Though USSTRICOM, utilizing the communications annex to High Beam, deployed joint communications support elements (JCSE) to Ascension, Kamina, and Leopoldville, the JCSE dispatched to Ascension did not arrive in time to be of use. Erdmann's struggle with the airwaves dogged his stay on Ascension. Furthermore, although USEUCOM had agreed to pass operational control to USSTRICOM upon closure at Ascension Island, Gradwell, as airlift commander, remained under the operational control of USEUCOM until 20 November. In the interim, Gradwell worked directly with Lieutenant Colonel Merrit, JTF LEO's liaison officer, and with the Belgians.[21] During the next three days, Gradwell became used to his direct relationship with Laurent, a relationship yet uncluttered by the change to USSTRICOM's operational control.

Colonel Laurent, satisfied with the airborne procedures agreed upon on the flight to Ascension, now worked to finalize his operational concept. By 1530Z, Laurent was ready, and he explained the changes in the plan to his regimental staff. Briefly, he told them that the change to a single pass over the airfield, preceded by the B-26s to neutralize enemy fire, would allow them to seize the airfield more quickly and prepare for the next phase of taking the city.[22]

Laurent's ground plan contained three phases. First, after an initial pass by B-26s, five C-130s would deliver 340 paras and door bundles. The Headquarters, Paracommando Regiment; the Headquarters Company, 1st Battalion; and the 11th and the 13th Companies would all make the jump on the first pass, followed by their bundles and the jumpmasters on the second and third passes. The paras were to seize the airfield and clear it for the airlanding of the four armored and four radio jeeps thirty minutes later. One hour afterwards, the 12th Company would airland, if possible, followed by the remaining personnel and twelve AS-24s to complete phase one.[23]

For phase two, Laurent planned to move on the city with two companies, penetrating along its northern and southern fringes. These companies would block the northern escape route across the Tshopo River bridge and the eastern route out of Camp Ketele. Once the city was sealed off, the third company would penetrate its center to locate and evacuate the hostages (see map 9).[24]

Laurent's plan showed the weaknesses pointed out in Adams' critical message on 16 November. Laurent would have to seize and clear the airport with only part of his battalion. Once all the men were on the ground, they would have to move on foot the three kilometers into the city behind the

Map 9. Colonel Laurent's concept for Dragon Rouge

armored jeeps. It would require the paras at least one to two hours to reach Camp Ketele, some six kilometers away, and the Tshopo Bridge, some five kilometers distant, even if they did not encounter heavy resistance. While his rifle companies searched the city, Laurent would have to maintain control of the airport. With such a small force at the airport, Laurent's men would be severely challenged. Clearly Adams' criticism of this plan made military sense. By using the drop zones suggested in High Beam, Laurent could have had his units in position immediately, while the remainder of the unit dropped on the airfield to seize it.

But Laurent had to operate in accordance with the political restrictions on his mission. He could not risk his young draftees in airborne assaults north and east of the city, where they might be overwhelmed by a determined assault. Nor could he use firepower to make up for his small ground strength; his mission was not to slaughter the Simbas but to conduct a humanitarian rescue without the benefit of Vandewalle's column.

However, part of Laurent's plan had a definite nonhumanitarian flavor. After clearing the center of the airfield, the mission of the 13th Company was "to remain ready on order to seize the residence [of Gbenye (near the airport)] and *its occupants.*" The rationales for this mission—given after the fact—have not been consistent. When interviewed by David Reed, the Belgian officers—in particular Laurent and Mine—indicated that the mission to capture Gbenye came from Clingerman. Laurent and Mine felt that by grabbing Gbenye, the back of the rebels might be broken. In addition, the action might uncover detailed information on the hostages. Later, Laurent took a different tack and indicated that the mission was intended to clear his flanks of possible enemy resistance that might threaten the American aircraft as they landed. The distance of the residence from the airfield—approximately one kilometer without direct line of sight—tends to weigh against this argument. Furthermore, if this mission succeeded, it risked changing the tenor of the operation from a humanitarian rescue to one of intervention against the rebel government. It also entailed a cost in time in reaching the possible locations of the hostages inside Stanleyville.[25]

At 1000Z on 19 November, John Clingerman, recently arrived from Brussels, briefed the assembled staffs of Laurent and Gradwell on the hostage situation in Stanleyville. His briefing consisted of the "hard intelligence" on the situation inside Stanleyville. After providing corrections to their TACTA maps, the former consul to Stanleyville began the meaty portion of his briefing. He emphasized the likelihood that all military camps and jails had to be considered as possible, if not probable, locations of the hostages, thus presenting the Belgians with thirteen sites to search (see map 10). Clingerman assumed the hostages numbered 550 Belgians, 30 Americans, 4 Italians, and 90 other European hostages; but he stated that with the Asian population, the number of hostages could exceed 1,000.[26]

Clingerman gave the assembled officers three lists: one of Americans inside the city, one of subversive personalities associated with the Red Chinese (as of September 1964), and one of missionaries stationed in the

Map 10. Suspected hostage locations, 19 November 1964

Congo—a list that did not include Dr. Paul Carlson. He next provided information on the haunts of the rebel leaders that included the residence of Gbenye, the Hotel Congo Palace, the old headquarters of the Force Publique, and the American consulate. He even warned the Belgians to be on the lookout for a black Mercedes and a white Rambler, often used by the rebel elite; these vehicles, along with the other locations, were expected to be heavily guarded.[27]

As to the enemy forces in the area, Clingerman told the paras that at the airfield, they could expect to find at least one .50-caliber machine gun, this at the control tower. He also asserted that the Simbas might have armored cars they had taken from the ANC. He expected the rebel population to approach 10,000, with perhaps 2,000 of the Simbas well armed. Warning against the fanatic *jeunesse*, Clingerman described the "uniforms" of the Simbas and stated that they might have Chinese advisory support. He predicted that the native population inside Stanleyville would be relatively friendly to the Belgians in contrast to the neighboring areas.[28]

In any case, Clingerman told the Belgians that the likely rebel reaction to an attack would be to kill the Americans but not to harm the Belgians. Clingerman felt that Radio Stanleyville should be used to warn the population to remain indoors and to advertise the reputation of the Paracommandos; this precaution would do much to stabilize the situation. To further aid the soldiers in gathering information on the hostages, Clingerman provided a list of five individuals in Stanleyville who could be approached with confidence.[29]

Clingerman's intelligence briefing on Ascension had several flaws. First, at the time of the briefing, the Belgians had already designed their ground tactical plan, so the intelligence briefing was regarded as just an adjunct to that plan, rather than its basis. Second, the briefing did not address the established pattern of behavior of the rebels while under air attack. The evacuation of the hostages before Lemercier's Ops Tshuapa and the killing of hostages in retribution for previous air attacks were not addressed. Most important, the pattern of rebel reaction to a concerted ground-air attack—specifically, the period of confusion and fear exhibited by the rebels at Kindu—was not even mentioned. In short, the briefing on the hostages emphasized thirteen probable locations of the hostages without providing equal emphasis on probable rebel reactions. The only exception to this was Clingerman's prediction that the Americans were in greater danger than the Belgians, a prediction that was totally in keeping with his mission.[30] The results of this briefing were mixed, but each side took away certain conclusions from its content.

During Clingerman's briefing, one thing rapidly became clear. Both the Americans and the Belgians assumed that the other would provide the critical knowledge concerning the city. The American planners believed that the Belgians would be familiar with the city and would not need additional expertise. While it was true that several of the Belgians had been in the city during the colonial era, none had set foot in the Congo since its early postindependence troubles. The Belgians believed that the embassies in Leopoldville would provide the latest possible information and perhaps ground guides to assist the soldiers in the rescue.

Clingerman, whose mission it was to reinforce the priority attached by the United States to its diplomats, recognized the problem.[31] He cabled Leopoldville almost immediately after conducting his briefing and requested that large-scale maps of Stanleyville be prepared and that available information on "lock-ups" in the city be forwarded. In the next part of his message, Clingerman articulated a number of serious concerns:

> Have briefed task force officers stop four on location U.S. nationals and am assured they realize importance getting to consular personnel fast. Camp Ketele first seizure objective after airfield. But forty-five minutes to do is best time expected since no force personnel have been in Stan last two years and none know local area thoroughly, under circumstances where minutes will count and because my familiarity local areas recommend be authorized go in Stan with last AC carrying surgeon and med supplies to assist task force commander in locating and documenting evacuees. If approve request sec state relay permission to Am Embassy Leo.[32]

Clingerman's request to go into Stanleyville opened another battle between the CWG and Ambassador Godley. Godley immediately grasped the critical nature of the problem and supported Clingerman. The CWG, already profoundly concerned over the use of the military to rescue five official Americans, was not enchanted with the thought of risking a sixth American diplomat (Clingerman) and denied the request. The CWG recommended that Godley pursue an alternative solution with the Belgians, specifically that he get the Belgians to send in an official to act as a guide. Nonetheless, when Godley pointed out that an American official was needed to fulfill American responsibilities in Stanleyville, the CWG relented; Clingerman could accompany the Dragon force into Stanleyville.[33] In retrospect, Clingerman's fears, derived from his consultations with the Belgians at Ascension, provided positive benefits.

Unfortunately, Clingerman's apprehensions made little impression on the Belgian's self-confidence. When Colonel Charles Laurent had boarded the aircraft at Kleine-Brogel, he had several long discussions with Gradwell and Poore in regard to the small size of his unit in comparison with the rebel strength in Stanleyville. When the Americans expressed concern over the unfavorable strength ratio of 600 Belgian paras to 10,000 rebels, Laurent looked at Major Poore and confidently stated, "You know, Major, with my regiment, I could be King of the Congo." That perception, the result of almost 100 years of Belgian supremacy in the Congo, was a natural, but dangerous, conclusion for Laurent. Nonetheless, the last time he had been in the Congo, the opposition had surrendered without firing a shot. Laurent's belief that the paras could reach Camp Ketele in forty-five minutes was prompted by his expectation of a repeat of 1960. Clingerman's briefing, occurring after the tactical plans had been issued for the operation and without mentioning the seizure of Kindu, only served to reinforce Belgian confidence. Despite the hampering political restrictions imposed on Laurent to kill few natives and lose few draftees, Clingerman's briefing had little effect on the colonel's self-assurance. In remarking "I say we jump and take them [the hostages] out," Laurent had stated the fundamental basis of his operational design. He believed that the appearance of his paras would stop all rebel activity in Stanleyville. Even today, neither Laurent nor his former subordinate officers question this belief.[34]

The paucity of aerial photography to support the Belgian planning was another gap in the intelligence picture. While the Belgians did have photography (taken on 6 November), its poor quality and oblique angle rendered it useless, if not detrimental, to planning. Captain Defreyne analyzed the pictures and told Laurent that the Simbas had helicopters. The disbelieving Laurent asked him to wait for new imagery; Defreyne had to wait until he returned to Brussels. To fill this vacuum, a USAFE RC-97 reconnaissance mission under the code name Running Bear deployed to the Congo at the request of the Belgian-American planning group in Brussels. This medium-altitude mission produced film that the embassy forwarded to Wiesbaden Air Base, Germany, on 16 November. There, the film was developed and dispatched to Morón, Spain, to link up with the task force as it staged to Ascension Island. Unfortunately, the film, addressed to Dragon Rouge in care of Lieutenant Colonel Erdmann, never made it past the Morón message center, which did not have any inkling as to whom it might belong. Since Erdmann did not know about the Running Bear mission or the film, he did not look for the film at Morón. Consequently, Morón returned the film to Wiesbaden, where it remained until after the task force returned to Europe. It was just another instance where hasty planning resulted in poor coordination and forced the Belgians to work off of aerial mosaics from 1960.[35]

While the Belgian officers planned for Dragon Rouge, other members of the staff drilled the soldiers on various aspects of the operation. In cooperation with Captain Donald Strobaugh, Ledant's jumpmasters conducted classes and drills on the proper techniques for jumping from C-130s. After training all members of the regiment, the instructors concentrated on teaching the 12th Company, 2d Commando Battalion, how to rig and jump with their equipment.[36]

Strobaugh was so well received by the Belgians that they designated him a static jumpmaster in case the 12th Company did actually jump. Strobaugh wanted to jump, as did Poore, but Gradwell's instructions were firm: the United States did not need an American jumping over Stanleyville, as his possible death or injury would be difficult to explain. Since Strobaugh could not jump, he and Sergeant Dias worked closely with Major Hardenne on the operation of the American-made ground-to-air radios. Again, like Laurent and Gradwell, Strobaugh's relationship with his Belgian counterparts worked to the benefit of the operation.[37]

Once the airborne training and tactical plans were complete, the Belgians rehearsed the operation. After memorizing his portion of the plan, each soldier recited his mission to his superiors. The soldiers then conducted full rehearsals, including ground exits from the C-130s, seizure of an unspecified airport, assembly, and movement toward an objective. By 20 November, Laurent's men knew their plan and how to accomplish it. They were ready, though they still did not know where they were going.[38]

The CWG, nonetheless, still aspired to attain a diplomatic solution to the situation in Stanleyville. Indeed, its soul-searching had led it to propose new negotiations with the rebels, which it hoped might impose a complete cease-fire in the Congo. Spaak, however, was convinced by his own and other Belgian efforts that such negotiations only served rebel interests and grew angry over the CWG proposal. He felt the latest threats from the rebels were serious; they might be moving their hostages. Vandewalle, in the meantime, was ready to move. Neither Spaak nor Tshombe was ready to postpone L'Ommengang in favor of a new round of fruitless international efforts. It was time to act.[39]

On 20 November, Spaak obliterated the CWG's chances for diplomatic overtures by publicly announcing the presence of the Dragon force on Ascension Island. Simultaneously, the Belgian Joint Staff alerted the Paracommando Regiment. Next, Spaak formally proposed moving the Dragon force to Kamina and signaled Belgium's willingness to initiate the move through the combined execution apparatus.[40]

Spaak's unilateral disclosure of the Dragon force's presence on Ascension stunned Washington. His proposal to move the force to Kamina increased the desperation of the CWG, but other factors intervened to overcome its reluctance to comply with Spaak's proposal. Vandewalle reported that crucial bridges were out and might delay his arrival in Stanleyville past 23 November, the announced date of Dr. Carlson's execution. When the CWG met on 21 November, the latest threat from the rebels included a promise to eat their hostages if attacked. The Dragon force's distance from Stanleyville argued in favor of a second move. But even if the force reached Kamina—some nine hours' flight time—by 0700Z on the 22d, Laurent's troops could not jump on Stanleyville until 0600Z on the 23d. Considering the five hours' time difference between Washington and Ascension—coupled with the flight time to Kamina—the CWG had to make a decision.[41]

On 21 November 1964, at 1820Z, the JCS flashed the order to move to Kamina. The order, due to the cryptographic backlog, came in the clear via the Twilight communications net. Quickly, Gradwell and Laurent acted to assemble crews and troops for boarding and takeoff. Shortly afterward, further word arrived from USSTRICOM that the force might have to execute the mission directly from Ascension. Fortunately, the paras were tactically loaded so that when Erdmann reached Gradwell—again via clear radio channels—the airlift commander was able to comply, if necessary, with a direct approach into Stanleyville.[42]

With the deployment to Kamina, planners in Washington shifted their attention from strategic-level hopes for a negotiated settlement to tactical maneuvers designed to forestall any rebel retaliation against the hostages in Stanleyville. While secret, the deployment into the Congo committed the United States and Belgium to Dragon Rouge. On 20 November, Ambassador

William Attwood had formally notified Jomo Kenyatta that he would discuss the Congo situation with the rebels' Nairobi representative. Unless the rebels gave into demands to release the hostages, Attwood's mission was to delay Carlson's execution past 23 November. Underlying these diplomatic maneuvers, the United States and Belgium sought to arrive at an agreement on the best timing for Dragon Rouge in relation to Vandewalle's movement. Further information on the deteriorating conditions in Stanleyville led to last-minute worries in both Brussels and Washington.[43]

Faced with the possibility that the Belgians might have to take Stanleyville unaided by Vandewalle, certain members of the CWG began having second thoughts about the Belgians' troop strength. Incredibly, it was not until 22 November that the CWG bothered to examine a map of Stanleyville, which, when balanced against the reported strength of the rebels, made the Dragon force seem inadequate.[44]

In response to this weakness, Secretary of State Dean Rusk asked General Wheeler if the JCS had any plan to reinforce the Belgians with American troops. Though Wheeler replied negatively, he suggested to Secretary of Defense Robert McNamara that a variation of High Beam be used to back up Dragon Rouge. But McNamara refused to discuss any use of American troops in the operation. On 22 November, Cyrus Vance requested that a second squadron of C-130Es be deployed to Morón, Spain. Faced with McNamara's refusal to use American ground forces, Vance wanted the second squadron close at hand to lift French or perhaps British troops as reinforcements to Dragon Rouge. Though he felt that such allied involvement was unlikely, McNamara agreed, and the orders went out. The JCS then directed CINCSTRIKE to deploy the squadron from the 464th Tactical Airlift Wing to Morón by 231355Z. This squadron closed on Morón on 23 November and remained on two-hour standby for the duration of the Dragon operations. The squadron's arrival in Spain without the proper diplomatic clearances later led the Spanish government to refuse to allow the return of the Dragon force through Spanish airspace.[45] In the interim, the State Department began looking for alternatives for use as reinforcements to Dragon Rouge.

Secretary of State Dean Rusk fastened on the British or the French as the most likely candidates for use in Dragon Rouge. The French had a special force at Toulon designated for employment in Africa, and they had other forces throughout West and Central Africa. However, the traditional Belgian-French rivalry over influence in Africa made the use of French forces unlikely. In fact, Washington had been pleasantly surprised when the French had granted overflight clearances to the Dragon force as it flew to Ascension. The British, on their part, had forces in East Africa in addition to the two battalions they had earlier volunteered to commit into Stanleyville. In pursuit of this possible reinforcement of the Dragon force, Rusk directed MacArthur at 221500Z to deliver the following message to Spaak:

> Perhaps in an excess of caution, I have been considering the contingency, however remote, that unanticipated difficulties might arise at the time the DRAGON ROUGE force assaults Stanleyville.

> In such an event, it might be preferable to have French or British military assistance as first follow-up in preference to further Belgian or US forces. I hope you can give some thought to this as the quickest available resource, since French and British forces are stationed in nearby areas. It would have the advantage of emphasizing the broadly based humanitarian mission.[46]

Taking his career as a foreign service officer literally into his own hands, MacArthur sat on the message rather than disrupt Spaak's determination. Only after favorable news about Dragon Rouge was received did the American ambassador inform Washington that he had not passed the message to Spaak. His action or inaction ultimately sealed the fate of the hostages in the Congo.[47]

It is difficult to understand this sudden and belated realization that the Dragon force might be inadequate for its tasks. That inadequacy was certainly pointed out by the force structure envisioned under High Beam or under the British plan for taking the city. Both concepts had called for a minimum strength of two battalions, and the CWG considered both plans to be examples of military overkill. Now, the very people who had dubbed Adams the "Big Hawk" and who had questioned the use of more than one Belgian company wanted to have a second battalion available for use. One report analyzing the question states:

> Participants in the decision-making deliberations of the weekend insist that it was not realized at the time that the Dragon force would not have enough strength to secure the airfield and also to seize the city. There was certainly a shortage of transport which would permit the paratroops to fan out through the city in search of hostages.[48]

When viewed within the context of Adams' criticisms of OPLAN 319/64 and the remark that his comments were of no substance, this statement is clearly not justifiable. The CWG had every opportunity to examine the military requirements for taking Stanleyville. That it failed to do so in a timely manner constituted negligence of the highest order.

In the meantime, the situation in the Congo began to clarify. Two major breaks developed: Attwood's negotiations with Kanza had apparently succeeded in delaying Carlson's execution, and Vandewalle met with all the principal military leaders involved in Dragon Rouge on 22 November.[49]

Vandewalle's consultations were absolutely critical to the events which unfolded shortly afterward, and they revolved around two principal alternatives: the execution of Dragon Rouge on 23 November, with follow-on operations at Paulis and Bunia on 25 November; or Dragon Rouge on 24 November, with follow-on operations at Paulis and Bunia on 26 November. After stating that he would arrive in Stanleyville on the morning of 24 November, Vandewalle argued in favor of the second alternative. Originally in favor of the 23 November option, Laurent agreed with him. In contrast, Colonel Isaacson, commander of JTF LEO, was in favor of an immediate operation the next morning as a method of speeding up the follow-on operations. In passing these views on to Washington, Godley reported that Colonels Monmaert and Williams, De Kerchove, and he were all firmly in favor of the 24 November solution. Nevertheless, the JCS placed the Dragon force on standby alert to meet a 230100Z launch for Stanleyville, an alert which they finally canceled at 222310Z.[50]

Strangely, the hesitancy so characteristic of the American decision-making process—in contrast to Spaak's hard line approach—now seemed to reverse itself. This early hesitation had led MacArthur to hold back Rusk's message on the use of French or British troops. On 23 November, Spaak told MacArthur that the Belgians in the Congo seemed to regard the decision to intervene as a fait accompli and were now only concerned with its timing. Spaak still had reservations over the linkage of Vandewalle's operations with Dragon Rouge, and he remained in favor of Vandewalle's seizure of the city without the use of the paras if L'Ommengang could liberate the hostages. To support a final Belgian review of the situation, Spaak cabled De Kerchove three questions: would Vandewalle hold to his schedule? did he feel that Dragon Rouge was necessary? and if Dragon Rouge did not take place, could operations be mounted on Bunia and Paulis on 24 November? Reporting these questions to Washington, MacArthur pointed out that Spaak was very concerned over the impact Dragon Rouge might have on the hostages held outside of Stanleyville.[51]

Ambassador Godley responded immediately to Spaak's queries. Godley agreed that linkage with Vandewalle's assault would somewhat color the character of Dragon Rouge, but he felt that could be offset by allocating geographic sectors to the two forces. Godley pointed out that cancellation of Dragon Rouge at this late date would not counteract its political effects. Once the presence of the force at Kamina became known, hostile propaganda would tie it to the ultimate fall of the rebel regime. Indeed, Godley was already dealing with press inquiries on the paras' current location.[52]

Godley reinforced his arguments with purely military considerations. Vandewalle would probably need several hours to secure the city before he could retrieve the hostages, and Godley feared that any delay would allow the rebels to kill or spirit away the hostages. Furthermore, as reports now indicated that a substantial number of hostages were being held on the south side of the Congo River, Vandewalle's tasks in securing both halves of the city were even more complicated.[53]

Godley also feared the political costs to Western-Congolese relations if, after convincing Tshombe to allow Western forces on Congolese soil, the United States and Belgium backed away from Dragon Rouge. After fending off pressure from Tshombe and Mobutu on 22 November to use the paras on 23 November, Godley reported that the Congolese would say that "we led them up [a] garden path" with a decision to cancel Dragon Rouge. Thus, Godley remained firmly in favor of Dragon Rouge. Spaak, however, continued to hesitate.[54]

MacArthur reported at 231920Z that he had met with Spaak to discuss the following options with the foreign minister:

(1) VDW [Vandewalle] column assault on the 23rd (that same day) without Dragon Rouge.

   (2) Dragon Rouge 24 November coupled with VDW arrival sometime the same day.

   (3) Dragon Rouge 24 November with VDW's arrival suspended until 25 November.[55]

Spaak considered the first option unworkable, since Vandewalle could hardly make his assault on such a short notice, and he would require some rest before attacking the city. Without Dragon Rouge, Vandewalle would also face the tactical problem of securing the city before any rescue of the hostages could be contemplated. Spaak did not hold option three to be realistic, as neither Vandewalle nor Leopoldville was likely to support such a delay. Spaak fastened on the second option as the best solution to the hostage question, since he "felt it would be 'grotesque' to allow our concern for international feelings to jeopardize the lives of more than a thousand people." On receiving Spaak's decision, Washington concurred, and the JCS at 231900Z directed the execution of Dragon Rouge.[56]

Stanleyville was now the focus of the Congo crisis. While Washington and Brussels had anguished over the necessity of Dragon Rouge, Vandewalle was pushing toward the city. On 21 November, L'Ommengang was joined by the Low Beam force, led by CIA agent William "Rip" Robertson, which consisted of eighteen Cuban exiles armed with sixty-eight different weapons. Robertson's team, along with Rattan and Weisel, made up the American contingent of L'Ommengang.[57] In the meantime, the rebels, after a futile attempt to spirit their hostages northward as a bargaining chip on 21 November, returned them to Stanleyville.[58] The evening of 23 November was hardly restful for the Westerners inside the rebel bastion. On the eve of Dragon Rouge, Radio Stanleyville sent the 200 hostages inside the Hotel Victoria to bed with these chilling instructions to their hosts: "Sharpen your knives! Sharpen your machetes! Sharpen your spears! If the paras drop from the sky, kill the foreigners. Do not wait for orders. You have your orders now: Kill, kill, kill!"[59]

   The paras were coming, but they were already tired. Following their flight to Kamina, the Dragon force had remained on semialert in case an immediate move was ordered. The following evening, the 22d, they went on full alert, as Washington and Brussels debated on whether to order the operation. Fortunately, no execution decision was reached; the communications network was out of order. When it became apparent that a surprise drop on 23 November was no longer possible, Laurent ordered his troops off the aircraft.[60]

   In addition to costing Laurent's men valuable sleep, this last delay had other negative effects. One of these was in the person of Colonel Isaacson, who met the force at Kamina to coordinate close air support. Laurent and Gradwell's men, by this time, had second thoughts over the utility of the B-26s provided by Isaacson; they feared that the fighters might simply alert any enemy defenses around the field. But operating on instructions from

Paratroops preparing to load gear at Ascension Island

Adams, Isaacson overcame the Belgians' reluctance to use the B-26s. Nonetheless, Isaacson had similar doubts about the planes—reservations that influenced him to lead the weather reconnaissance mission ahead of the force using a C-130 from JTF LEO, rather than employing one of the B-26s. But as Adams' subordinate, Isaacson had no choice: he insisted that the B-26s be included in the operation.[61]

Isaacson's debate with the Belgians and Americans in the Dragon force over these matters led to friction. As airlift commander, Gradwell held equal rank to Isaacson, and resentment developed over what the USEUCOM crews viewed as Isaacson's superfluous position. Moreover, after six days of close contact with Gradwell, Laurent continued to consult him, only grudgingly recognizing Isaacson. The conflict, essentially command rivalry between USEUCOM and USSTRICOM, added an unnecessary element of agitation within the airlift force that, after all, came from the same squadrons in the United States.[62]

Similar tensions had developed on the Belgian side between Vandewalle and Laurent when the former arrived at Kamina on 22 November. Now firmly in charge of L'Ommengang and pushing toward Stanleyville, Vandewalle regarded Laurent's mission with doubt. He felt that he could take Stanleyville on his own and that Laurent's men could be better utilized in the outlying regions of the Congo. Laurent, on the other hand, doubted the capabilities of Vandewalle's L'Ommengang to seize Stanleyville. Furthermore, he feared that his young draftees might become as bloodthirsty as Vandewalle's mercenaries once they were exposed to them in Stanleyville.[63]

Belgian paras loading up for Stanleyville from Kamina airfield

In both cases of rivalry, the causes lay in the hasty, improvisational nature of Dragon Rouge. As a representative of USSTRICOM, Isaacson had been in the Congo for a month. As Spaak's front man in the crisis, Vandewalle was the most informed Belgian on the situation. Neither man was consulted in the planning for Dragon Rouge until 14 November. The same held true for Gradwell and Laurent; both had operated in the dark since they had met on 17 November. Now on 22 November, they had to adjust and coordinate their actions in an extremely delicate situation. All were professionals, and they worked to overcome these liabilities. But they were human; the tensions remained.

The next day consisted of putting the finishing touches on an otherwise ready operation. Intelligence from the Running Bear mission confirmed earlier reports that the airfield was blocked with oil drums and junk cars. Speculative reports also surfaced that some of the hostages might have been removed to the island of Basoko or north to Banalia. News of L'Ommengang arrived in the afternoon with a report that Vandewalle was moving and expected no resistance. Tension began to build, as it seemed by now that

Dragon Rouge was inevitable. That suspicion became fact when CINCSTRIKE at 232100Z flashed the long awaited "Big Punch." Dragon Rouge was on![64]

The Dragon Roars

To ensure that he arrived simultaneously with Dragon Rouge, Vandewalle intended to emulate Liegeois' night march on Kindu. With this plan in mind, L'Ommengang resumed its drive on 23 November, at 1500*; Vandewalle, however, was prepared to seize Stanleyville even if Dragon Rouge was canceled.

Vandewalle's plan to seize Stanleyville—an expanded version of the assault on Kindu—was to be independent of any assistance from the Paracommandos. From Wanie Rukulu, Vandewalle planned to dash full tilt into the city with Lima I. Liegeois was to fan out from the center, with one platoon to seize the airfield and a second to seize the Tshopo Bridge. Meanwhile, Lima II, the second half of L'Ommengang under Lieutenant Colonel Lamouline, was to follow in trail to occupy Camp Ketele and seal off the city's eastern exits. Once inside the city, Vandewalle planned to develop the situation and ultimately to rescue the non-Congolese.

At Vandewalle's disposal was a mixed force of Belgian advisers, Hoare's mercenaries, Rattan, Robertson's Low Beam team, and nearly 1,000 native troops. Led by Ferret armored cars, L'Ommengang was crammed into 100 vehicles along with its fuel and ammunition. Vandewalle would have preferred to have Katangan gendarmes airlifted into the city to aid in its occupation, but all airlift support was now being given to the Paracommandos. Still, he was satisfied with the plan, and L'Ommengang rolled toward Stanleyville at 1500 hours. Almost immediately, an African thunderstorm drenched the column. It was going to be a long night for Vandewalle's force.[1]

Though its initial movement toward Stanleyville went well, L'Ommengang ran into problems around midnight. Frenchy, the mercenary gunner in the lead Ferret, thought he saw an approaching armored car, and after he had halted the column, called for a bazooka team. Hoare responded quickly; a team went forward and, using matches to illuminate their sights, put two rockets into the enemy vehicle. Explosions illuminated the sky as the vehicle—which turned out to be a Mercedes loaded with

---

*All Stanleyville times are local.

explosives and ammunition—erupted in flames. Once the fireworks display died down, the column eased past the glowing hulk to continue its march. Things really began to heat up shortly afterward.[2]

About an hour after the initial halt, the column ran into a Simba ambush. Several mercenaries were hit: Freddy Basson died instantly, and Bruce Harper was wounded, along with a couple of the Low Beam Cubans. After providing limited care to the wounded (there was no doctor), L'Ommengang moved forward. An hour later, a second fusillade ripped into the column, killing another of its members. This time, the dead man was George Clay, a South African NBC correspondent who had slipped into Lubutu the previous day to join the column. Once again, the convoy moved forward, with the bodies of Basson and Clay in a bus. At 0330, the convoy hit a third ambush, and Vandewalle halted the column for the night. With each of its vehicles loaded with extra fifty-five-gallon fuel drums and ammunition, another ambush held promise of a disaster. Consequently, L'Ommengang did not resume its march until 0530; by then Dragon Rouge had become a reality.[3]

In keeping with OPLAN 319/64, Colonel Isaacson launched from Kamina at 232345Z to conduct the weather reconaissance. As he flew the designated route to Stanleyville, Isaacson carefully checked weather conditions. In the vicinity of the target, he remained at the same altitude,

L'Ommengang in the advance to Stanleyville

keeping a minimum of twenty-five miles from Stanleyville. Satisfied that weather conditions were suitable, Isaacson returned west along the Congo River, where at twenty minutes before dawn, he sighted Gradwell's C-130s.[4]

The first five C-130s had launched in ten-minute intervals beginning at 240046Z. In the lead, Gradwell ordered all aircraft to form on him and informed Colonel Laurent that all of the assault wave was airborne. Based on Isaacson's weather report, Gradwell knew that he would have to circumnavigate a line of thunderstorms by flying fifty miles west of their planned course. To compensate for this detour, the force had launched early; the lead navigator was responsible for getting them back on schedule. It was a challenge met easily. The C-130s arrived at Basoko on time. There, they picked up their B-26 escort and turned east toward Stanleyville. At Basoko, Gradwell's planes had dropped to low altitude in preparation for the assault. Isaacson, who was directing the B-26s, had difficulty communicating with his pilots, Spanish-speaking Cubans. He wanted them down low, where they could spot Simba positions. As the B-26s bored in on the airfield, expectantly testing the enemy air defenses, they were too fast and too high; no fire rose to meet them, and they radioed back for the C-130s. Gradwell's ships popped up to 700 feet, and 60 seconds after the B-26s crossed the airfield, the 5 C-130s reached the target.[5]

Inside these aircraft, the Belgians had been on standby since 0555, when the loadmaster had opened the doors. In each aircraft, jumpmasters made their checks, and the lead troopers shuffled forward. At 0600, with the Stanleyville Airport visible below, the red warning lights turned green.

The night march on Stanleyville

Cuban-exile pilots

Laurent's troopers leapt into the morning sky, and within sixty seconds, all the men of the first pass were on the ground. Gradwell's crews, unlike those in the B-26s, received hostile fire from the Simbas; on their initial pass, four of the five C-130s were hit by light antiaircraft fire. Gratefully, there was no sign of the expected 20-mm gun, and the C-130s swung around for their second pass over the drop zone. Now Ledant's jumpmasters, after shoving their bundles out, leapt into the air. With all the assault wave out, the aircrews turned toward Leopoldville at the order of Colonel Gradwell. Stacked above and behind the formation of C-130s, Colonel Isaacson had monitored the airborne assault. At its conclusion, he made one low pass over the airfield and turned to follow the C-130s back to Leopoldville, leaving Gradwell in orbit above the city.[6]

On the ground, the Paracommando Regiment had landed precisely on target. Both Colonel Laurent and Major Mine were surprised by the accuracy of the drop. Indeed, Mine did a stand-up landing within fifty meters of his planned impact point. Moreover, all of the troopers and most of the door bundles had landed on the drop zone. While eight of the paras were injured, only three—Corporal Andre Daubercy and troopers Yves Warshotte and Franz Vanaelten—were out of action.[7]

As the paras shrugged out of their harnesses and set to work, feverish activity engulfed the airfield. Members of the Headquarters Company and

Paracommandos on the edge of the Stanleyville airfield after parachuting

the jumpmasters cleared the strip of some 400 fifty-five-gallon drums and around 10 wrecked cars. It was an enormous task; the drums were filled with water, the wrecked vehicles had no wheels, and all had to be manhandled a safe distance away from the strip. What made it all the more remarkable was that it had to be done under hostile fire.

In response to Spaak's announcement on the presence of the Dragon force at Ascension Island, the Simbas had reinforced the airfield defenses with around 200 men. With the end of the airborne operation, the Simbas shifted their attention from the disappearing C-130s to the Belgian Paracommandos. Though many of these rebels fled or hid from the Belgians, the remainder put up a surprisingly intense, but inaccurate, fire around the airfield. Even as the Headquarters Company and Ledant's jumpmasters busily cleared the runway, the other units moved to silence the rebel guns.[8]

The 11th Company, under Captain Emiel Pierlinck, had the mission of securing the control tower, the Sabena Guest House, and the terminal building. Master Sergeant Max De Haes, the company sergeant major, was to seize the control tower. As he exited his aircraft, De Haes spotted a machine gun firing from the eastern end of the runway. After mentally marking the gun position, he gathered up a small assault team and stormed the tower. De Haes' assault team drove off the thirty or so rebels in the tower, wounding several and capturing two prisoners. When De Haes grabbed one and demanded, "Where are the Europeans?" both answered, "They are at the Hotel Victoria!" It was the first break on the location of the hostages. De Haes turned the critical intelligence and the prisoners over to a subordinate before he moved off to clear out the machine-gun nest east of the runway.[9]

It did not take much time for De Haes to reach the tree line east of the runway. There, he met Captain Huyberechts, whose mission it was to lay out air identification panels once the field was secured. Both men recognized the machine gun as a major threat to the expected airland element and decided to cover each other as they took it. De Haes eased forward till he spotted a tent by the gun position and opened fire. No return fire answered him, and both Belgians rushed the position. There, they found two ammunition boxes, a Mauser rifle, and the tripod to a heavy machine gun. Unable to locate the machine gun, they seized its ammunition, the rifle, and returned to the control tower. The eastern end of the airfield was temporarily secure by 0630.[10]

Headquarters Company was to secure the western end of the field after clearing the runway. During its actions in clearing the strip, the company rescued a Dutch missionary who had fled to the field during the morning's confusion. He told his rescuers that the Europeans were gathered in the Hotel Victoria and the Procure, a Catholic administrative center along the Congo River. It was the second bit of intelligence on the hostages, and the paras dispatched the Dutchman to the control tower under escort.[11]

Sergeants Julian Derwaerder and Marcel Dominique were the first paras to land on the field. While the bulk of their company was engaged on the airfield, the two sergeants had the mission of providing initial cover. Immediately, they secured their two machine guns and assistant gunners and established blocking positions west and southwest of the field. By 0640, the western end of the field was also clear. Meanwhile, the 11th and the 13th Companies had been seeking out their initial objectives.[12]

The mission of the 3d Platoon, 11th Company—that of seizing the control tower—has already been discussed. The other platoons were equally successful; the 1st Platoon's capture of the hangars occurred without opposition as did the 2d Platoon's clearing of the Sabena Guest House just south of the main road into Stanleyville. While the 2d Platoon returned to the airfield for assembly and movement into Stanleyville, it aided the 13th Company in achieving its objective.[13]

The 13th Company had moved off on its objective, the Residence, where it hoped to capture Gbenye and possibly Soumialot. Soon after the 0600 drop, Lieutenant Andre Patte, 13th Company commander, had his unit assembled and moving on its objective. To effect a rapid assault on the Residence, Patte left his mortar section behind to recover its equipment. Despite his desire for speed, Patte ran into navigational difficulties: the thick vegetation and the lack of an accurate map slowed the company's progress. After about twenty-five minutes, Patte reached a building that he thought might be the Residence. Instead of a plush estate, however, Patte

Corporal Warschotte, wrapped in his reserve parachute awaiting medics after breaking his leg in landing had stumbled on a ruins where he found an elderly Congolese—not the "Venerable One," Gbenye. The old man told the frustrated Belgian commander that he had missed the Residence, which was located back by the airfield. Patte believed his mission of removing the Simbas' political leadership in one fell swoop had failed, so he rallied his company and returned to the airfield. En route, he came close to nabbing the elusive Gbenye.[14]

Between Patte's fruitless search for the Residence and the 11th Company's seizure of the Sabena Guest House, the two units succeeded in flushing out three Simba vehicles, one of which was the Rambler mentioned in Clingerman's briefing. The Simba vehicles drove into a roadblock established by Lieutenant Gustaaf Mertens of 11th Company. When the Simba vehicles failed to halt on command, the paras opened fire. Two of the three vehicles were destroyed; in one, the paras found Gbenye's identification papers, health card, passport, and a sizable roll of Congolese francs. Cowering in the third car, the paras discovered Hugh Scotland, a Jamaican with a British passport. Scotland, who had come into Stanleyville as a journalist, found himself a prisoner. As for Gbenye, the paras later learned that the wily leader slept in the native villages to avoid a capture attempt. All of the material, along with Scotland, were returned to the control tower.[15]

Back at the airfield, Major Mine had established his battalion command post by 0630. Mine concentrated on monitoring his unit's progress while he awaited information on the hostages. At 0635, shortly after Mine received

After the jump on the Stanleyville airfield, rebels who formerly controlled the tower are held on the ground as prisoners

the information from De Haes' field interrogation of the Simbas, the phone rang in his command post. Lieutenant Matten answered the phone. An unidentified French speaker quickly said that all the hostages who were held in the Hotel Victoria and the Hotel des Chutes were in danger of immediate slaughter. Five minutes later, the Dutch missionary rescued by Headquarters Company confirmed the two reports. Mine now had a definite objective and, at Laurent's instructions, gave orders for the immediate assembly of the 11th and 13th Companies. Following their assembly, 11th Company was to lead the advance directly into the city to the Hotel Victoria and the Congo Palace. The 13th Company, after initially following in trail, was to turn south to the Procure, the Hotel des Chutes, and its ultimate objective, Camp Ketele. Laurent's plan, however, still depended on the armored jeeps and the additional manpower of the 12th Company, all of which were still in the air. By 0650, the airfield was clear, and Major Roger Hardenne of Dragon Control passed the clearance for airland operations to begin.[16] Things began to go wrong almost immediately.

In fact, one mishap had already occurred when Chalk Six took to the air with Captain "Mac" Secord at the controls. Less than five minutes after take off, the starboard fillet on the left wing opened and dumped an inflating life raft into the wind stream. The flapping raft, which wrapped itself around part of the controls, severed the radio antenna and damaged the inboard prop on the starboard side. Either the cable or a piece of the prop tore a thirty-six-inch gash in the aircraft skin. Consequently, at less than 1,500 feet altitude and at night over the jungle, Secord found himself in a fully loaded C-130 trying to bring his damaged aircraft back under control.[17]

Mac Secord was a hot pilot; his commander had deliberately picked him to land the initial aircraft into Stanleyville. Now Secord was to prove his abilities: he stabilized the bucking C-130, declared an emergency, and brought his ship back into Kamina without further damage. It was quite a feat of airmanship, and it won him the Distinguished Flying Cross. Secord did not waste any time getting back in the air; he taxied up to the spare C-130, and with a tremendous effort, the new Chalk Six was en route to Stanleyville within the hour. Nevertheless, when Hardenne radioed Gradwell to send in the first aircraft, Chalk Seven came into land; Laurent's second element of armored jeeps would be late for the move into Stanleyville.[18]

Even as the first C-130 landed, harassing fire by the Simbas reappeared. Lieutenant Walter Mertens, one of Ledant's jumpmasters, was in position along the eastern end of the field when the firing broke out at around 0700. Like Huyberechts, Mertens gathered several of his men and moved to the sound of the guns. This time, the firing came from the northern wood line of the airfield, and as Mertens advanced, he heard a heavy machine gun firing at the incoming aircraft. The paras fired on the position and overran it without casualty. Along the wood line, they found a 12.7-mm Chinese Communist heavy machine gun and tripod dug in and camouflaged. Though the paras found no rebels, the gun had been fired; one ammo box was empty, and cartridge cases were scattered over the ground. Mertens' men loaded the gun on one of the AS-24s that had just arrived and took it

Major Mine and Lieutenant Legrelle confer, Stanleyville airfield

to the control tower. Laurent's units had problems with several machine guns around the airfield. Huyberechts located one gun, Mertens captured a second, while a third periodically fired from another position but was never located.[19] While the Simba gunners were unskilled with their weapons, they still played havoc with the airland operations.

Chalk Seven, followed by Chalks Eight, Nine, Eleven, and Ten, flew into the airport. Eight and Nine held the men of 12th Company, who were welcome reinforcements for Colonel Laurent. Laurent wanted his units to step out. The short, doughty colonel moved up and down the line exhorting his companies to hurry their assembly. Finally at 0715, the 11th Company jumped off, led by a two-jeep element under Sergeant Spillebeen. The 1st Parachute Battalion command post of Majors Mine and Andre Anne de Molina, followed by the 13th Company, trailed the lead unit. Even as the 12th Company off-loaded from the C-130s at 0720, Laurent was pushing it into formation. Captain Raes then led it toward Stanleyville. Next, Chalk Six landed with the last two armored jeeps, and Laurent ordered their section chief, Sergeant Luc Goris, to catch the 13th Company on its way into the city. Chalk Twelve followed Secord onto the field. Both Chalk Twelve and Secord's aircraft were to wait for the arrival of the hostages. Laurent was not waiting for anyone; shortly after all his units set off, he grabbed an AS-24 and, in the company of John Clingerman and a couple of jumpmaster teams, sped off into the city on the handy tricycles.[20]

As the Paracommandos moved toward Stanleyville, Sergeant Spillebeen's reconnaissance section, in its armored jeeps, led the way along the tree-lined route. Each jeep leapfrogged ahead of the troop column, one providing covering fire as the other moved. Sporadic fire ripped overhead from the bush, but generally unaimed, it caused no casualties. Nevertheless, it slowed the column, since the paras, most of whom had never been under hostile fire, could not identify targets for return fire. Unable to respond to the Simba harassment and weighed down by their heavy loads of equipment and ammunition, the column moved slowly—more slowly than Laurent wished.[21]

It was 0740 before the 11th Company penetrated the outskirts of Stanleyville. On the city's western limit, the paras sought out Mr. Gerlache, who according to Clingerman could provide current information about the

An AS-21 tricycle moves troops into place around Stanleyville airport

hostages. When they located Gerlache, he could not help them; the Simbas had severely beaten the unfortunate Belgian the previous evening, and he was unable to speak. As the column pressed on, encouraged by Gerlache's gesturing, Spillebeen's jeeps cleared each intersection and provided cover as the 11th Company passed. Moving eastward along Avenue Monseigneur Grison, the 11th Company turned on to Avenue Gouverneur Moeller (see map 11). Spillebeen's jeeps moved forward one block to Avenue De L'Eglise and took up blocking positions against rebels fleeing to the southeast. Lieutenant Gustaaf Mertens, at the lead in front of the 11th Company, led the company north towards Avenue Lothaire. As he reached the intersection, he heard firing to the south. The paras ran toward the shooting, firing at the rebels fleeing in front of them. At 0750, Lieutenant Mertens and Major Mine turned the corner onto Avenue Sergeant Ketele, only to be greeted by a scene of horror.[22] For many of the hostages in the Hotel Victoria, the red berets were minutes too late. Hoyt and Grinwis recorded the nightmare:

> *24 November* - At 0600, the hostages in the Residence Victoria were awakened by the sound of a number of planes overflying the city. Speculation began immediately that this represented the Belgian paratroop drop, which had been reported as a possibility on the international radio. There was very little traffic in the town, but at 0700, the guards at the Residence Victoria knocked on all the doors and ordered all men, women, and children down into the street. Columns began to form up of ranks of three abreast, then Col. Opepe arrived and announced that all the men, women, and children were going to be taken to Stanleyville Airport to prevent its bombardment by American and Belgian planes.
>
> There was considerable confusion in organizing the files of hostages, which were directed by perhaps ten Simbas. Hoyt and Grinwis were in the third rank at the head of the line, but other Americans, including Dr. Carlson and the other three members of the Consulate staff, were scattered back almost to the end of the long triple files. We began walking from the Victoria toward the airport with frequent halts. At a point two blocks from the Victoria, near the Congo Palace Hotel, the column made a right turn in order to go towards the main road to the airport. However, when only half the column had made the turn, leaving the column in an L-shape, we were told to halt. The armed Simba guards took up positions on the inside of this L with Col. Opepe standing more or less near the base of the L. Firing was heard from the direction of the airport throughout these maneuvers.
>
> Opepe then made a small speech in Swahili, in which he said that he had attempted to protect the Belgians and Americans and that now he believed he was betrayed by these same people who only pretended to be negotiating with the leaders of the revolutionary government.
>
> At this point, a truck of Simbas arrived from the airport crying out that Belgian paratroopers had landed and infested the airport. Col. Opepe, who had not realized until that moment a parachute drop had occurred, then ordered us to sit down in the street where we were. Considerable confusion ensued among the Simbas for the next two or three minutes. Soon, however, very heavy firing was suddenly heard from close by. It is not clear at this point if Opepe ordered his Simbas to fire on the seated people or if a single Simba

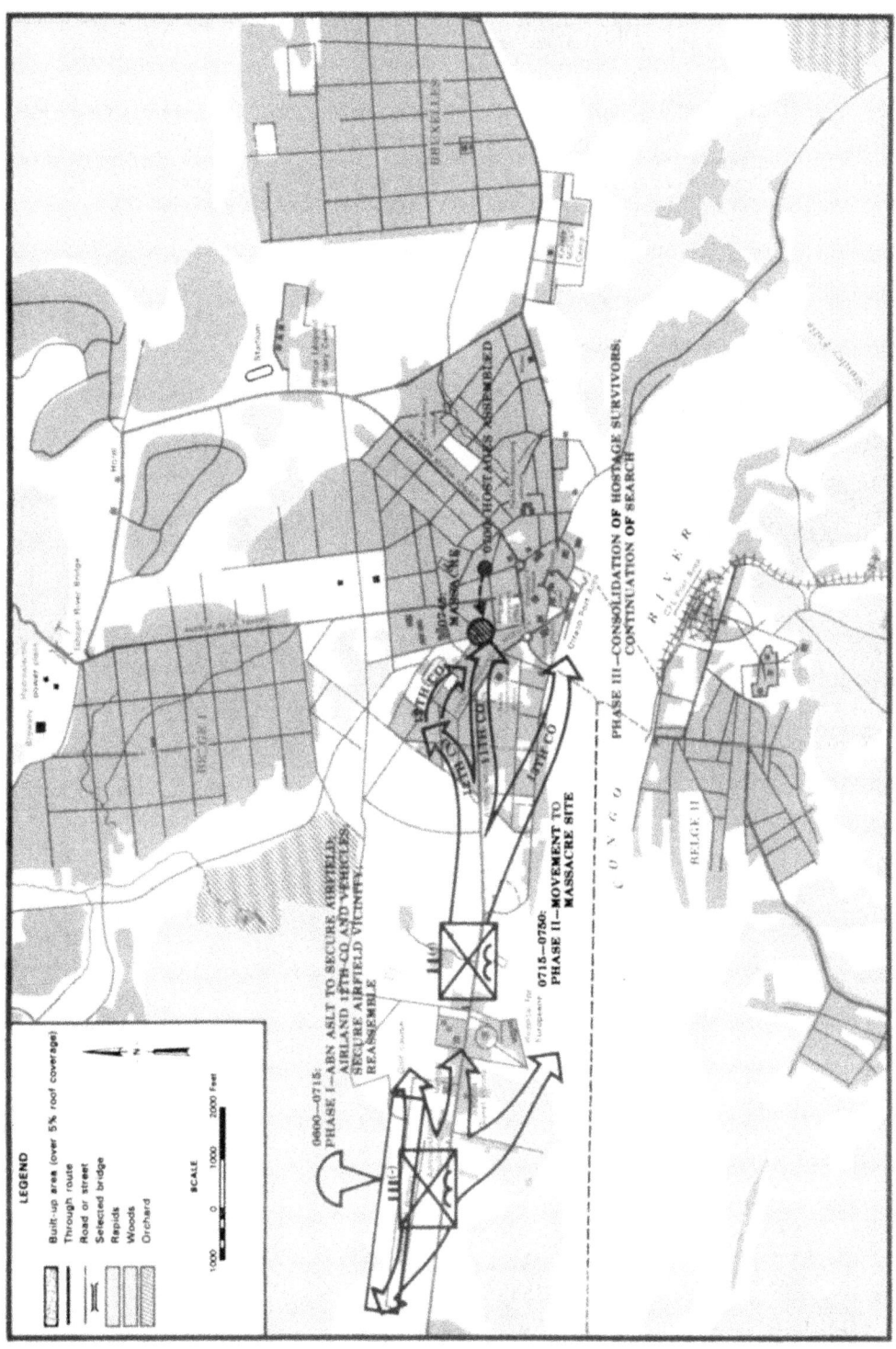

Map 11. Dragon Rouge, Phases I and II, 0600—0750

started the firing and all the others followed suit. In any case, the Simbas deliberately began firing with their automatic weapons on the seated Belgians and Americans. During the next five minutes, before the arrival on the spot of the Belgian paratroopers, the Simbas chased and shot all those Europeans who were on the street and those who were attempting to escape from the initial Simba field of fire. Hoyt and Grinwis, being at the head of the line, were by accident able to run up a nearby driveway. Mr. Houle remained lying in the street until the paratroopers actually appeared on the scene. Most of the Belgians and Americans, however, attempted to run away from the scene and hide in houses or behind walls and any other place that would hide them from the Simbas. It is during this five minute period that Dr. Carlson and the other victims were shot by pursuing Simbas.[23]

Belgian paratrooper rigging for Stanleyville jump

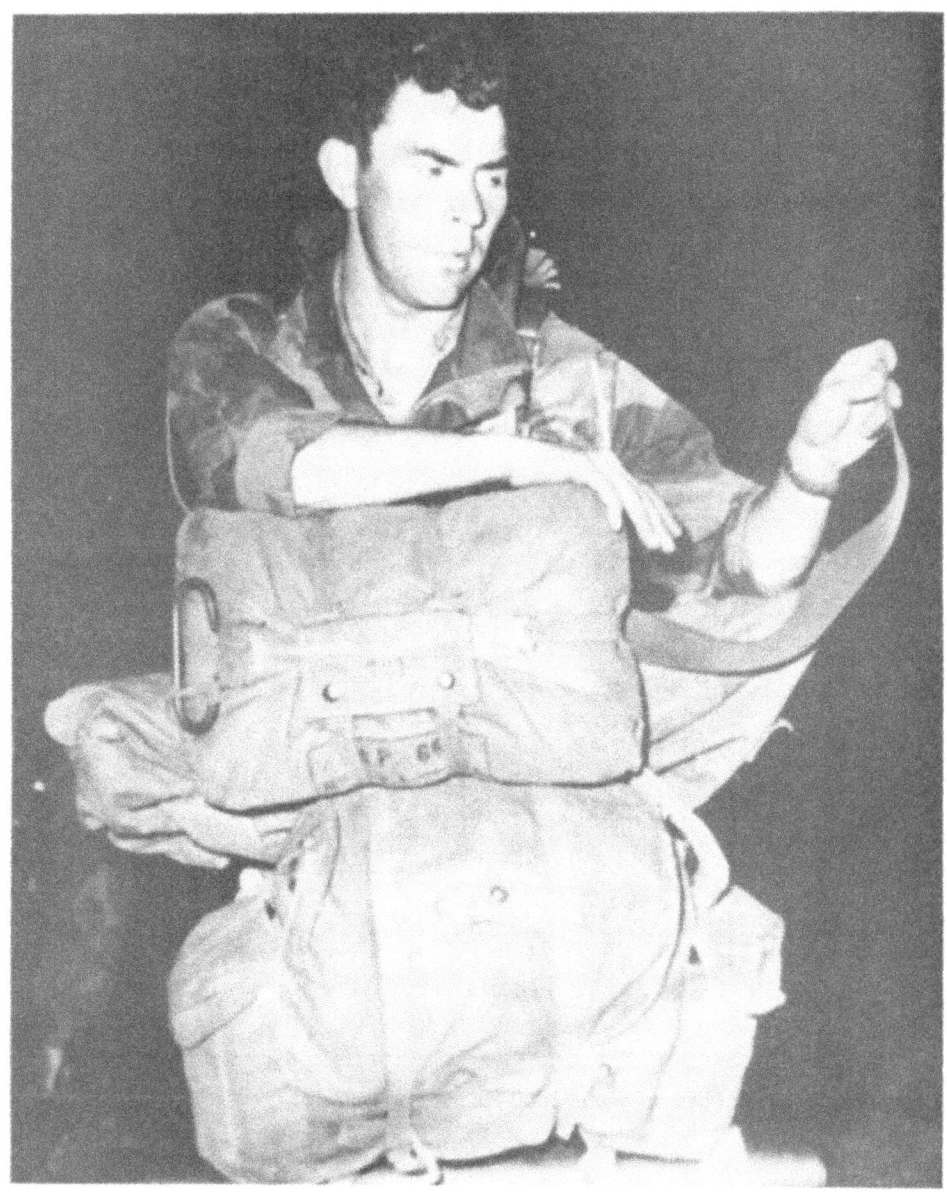

U.S. aircrews and Paracommandos at Kamina airfield prior to Stanleyville flight

Belgian Paracommandos en route to Ascension Island

Some of the hostages after the terrible shooting by the rebels

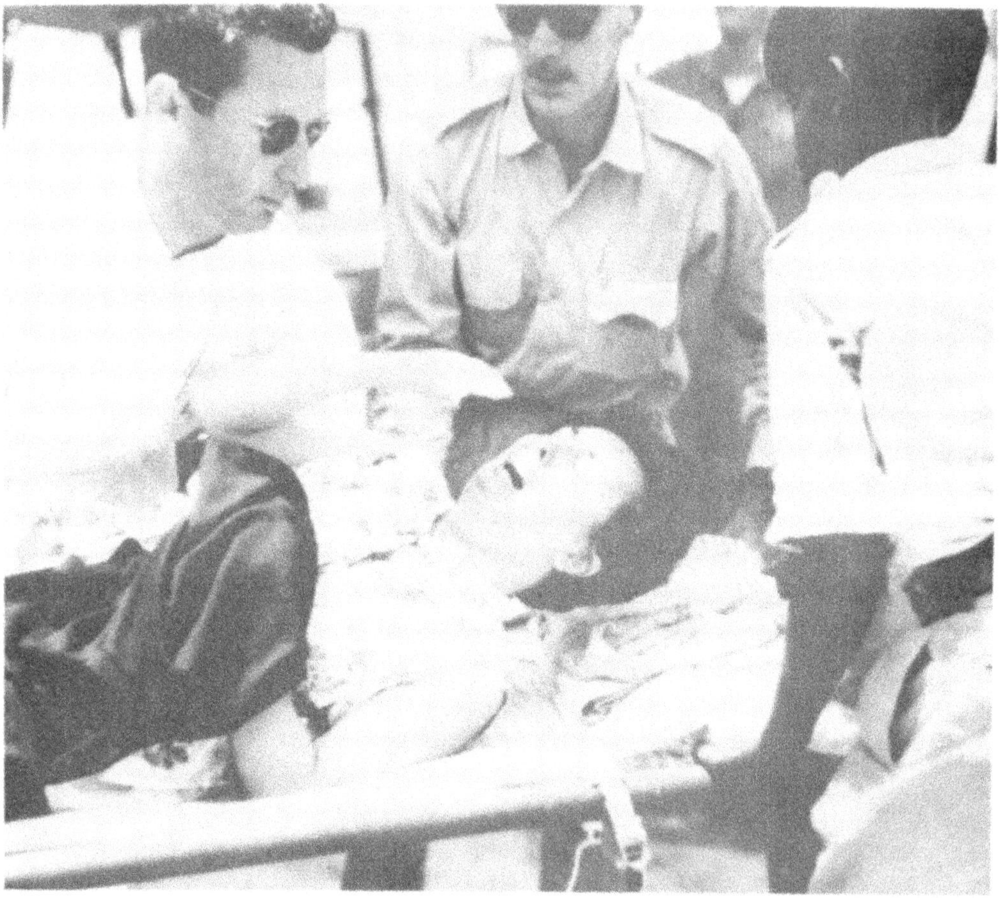

A Belgian woman in hysterics as she is transported to a departing C-130

U.S. Air Force photo

Belgian paratrooper escorting a captured Simba, Stanleyville Airport

Refugees moving toward the Stanleyville airfield

First evacuees from the massacre at Stanleyville, 24 November

Refugees on the road to the airfield

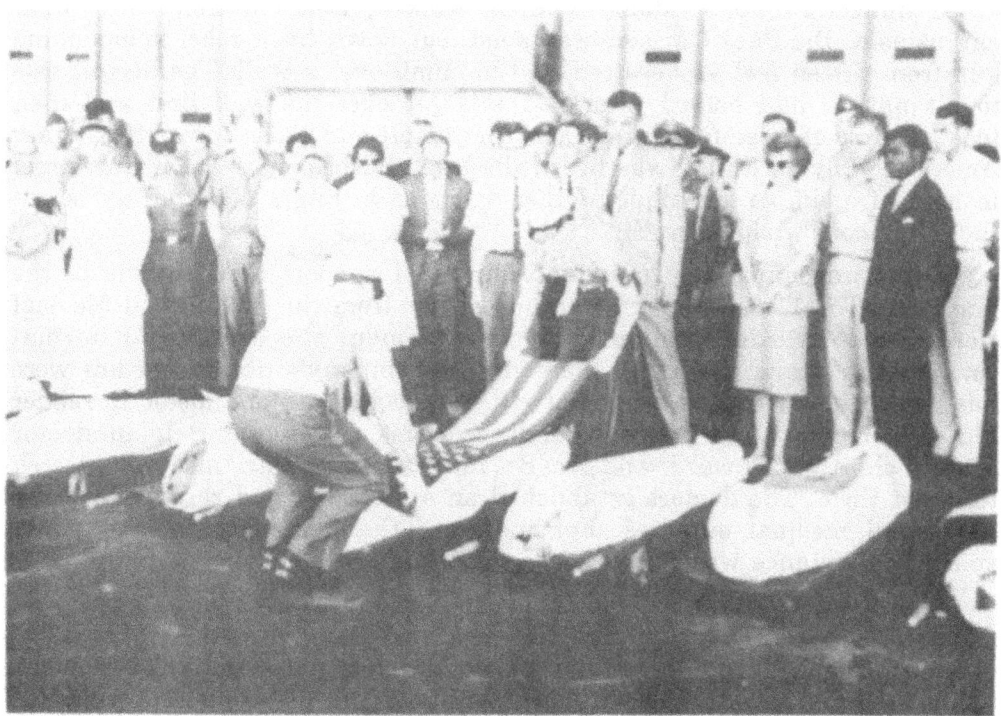

An American flag is placed over the body of Dr. Paul Carlson during services at Leopoldville

There were well over 300 hostages inside the Hotel Victoria, and their waking reactions to the noise of the aircraft were mixed. Most knew that the roar of aircraft around the airfield signified the arrival of the Belgian paras; a French secretary from the consulate had told James Stauffer the previous day that the paras were on their way. Some of the hostages, attracted by the spectacle, went up on the roof to watch the show, noting that as long as the aircraft were visible over the city, the rebels remained hidden. Others, in an effort to calm their nerves, prepared and ate their breakfasts, avoiding all speculation on their immediate future. Others simply prayed. Those who listened to Radio Stanleyville had heard the order at 0630 to kill all foreigners. When Colonel Opepe ordered them out into the streets at 0700, not all of them obeyed. Some barricaded themselves in their rooms and hid under beds or in closets.[24] Most, however, obediently moved into the street and marched to the massacre at the corner of Avenue Sergeant Ketele.

Major Mine reacted immediately to the scene before him. Making the almost inevitable comment, "C'est le Congo!" Mine urged the 11th Company forward to its objectives, the Hotel Victoria, the Congo Palace, and the prison. Meanwhile, members of Lieutenant Mertens' platoon and the battalion staff began stabilizing the local situation.[25]

Of the roughly 250 hostages gathered by the Simbas that morning, 18 were already dead, and another 40 were severely wounded. The Simbas had killed indiscriminately, shooting men, women, and children with equal enthusiasm. Dr. Paul Carlson was dead, cut down by a rebel submachine gun from fifteen feet as he attempted to climb over a wall. The doctor, true to his nature, had helped Charles Davis get over the wall first and then took a burst of over fifty slugs as he attempted to cross himself. Another American, Phyllis Rhine, was hit in the legs and bled to death in the street in need of a simple tourniquet. Other wounded hostages died quickly before the paras could help them.[26]

The Paracommandos had limited medical support at the scene of the massacre. The 11th Company had one doctor from the Regimental Medical Center and an additional medic to supplement the company's normal complement of one medic per platoon. The company's normal medics were busy with their platoons, and that left one doctor and one medic to render aid to some forty seriously wounded victims. A second Belgian doctor arrived shortly afterward, and Dr. Brevant, a Frenchman, also volunteered to assist them. The doctors established an aid station and radioed back for additional medical supplies. For many of the hostages, however, only spiritual assistance was available.[27]

Padre [father] Van der Goten of the 1st Parachute Battalion, an old soldier and veteran of the fighting in World War II, had seen a lot of deaths, particularly fatalities among the civilian population. He now moved among the dead and the dying to administer the last rites. He made no effort to distinguish between Protestants or Catholics, blacks or whites, as he granted absolution and final comfort to over fifty people lying in the street.[28]

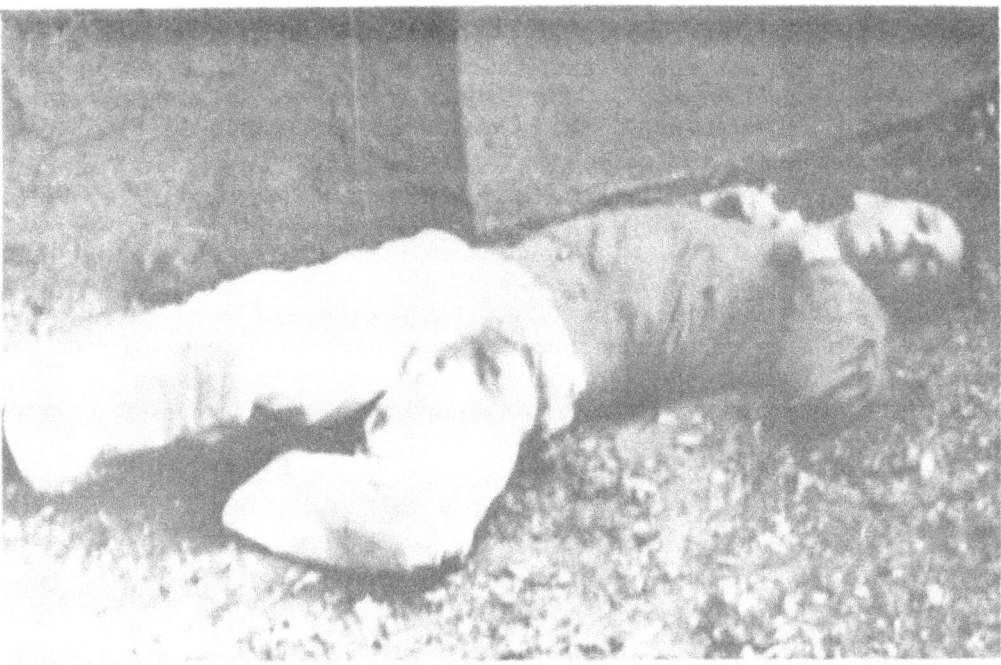

The corpse of Dr. Carlson

Off-loading medical supplies and food at Stanleyville

The paras' assembly of the survivors was made all the more difficult by the mental state of those fortunate enough to be alive. Families had broken apart in the scramble to avoid the rebels' fire. Some families, in attempting to rally to one another, had been cut down one by one. For other families, there were joyous reunions in the street, at the airport, or later back in Leopoldville. For many, the only reunion was to be in the painful experience of identifying the remains of a loved one. Most of the hostages were in shock, and some were near madness. One unfortunate mother staggered around the street holding her dead child until a soldier took it from her and her husband led her away. It was this pitiful group that the paras had to get to the airport.[29]

Major Anne de Molina, the 1st Parachute Battalion's S3, established the forward command post in a concrete building off the intersection. As the paras assembled the refugees, they moved them into the building for protection. Within minutes, Simba rifle fire and an occasional mortar round began to pepper the area. Not all the Simbas in the area had succeeded in getting away; one unlucky rebel tried hiding under the paras' radio jeep, where he was soon discovered and captured. He later met his fate at the less gentle hands of the ANC. As the numbers of refugees grew, Anne de Molina's task became increasingly difficult.[30]

Anne de Molina organized successive columns of evacuees. As he gathered in a group of 100 to 200 refugees, he placed them under the escort of Ledant's jumpmasters or Sergeant Spillebeen's reconnaissance jeeps. Ledant had separated his jumpmasters into several teams. Some, namely Mertens and Huyberechts, were back at the airfield. Others, under Captains Vanderperre and Lauwers and Lieutenant Mousset, provided column escort mounted on AS-24s. Most of the refugees walked the three kilometers [nearly two miles] back to the airfield; the exceptions were the seriously wounded that Anne de Molina evacuated on confiscated transport. While the S3 worked on the refugee problem, his battalion commander continued to direct the unit's operations.[31]

Inside the command post, Mine recognized that if further slaughter was to be avoided, haste was necessary. He directed the 11th Company to continue its operations in the center of the city, while the 13th Company moved along the Congo River. Though the 12th Company had been moving in accordance with its original orders to screen the northern flank of the city, Mine changed its mission. He directed Captain Raes to move into the vicinity of the command post to protect the hostage assembly area. Even as Mine and his S3 brought some order into the chaos of Avenue Sergeant Ketele, further assistance arrived in the form of their regimental commander.[32]

About one-half hour after the paras' arrival at the massacre site, Colonel Laurent arrived via an AS-24. Laurent quickly reviewed the situation with his battalion commander. He approved the dispositions but ordered that one platoon of the 12th Company be sent to clear the route back to the airfield, already under increasingly heavy harassment by the Simbas. Satisfied, Laurent set off with Majors Ledant and Rousseaux to swing through the city, leaving behind his other traveling companion, John Clingerman.[33]

John Clingerman was in the center of Stanleyville looking for the American hostages. Wearing a .45 on his hip, the former consul was extremely worried about their fate when he arrived with Colonel Laurent. Though dismayed by the deaths of Dr. Carlson and Miss Rhine, Clingerman was greatly relieved to find all five American officials alive and in relatively good condition. He hustled them into the evacuation columns for the airport, though he met some resistance from Grinwis.[34]

In his capacity as CIA agent cum vice consul, Grinwis had readily grasped the significance of controlling Radio Stanleyville. Therefore, he wanted the Belgians to secure its downtown office in order to broadcast instructions to all non-Congolese to move to the center of the city for evacuation. For some reason, the Belgians refused to comply, though Grinwis' wishes were in keeping with their operations order. Clingerman ordered Grinwis back to the airfield, leaving his suggestion unheeded by the paras, a suggestion that would have made their search of the city all the easier.[35]

The 11th Company had continued its clearing and search operations inside Stanleyville (see map 12). Each of its platoons broke off from the company and operated as independent units. Lieutenant Mertens' platoon

Map 12. Dragon Rouge, Phase III, search and evacuation, 0750—1400

had moved off ten minutes after it reached the massacre site. On the way to its original objective, the platoon ran into a pickup truck full of Simbas. Having just seen the victims of the Simbas' bloody nature, the paras were not in a merciful mood. They opened fire immediately, killing several rebels and wounding others before the remainder fled. Mertens moved his platoon on to the Victoria Hotel, where they found two more non-Congolese casualties, this time one dead and another wounded outside the building. Mertens deployed two sections to cover his movement and took one section inside to search the hotel. They found around fifty hostages, who had remained hidden inside when Colonel Opepe had ordered the group into the street. Mertens' men had to coax them out. Once assembled, he sent them to the battalion command post before continuing his mission.[36]

In the vicinity of the Place du Canon, Mertens' platoon began house-to-house searches. It was dangerous work. In clearing the houses, his men had to announce their presence to draw the Europeans out of hiding. Often the Europeans remained inside, and the paras had to go into the houses and get them. Though trained in clearing buildings by assault, the soldiers could hardly toss a grenade into a building that might hold innocent civilians. Instead, they called out in French and Flemish that they were coming in before entering each house; one soldier, De Waegeneer, was cut down by a Simba just as he entered the front door of a house. He was the first para wounded in the operation, and his name was the first name entered in red in Laurent's journal. Mertens evacuated him to the airport for immediate medical attention and grimly pressed on with his mission.[37]

Mertens' platoon continued along Avenue Major Massart to Avenue Bernart. In the vicinity of Avenue Bernart, a refugee informed Mertens that more hostages were located near the Public Market. Since he had his own sector to search, Mertens passed the information back to the 1st Parachute Battalion command post and kept moving. His next objective was the prison; his platoon secured the prison without finding any non-Congolese prisoners. Satisfied that his sector was cleared of refugees, the platoon leader established a blocking position at the Place du Canon and remained there till 1530.[38]

The other two platoons of 11th Company were engaged in similar operations. Lieutenant Hardy, with the 2d Platoon, moved north from Avenue Sergeant Ketele to clean out a factory behind the Palace Hotel. His subsequent objectives were the local brewery and, finally, the Ecole des Soeurs Franciscaines. As Hardy's and Mertens' platoons moved, they came under sporadic, harassing fire. By 0815, Hardy had reached his final objective and rescued a total of 150 refugees, all of whom he returned to the battalion command post. The 1st Platoon, 11th Company, under Lieutenant Wittemans, moved eastward via the radio station, Place Leopold II, and, finally, the Place de la Victoria. Again, as the soldiers gathered in refugees, they directed them eastward to the battalion command post for evacuation. By 1300, Captain Pierlinck's 11th Company had accomplished its mission inside the city. It remained there in blocking positions until

1530.³⁹ Meanwhile, both the 12th and the 13th Companies were engaged in their own operations.

Lieutenant Patte, at the head of 13th Company, had followed the 11th Company as it approached Stanleyville. As the 13th Company moved, Sergeant Goris, with the second section of armored vehicles, caught up with the company. Goris, delayed by the mishap with Chalk Six, raced past the company and shifted into tactical movement. Like Spillebeen, Goris leapfrogged his two jeeps forward, successively clearing each intersection. Patte's company, with Goris out front, was organized in accordance with its mission. His lead platoon, under Lieutenant Kovilic, had specific instructions to move as fast as possible behind the reconnaissance jeeps, while the trail platoons, the 1st Platoon and the 4.2-inch Mortar Platoon, gathered in the refugees. At the junction of Avenue Maréchal Montgomery, Patte's company veered southward to Avenue Reine Elisabeth to cover the southern flank of the city.⁴⁰

Escorted by the Dutch missionary, Patte's first objective was the Procure at the Mission du Sacré Coeur. At 0750, Patte's lead platoon reached the objective and found around fifty nuns and missionaries. Though unharmed, these people were more than willing to evacuate, and Patte sent them under escort to the airfield. Shortly afterward, the 13th Company received orders to proceed to the Hotel des Chutes, where they found another three refugees and a large quantity of arms and ammunition. Once again, Patte moved off on the route to Camp Ketele.⁴¹

As the 13th Company departed the Hotel des Chutes, Sergeant Goris ran into a truck full of Simbas, who fired wildly in his direction. Goris' return fire was deadly; he killed one Simba and wounded several more in the exchange. Despite this brief firefight, the column continued until 0810, when it received an incoming rocket; fortunately, Simba gunnery remained poor, and the rocket missed. During the pause, Colonel Laurent and his companions, Majors Ledant and Rousseaux, stopped on their way back from the eastern part of the city. Laurent urged Patte and the 13th Company to move out. Patte obeyed and increased his rate of march, passing numerous houses with Europeans visible inside. The paras called to them to move toward the airfield and pressed on to Camp Ketele, where the 13th Company arrived at 0900.⁴²

Patte's company occupied the camp quickly, thus closing the eastern exit of Stanleyville three hours after the airborne operation began. Patte sent one section in to search the camp area; they found it empty of life but seized two vehicles and another 12.7-mm Chinese machine gun. Meanwhile, Patte dispatched Goris and the company mortar section to the eastern edge of the camp to establish blocking positions. On the same road, he installed Lieutenant Kovilic's 2d Platoon facing the native quarters, Bruxelles, to the north. Farther west, the 4.2-inch Mortar Platoon, under Captain Ramaeckers, established the northwest blocking position. Patte then sent Lieutenant Bourgeois and the 1st Platoon to the east-west road south of Camp Ketele to secure it by 1030.⁴³

Patte's northern positions soon became the objective of several Simba attacks originating from a native village. The northern road between Camp Ketele and the village was screened by heavy brush. Simba infiltrators used the abundant cover to creep undetected to within bow range of the Paracommandos. They would then open fire with small arms, bows and arrows, and even spears. Trooper Closset of the company mortar section took a round through the back at 1030 and was evacuated to the airfield; his was the second name in red in Laurent's journal. To discourage further attacks and "to calm" the rebels, the paras began tossing a couple of grenades into the bush at the first sign of hostile activity. The paras found that each grenade shower was worth about a quarter of an hour of peace before the Simbas again grew restless. While Patte's company traded grenades for arrows with the Simbas around Camp Ketele, the 12th Company had gone into action.[44]

At 0930, Major Mine gave Captain Raes new orders based on his original mission. Mine directed that 12th Company move to the northwest of the European sector of the city toward the native quarter, Belge I, and westward to Camp Prince Leopoldville II. Raes was to cut off Simba infiltration routes toward the airfield road and the city's center.[45]

Raes' unit, in reserve at the battalion command post since 0815, moved off on two axes in the direction of the Atheneé Royal Stad. One platoon moved northwest along Avenue Chaltin, while the other platoon paralleled its movement along Avenues Lothaire and Binnie. In the vicinity of the stadium, Raes' young Paracommandos ran into heavy resistance, which they answered with grenades and their bazookas. By 1200, Raes had moved along Boulevard Ryckmans to the main route leading north to the Tshopo Bridge. Again, they ran into heavy resistance centered around a second stadium to their north. One 12th Company soldier, Nobels, was wounded, providing a third name in red for Laurent's journal. Raes radioed his position, and Mine ordered him to hold in place, where he remained until 1600. Confirmed in person by Colonel Laurent, the order to halt prevented useless casualties. Raes had accomplished his objective of halting Simba movement toward the airfield.[46]

Operations at the airport had continued after the departure of the paras for Stanleyville. Gradwell continued to orbit the field, while down in the control tower, Major Hardenne passed information to him. Chalks Six and Twelve remained on the ground waiting for evacuees, but for almost an hour, nothing seemed to happen. Gradwell, concerned by a low fog bank which blocked visibility, had his pilot, Captain William Long, fly lower underneath the scud. Soon the C-130 was down below 500 feet, and the Simbas reacted immediately. The rebels hit Gradwell's C-130 seven times with small arms, and the crew chief reported serious fuel and hydraulic leaks. Gradwell knew he would have to turn for Leopoldville or Kamina. Before he could do that, however, he had to make a decision about his two aircraft on the ground.[47]

About 0800, Hardenne radioed Gradwell, "Do you see any smoke on any of the buildings any place? And can you direct us to their area. We are amazed that there are no hostages. There are no people for us to load as yet."[48] Hardenne's question almost decided the issue. Gradwell had fulfilled his mission, and he did not want to leave his aircraft on the ground exposed to hostile fire. He knew that the C-130s of JTF LEO were on standby, waiting to begin the air evacuation. Gradwell began to order Captain Secord to take off, then stopped. Canceling the order, Gradwell instinctively felt that both Chalks Six and Twelve would be needed. Reluctantly, he turned toward Leopoldville with the two C-130s still on the ground.[49]

Defending the airfield at Stanleyville

On the airfield, the Belgians were organized and waiting for news from Stanleyville. Hardenne had been running the ground-to-air liaison net but found that his limited English did not meet the strain of the fast-talking American pilots. Consequently, he asked Captain Strobaugh and Sergeant Dias to take over the air-operations net. Hardenne then went to assist Commandant Jacques Holvoet. Holvoet was the Belgian officer responsible for the evacuation of the refugees. He and three jumpmasters, Coremans, Pattyn, and Gillet, established a control point near the tower to process the civilians. Shortly after 0800, Holvoet and Hardenne received word that refugees were en route to the field. Neither officer was prepared for the throng that soon descended on the airport.[50]

The first refugees arrived at the airfield at 0830. Guarded by jumpmasters and men from the 1st Parachute Battalion, they had walked the three kilometers from the city. The condition of the survivors was a mixture of shock and despair. Holvoet's men attempted to process them but gave up and merely pushed them onto Mac Secord's C-130. Watching from the ramp of the second C-130, Lieutenant Colonel George Banning and Captain May, Detachment 1's flight surgeon, waited for any casualties. Shortly after the first hostages arrived at the field, three trucks with yellow crosses drove onto the tarmac and headed for Chalk Twelve. The doctor's wait was over; they were soon overwhelmed with work. As the trucks pulled up, the Belgians began unloading wounded civilians. Major Robinson's public affairs team had been filming the scene, but they stopped, as everyone available tried to help with the casualties.[51]

These people were the twenty most critically wounded during the massacre. One victim, a man, had been shot through the chest; the bullet had exited through the side of his mouth. Another, a woman, had been shot in her left leg, the bullet also shattering her pelvis and lodging in her abdomen. A third victim, this one a young man, had his arm virtually shot off; the arm hung from his shoulder, held by a flap of skin, arteries, veins, and nerves. While these three represented some of the most severe cases, the others were also in serious condition. The floor of the aircraft was soon covered with their blood.[52]

Banning and May worked feverishly to save lives. With so many wounded, the doctors could provide only limited care to each individual. Their corpsman, Charles Terrell, assisted, helped by Robinson's team and the crew chief. One Belgian soldier, seeing a need for some sort of sheet to lay on the floor of the aircraft, pulled the exterior wrap off a Congolese woman and gave the almost nine yards of cloth to the crew chief. Banning and May used morphine to quiet the wounded and hung i.v. bags along the side of the aircraft. Within minutes, the doctors were ready for the two and one-half hour flight to Leopoldville. In spite of their efforts, three of the victims died, one inflight and two in the hospital. Even as the ramp closed on the C-130, the Simbas took it under fire. The Belgians ordered it and the other C-130 to take off. Now with a load of 100 refugees, Secord's C-130 taxied to the eastern ramp, turned onto the strip, and with the sound of rounds peppering his ship, roared down the runway and into the air. Banning's aircraft immediately followed him.[53]

Banning's medical evacuation. Wounded hostages receive medical aid.

When Banning's C-130 launched from Stanleyville, its departure significantly reduced the medical capacity of Dragon Rouge. While Banning had twenty of the most serious cases with him, there were another thirty left behind who would be evacuated without the benefit of special medical care. Moreover, Banning's aircraft took off without unloading 600 pounds of medical supplies, supplies that would be needed in Stanleyville. But neither Banning nor the Belgians had the luxury of time in making the decision to take off; the rebel fire, originally only scattered harassment, had become a serious threat.[54]

Unknown to the Belgians, the Simbas had returned in force to the airfield. A group of around 150 rebels had closed in around the western end of the runway. Another force of approximately 180 men had occupied the northern border of the strip. These two groups had held their fire till 0830, when they took two C-130s full of refugees as targets.[55]

Even as they ordered the C-130s to launch, the Paracommandos responded to the Simbas' attack. Captain Huyberechts, who had been helping load the wounded on Banning's aircraft, took jumpmasters Smaers, Reniers, and Deschryver to answer the rebel threat. Huyberechts could hear a submachine gun firing from the wood line, and he moved toward its probable location. While his men laid down covering fire, Huyberechts flanked the position and forced the rebels to withdraw. The paras pursued, but the rebels continued to elude them. Soon Huyberechts found himself 500 meters into the wood line in a fruitless search for the Simbas. Before he could again make contact with this northern threat, Huyberechts received new orders recalling him to the airfield to answer a different attack.[56]

At 0850, Lieutenant Forman's 2d Platoon, 12th Company, had returned from the city on the orders of Colonel Laurent. The platoon had accomplished its mission of clearing the evacuation route before continuing to the airfield. Huyberechts met it at the control tower and took command. Pressure had built up on the eastern end of the airfield, and Huyberechts moved to drive the rebels back. After pushing the rebels back out of small-arms range, he put the Paracommandos into position along the eastern border of the airport. His mission completed, Huyberechts returned to the tower for further orders.[57]

Huyberechts' fire brigade defense of the eastern end of the airfield was symptomatic of the entire perimeter. At the western end of the field, Sergeant Derwaerder had countered three rebel probes before noon. Laurent and his men were learning the hard way that the Simbas were not the same as the Congolese of 1960. While the Simbas were unorganized, ill disciplined, and extremely poor marksmen, they did not quit. The rebels kept coming back, and with two-thirds of his men in the city, Laurent was unable to build a continuous perimeter around the airfield. This lack of security greatly complicated air evacuation operations.[58]

After the Simba attack at 0830, Strobaugh halted air operations for the next half hour. This suspension of air operations, however, did not stop the movement of refugees to the airfield. Whereas Hardenne had been concerned over an absence of hostages at 0800, by 0900, he and Holvoet were facing a flood of humanity. While Holvoet attempted to care for the refugees—providing food, water, and shelter from rebel fire—Strobaugh and the Belgians worked feverishly to get them safely out of Stanleyville.[59]

John Clingerman returned to the airport shortly after 1100. There, he worked with Holvoet in sorting out the refugees and debriefing them. Clingerman also turned the captured Hugh Scotland over to Grinwis to escort back to Leopoldville. Grinwis knew that the British embassy would be interested in the latest activities of the journalist. At 1145, Clingerman gave Strobaugh a message for immediate transmission. The message informed Leopoldville that the American officials were alive but that Carlson and Rhine were dead. Clingerman requested immediate assistance for the remaining wounded. Strobaugh got the message through with difficulty on the single-sideband net. To push the information through, Clingerman made a direct phone call to Washington and reported the details of the massacre. At this time, the Twilight network was oversaturated with signals, as a host of stations sought information on the situation, and net discipline had broken down. Refugees continued to stream into the airfield in groups of 100 to 200. Finally, at 1115, Strobaugh, again through the overloaded

A C-130 roars in low over Stanleyville before returning to Leopoldville

Twilight Net, passed a critical situation report that ended with: "Junction with Vandewalle made at Camp Ketele at 0900." Laurent's beleaguered troops had received vital reinforcements in the form of L'Ommengang.⁶⁰

At 1100, the eastern blocking position of the 13th Company on the Rue de L'Ituri reported contact with the 5th Brigade Mecanisée. In approaching the city, Vandewalle's men fired a flare as the recognition signal and proceeded into Camp Ketele. At the outskirts of the camp, Frenchy spotted several red berets behind a machine-gun position; the coordinated assault on Stanleyville, so long debated at the highest levels of three governments, was now a reality.⁶¹

Following their halt at 0330, Vandewalle's troops slept uneasily till 0530. Shortly afterward, the march resumed, led by Frenchy in his beloved Ferret. Around 0615, news of Dragon Rouge reached them, and the column, now covered by close air support, increased its pace. Once Vandewalle had reached the new tarmac road to Stanleyville, he put both his armored cars abreast in the lead for the last ninety kilometers into the city. The last barrier on the way was the Bailey bridge at Wanie Rukulu, thirty kilometers south of Stanleyville. The column slowed to cross the bridge, firing as it went at scattered rebel resistance. Twenty kilometers from the city, L'Ommengang ran into several groups of three to five cars filled with fleeing rebels. The armored cars and the air cover played havoc with these Simbas, who fortunately had not taken any hostages with them in their escape from Stanleyville.⁶²

Upon hitting Camp Ketele, Vandewalle's forces split up according to plan. Liegeois and Lamouline pursued their individual objectives. Lima I penetrated the city, occupying key crossroads, and by 1230, its 51st Commando controlled the Tshopo Bridge. Lima II dropped off the tail of L'Ommengang and occupied Camp Ketele. With these points now under control, the principal escape routes out of Stanleyville were finally closed.⁶³

Vandewalle, accompanied by Rattan, Robertson, and the Cuban exiles, proceeded at full speed to the airfield. At 1130, Vandewalle met with Major Hardenne to discuss operational boundaries. Vandewalle, with his greater mobility, assumed control of the city east of the Canal de la Kitenge. His troops were to secure the city and search its outlying areas for remaining hostages (see map 13). As of 1700, the Paracommandos would withdraw west of the canal and maintain control of the airfield. Hardenne agreed with the proposal, as it matched his commander's intent; Laurent wanted nothing to do with the government column's actions in Stanleyville. He expected savagery by the mercenary and native troops in retribution against the rebels.⁶⁴

While Hardenne and Vandewalle conferred, Rattan and Robertson met with Clingerman. Clingerman in his debriefings of American refugees had learned from Al Larson, an American missionary, that some twenty-five missionaries remained at his mission, referred to locally as the "Kilometer 8 mission." Larson knew that his companions were in grave danger. He had tried to get the Belgians to rescue them, but while sympathetic to his

Map 13. L'Ommengang's occupation of Stanleyville, 1100—1815

concerns, they just did not have the men or transport. Clingerman now turned to Rattan and Robertson to resolve the problem; both agreed to make the effort. Rattan went with Sam Weisel to find some transport, while Robertson, with Larson as a guide, proceeded to the mission.[65]

Robertson introduced himself to Larson as "Carlos" and led the group along the route specified by the missionary. Larson was impressed by the swarthy band, who were careful to describe themselves as "not Castro Cubans." The tiny force sped through the town in a jeep and a pickup truck, passed by Camp Prince Leopold II, and punched through two roadblocks to reach the mission. For one of the missionaries, they were three hours too late.[66]

That morning, the Simbas had arrived to arrest the remaining missionaries at Kilometer 8. Panicked by the news of Dragon Rouge, the Simbas shot two missionaries and two boys. One missionary, Hector McMillan, died shortly afterward, but the others survived. Larson and Robertson found the survivors shaken. The CIA agent wasted no time: his troops emptied their vehicles of everything that did not shoot and crammed the refugees in them. Robertson left McMillan's body behind, along with the refugees' baggage, and the overloaded vehicles roared back into Stanleyville without incident. Again, Robertson's men were at pains to clarify their political affiliations. One of the men, after taking a snapshot of a pig along the road, smiled and said, "Castro . . . someday we do that!"[67]

In the meantime, Rattan had been having his own adventures in just getting out of town. While he had succeeded in getting a truck, when he headed out of the city accompanied by Delbert Carper, they ran into a firefight. Carper, another missionary from Kilometer 8, was anxious to get to the mission, but their Congolese driver refused to continue, so Rattan decided to return to town. There, he picked up a squad of Hoare's men and a gun jeep and proceeded out to the mission. Rattan found the Cubans' gear and the missionaries' baggage and loaded it on the truck. However, he did not find McMillan's body. During the return to Stanleyville, Rattan's group came under fire from the ANC, some Belgian mercenaries, and a Simba. Fortunately, their aim was bad, and Rattan made it back to the airfield in one piece.[68]

At the airfield, the number of refugees grew as columns continued to arrive from the city. Other refugees, rescued by actions such as Robertson's, added to their number. Vandewalle had now established direct liaison with the Paracommandos; Captaine Commandant Armand Verdickt, Vandewalle's intelligence officer, who had just arrived from Kindu, coordinated mercenary rescue parties with Hardenne. By 1800, his teams had located and rescued over 200 refugees. By 1200, Laurent was back at the field; he was concerned by the number of refugees that had accumulated. At 1225, Laurent passed a message through Strobaugh demanding that the Belgian embassy charter at least two DC-6s for evacuation support. He further asked for maximum C-130 support for refugee airlift.[69] Laurent soon had the requested support.

In accordance with OPLAN 319/64, JTF LEO was to provide the C-130 support for airlift operations. Consequently, one C-130 from Kamina had flown in with emergency rations to Stanleyville and had taken off with a full load of refugees. The remaining two C-130s of JTF LEO at Kamina, responding to Laurent's call, also launched for Stanleyville. After their recovery at Kamina, the three Dragon aircraft flew back to Stanleyville. There, the aircrews ignored passenger limitations; load masters crammed in as many as 120 evacuees at a time. If a family member got left out, the Belgians just picked him up and crammed him into the plane. The American C-130s airlifted close to 800 refugees by the end of operations on 24 November. Aircraft belonging to Air Congo, Sabena Airlines, the Belgian Air Force, the United Kingdom, France, Italy, and the Red Cross: all responded to Laurent's demand for support.[70]

Strobaugh's responsibility was to bring all these aircraft into Stanleyville safely. Strobaugh also had other aircraft to handle besides the evacuation airlift; with the arrival of Vandewalle, Strobaugh had a large number of close air support aircraft flying in and out of the field. By late afternoon, there were four T-6s, two T-28s, and a number of B-26s flown by Cubans. The ever-changing tactical situation around the airfield complicated Strobaugh's job. Fortunately there was no wind, and as Simba pressure built up on one end of the field, he was able to shift the approach into the airport to the opposite end. At 1430, Strobaugh relinquished his long-range communications responsibility to USSTRICOM's joint communications support element, which had been flown in from Kamina. Teletype communications remained slow, with Flash messages taking three to seven hours to reach the United States. Further support came as the Belgian air traffic control team succeeded in getting the tower back in order. This team, composed of Lieutenant Colonel Cailleau and Lieutenant Dedoncker, took full control of the air operations beginning at 1700. By midafternoon, Stanleyville Airport had the appearance of a gargantuan wasp's nest, with air evacuation missions being conducted simultaneously with close air support.[71] Laurent, however, still needed additional forces to protect the critical field.

At 1300, almost all of the 1st Parachute Battalion was still committed inside Stanleyville. As mentioned earlier, Lieutenant Mertens of the 11th Company had learned that the Simbas still held a number of hostages in the area of the Public Market. When a patrol from the 11th Company failed to get through to the market, Major Mine ordered the 13th Company to move to the area to secure any hostages. The 13th Company was no longer needed at Camp Ketele, since Lima II was now in control of that cantonment. However, Lieutenant Patte experienced difficulty in regrouping the 13th; at the time, the native troops of Lima II were firing indiscriminately inside the camp, and Lieutenant Patte had lost radio contact with one of his platoons along the camp's southern border. Patte was forced to send a patrol through the camp to notify the platoon to reassemble at the company command post. At 1400, an hour after receiving Mine's orders, Patte moved out toward the Public Market.[72]

The 13th Company, again with Sergeant Goris in the vanguard, hit the market soon afterward. En route, Patte had met little resistance, and at the market, he found that the Simbas had disappeared after killing one Belgian shopkeeper. The 13th Company did find approximately forty refugees in hiding around the square and soon had them on the way to the airfield. Patte's rescue of these hostages was the final action of the 1st Parachute Battalion inside Stanleyville. At 1500, Colonel Laurent ordered the withdrawal of Mine's battalion. Within one-half hour, the three rifle companies broke contact with the rebels and moved to the west. By 1700, all of Mine's companies were back at the airfield; they were sorely needed.[73]

Lieutenant Le Grelle, Headquarters Company, was charged with the defense of the western end of the airfield. All morning, he and Sergeant Derwaerder had been fighting off attacks by the Simbas. Until midafternoon, these attacks had been relatively unorganized, with the Simbas content to periodically harass the paras with probing actions. Around 1600, however, the threat against Le Grelle's men grew serious. Simba pressure on the western end of the airfield had exploded shortly after 1530. Le Grelle had known since 0830 that there were well over 100 rebels concealed in the bush facing his men. But he did not have enough men to expand his perimeter, so the Paracommandos had merely responded to sporadic probes. Le Grelle became concerned, however, when he heard the Simbas begin chanting to build up their spirits for a major assault. The young paras, though chilled by the savage nature of their enemy, gripped their weapons more tightly and grimly waited for the attack.[74]

Just as the last C-130 came in to land at 1745, the Simbas threw up a heavy curtain of fire in front of Le Grelle's men. The C-130 aborted its landing, and all air operations halted. Le Grelle opened fire on the suspected rebel positions, but this time, the Simbas responded differently. Instead of fading back from the airfield, around 150 rebels came marching out of the bush. Led by a Simba witch doctor, the drugged attackers sang and danced as they came forward waving their weapons. It was a madcap attack, and the Belgians, surprised by its idiocy, briefly stopped firing. Just as they resumed firing, the paras came under mortar attack. Between twenty and thirty mortar rounds landed on the Belgian positions. Sergeant Derwaerder, holding the northwest flank of Le Grelle's defense, was slightly wounded. One surprised para had his shirt blown off but was otherwise unscathed. While Derwaerder's men laid down deadly fire on their mindless attackers, Le Grelle requested immediate reinforcements.[75]

Lieutenant Patte and the 13th Company had just gotten back to the airfield and received their defensive assignment. When Le Grelle's demand for reinforcements came in, Major Mine committed Patte's company against the attack. Patte ordered Lieutenant Kovilic's 2d Platoon to move against the Simbas on Le Grelle's northwest flank. Sergeant Goris and three armored jeeps roared up the runway, with Kovilic's men running behind them. Goris opened fire, killing the witch doctor, and broke up the assault. When the enemy mortar fire continued, Mine called in an airstrike by two

T-6s to silence the position. This airstrike ended the immediate threat to the western end of the airfield.[76]

While the paras fought off the Simbas west of the field, Captain Huyberechts was once again in action to the east. De Waegeneer, the 11th Company soldier wounded inside Stanleyville, was in too serious a condition to be evacuated back to Leopoldville. He required immediate surgery, and Colonel Laurent had ordered the Belgian surgical unit flown in from Kamina. It arrived at 1415, and Major Hardenne ordered Captain Huyberechts to seize the European hospital, east of the airfield, for its use. Huyberechts, along with Captain Vanderperre and the jumpmasters Reniers, Pieters, Deschryver, Wauters, and Aelbrecht, moved off on the mission.[77]

Huyberechts' team took the hospital in a short fight. Once inside, they cleared its operating room and captured several wounded rebels. The remaining Simbas hid in the hospital basement and on the second floor, but rather than risk his men, Huyberechts left them alone. He and his men held the Simbas at bay, while the surgeon, Dr. Moons, operated on De Waegeneer. The Belgian surgical unit and its small security team remained outside the airfield defensive perimeter until 1800, when Major Mine had enough forces to include the hospital in his defensive dispositions.[78]

By 1815, Mine had his battalion established in a defensive perimeter around the airfield. The 13th Company, supported by Le Grelle's platoon, occupied the western side of the perimeter, while the 11th Company protected the north. Captain Raes' 12th Company defended the eastern end of the field, including the hospital. Headquarters Company and an airfield defense company of Katanganese that had arrived from Kamina completed the southern boundary. Ledant's men, divided into two teams under Captains Huyberechts and Vanderperre, conducted roving patrols to maintain security against infiltrators. With the establishment of this defensive perimeter, the Paracommando Regiment marked the end of its mission inside Stanleyville.[79]

Vandewalle's forces assumed full responsibility for Stanleyville at 1700. His forces were fully occupied with maintaining control of the city. In addition to the commando holding the Tshopo Bridge, one commando had established a position along the Congo River and was engaged in an artillery and machine-gun exchange with Simbas on the Rive Gauche. Lamouline had control of Camp Ketele and was busy securing Camp Prince Leopold II. Neither Vandewalle nor Laurent made any real effort to move across the Congo River.[80]

Laurent had visited Vandewalle's headquarters at 1500 to confirm their areas of responsibility. Though both supported the withdrawal of Laurent's forces to the airfield, the question of the Rive Gauche has provided a source of controversy that remains active today. After their briefing at Kamina on 23 November, Vandewalle expected the Paracommandos to secure the ferry or a suitable substitute for crossing to the south bank of the Congo River. Laurent, who now states unequivocally that he never agreed to such a responsibility, had not given the matter any priority. Laurent had all the tactical requirements that he could handle. Vandewalle, after his arrival in the city, put off any serious attempt to cross the river. The ferry was inoperable (a fact disputed by Hoare) and would require several days to repair. After an abortive attempt to land an H-21 helicopter covered by T-28s, the crossing of the river was delayed until 27 November. The real losers in this dispute, which seemed to grow out of a personality conflict, were the hostages known to be in Simba hands on the Rive Gauche. Nevertheless, Laurent's and Vandewalle's agreement to divide their forces marked the end of Dragon Rouge. During the next thirty-six hours, Laurent focused on mounting Dragon Noir, while Vandewalle concentrated on securing Stanleyville for the central government.[81]

Last Gasp of the Dragon

The idea that a drop on Stanleyville might necessitate further operations had led to the second planning conference in Brussels. During 18 to 20 November, this conference had produced the necessary contingency plans for follow-on operations in Bunia (Dragon Blanc), Watsa (Dragon Vert), and Paulis (Dragon Noir).[1] Military leaders were already acting on these plans should their execution be necessary. Logistical and tactical planning could not be held in abeyance until a political decision to act was made. Because Simba retribution against the hostages in the outlying districts was an omnipresent threat, planning had to keep abreast of possible developments.[2] The decision to execute Dragon Rouge had been agonizing; the decision to execute Dragon Noir was equally painful. Consequently, the political decision-making process tied to Dragon Noir began almost as soon as Dragon Rouge was under way.

When the word to execute Dragon Rouge flashed to Kamina, planners in Washington, Brussels, and Leopoldville gathered expectantly to await the results of the operation.[3] In Washington, at 0705Z, the first word came from Godley, who reported by telephone of Isaacson's successful drop.[4] Twenty-five minutes later, Godley followed with a despairing cable: "FLASH JUST RECEIVED—Many refugees seeking attain airport were attacked. Fifty to seventy-five wounded. No Rpt. No further details. Endeavoring ascertain."[5] His cable brought visions of disaster to those waiting for further information. Although Godley attempted to speed up the slow communications, the State Department still had to wait until 0745Z to receive Clingerman's message concerning Carlson's death and 0750Z for word of Rhine's demise. Though Clingerman's message also contained news that Hoyt and all the official Americans were unharmed, the confusion existing as to what had actually happened led to impressions of disaster. Washington began calling Leopoldville to clarify the situation, but by 0848Z, message traffic was reporting that two massacres had occurred. One message erroneously reported a massacre at the airport hotel. Another message announced the actual massacre near the Hotel Victoria, though an earlier message reported it as having occurred at Lumumba Square.[6]

The communications problem created consternation between the National Military Command Center (NMCC), the State Department, USSTRICOM, and USEUCOM. The military was in contact with the State Department trying to find out about Godley's phone calls; the State Department complained about the delay in teletype communications; the NMCC called USSTRICOM and ordered that the teletype relay be improved; and USEUCOM called the NMCC to report that the needed information was coming in via the Twilight Net.[7]

The results of Dragon Rouge did not emerge until late in the evening, after Godley had debriefed Hoyt and Grinwis. The only good news during this period of doubt was that the 52d Commando had successfully taken Aketi, rescuing well over 100 non-Congolese without a loss. Coupled with the initial gloomy reporting out of Stanleyville was the expected international backlash. While the operation was supported in the United States and Belgium, Third World reaction was hostile and continued to grow in its ferocity. Planners in Washington and Brussels had approached the Dragon Rouge operation with trepidation; now, with the current feeling of gloom, they were hesitant to push for further operations.[8]

Perhaps sensing the mood in Washington and Brussels—and the developing inertia—Ambassador Godley was the first to go on record in support of follow-on operations. At 1800Z on 24 November, Godley cabled the views of the Americans and Belgians in Leopoldville, stating they "strongly" favored "proceeding with drops on Paulis and Bunia according to plan." Noting an absence of hard information on the fate of non-Congolese in the outlying districts, he stated it was the "unanimous belief of Belgians and Americans that all non-Congolese hostages in gravest danger." Godley pushed hard for the simultaneous execution of Dragon Blanc and Dragon Noir on Thursday. He suggested that the Paracommandos might be withdrawn to Kamina on Wednesday and launched from there. This would distance the new operations from ANC actions in Stanleyville.[9] With this reaction from the field, the high-level decision makers met in Washington and Brussels to discuss the issues.

A joint State Department and Department of Defense group met on the same evening as Godley's cable to discuss the issue of follow-on operations. The overriding question that dogged the meeting was the number of men necessary to implement the operation. While the group recognized the necessity for follow-on operations, the increasingly hostile world reaction to the Stanleyville operation colored their thinking. Secretary of State Dean Rusk questioned the justification for a rescue mission in Paulis, because the number of hostages and occurrences of atrocities there were unknown. Rusk pointed out that the execution of Dragon Rouge, already a source of international uproar, was prompted by knowledge of the number of hostages involved and on documented atrocities. The meeting broke up without a resolution of the issue, but that evening, the State Department stated its position in a paper to the Defense Department.[10]

The paper requested an American-Belgian study of the situation in Stanleyville and of the effect of an immediate withdrawal of the Paracommandos to Kamina. The State Department hoped a withdrawal would protect the hostages in Paulis, Bunia, and Watsa, thus making further interventions unnecessary. It felt such a withdrawal might also document the humanitarian nature of Dragon Rouge and quell rising Third World hostility.[11] When the business day ended in Washington on 24 November, the mood concerning further operations in the Congo was definitely pessimistic.

The mood in Brussels was equally dismal. Though opposition leaders had supported the operation in Stanleyville, Spaak remained hesitant concerning further operations. Like the secretary of state in Washington, Spaak could easily envisage Belgium being drawn into a damaging Congolese entanglement. How many more operations could Laurent complete without having Belgium held up to international scorn as a neocolonialist? Already Belgium was under fire from the Third World, and Spaak must have wondered how long he would have Belgian domestic support for continued operations. He had already risked the future of his political party by deciding to intervene in the Congo without formal approval of the Belgian Parliament. Could he do it again? Like those in Washington, Spaak suspended his decision until he received input from the field.[12]

In keeping with his personality, General Adams did not wait for Leopoldville's answer to the latest round of soul-searching in Washington and Brussels. At 0550Z on 25 November, Adams cabled the JCS expressing his opinions on the Congo. Adams came down firmly on the side of further operations. Like Godley, he pushed for the operations at Bunia and Paulis on 26 November, followed by Watsa as soon as it was feasible. Adams described the military situation in the Congo as "practically a rout," which demanded full-scale pursuit operations. While Adams' views were noted, Washington awaited the verdict from the Congo.[13]

Like Ambassador Godley, the military leaders inside the Congo had begun planning follow-on operations even before the Paracommandos withdrew to the airfield. At 1630 on 24 November, Colonels Logiest, Marliere, Laurent, and Vandewalle met to discuss the requirements for subsequent operations. The second Brussels conference had decided that the priority of targets would be Bunia, Paulis, and Watsa—in that order. In these later discussions, however, the priority changed. After initial objections by Colonel Laurent, the group agreed that Paulis should be the first target. The debriefing of the hostages rescued at Aketi that morning indicated that several hundred hostages in Paulis were in the hands of a particularly vicious group of Simbas. Consequently, Paulis would be the priority if follow-on operations were authorized. This accord received the further support of General Mobutu, who visited Laurent's headquarters at 1805; the ANC commander was more than willing to have the Belgians quell the rebellion in the northeastern Congo. With the priority of targets established, the meeting adjourned.[14]

At 2000, Laurent convened a staff meeting at his headquarters concerning the proposed operations. Laurent's S2 section had been busy assembling information on Paulis. They had aerial photography from the Running Bear RC-97 mission, but the only available map of the city was a ten centimeter by ten centimeter map in a tourist brochure (see map 14). Fortunately, José Romnée, an old SAS trooper rescued in Stanleyville, had provided critical information to fill in the gaps. Despite the focus on Paulis, however, Laurent still considered Bunia and Watsa as probable targets. He directed Major Mine to request two helicopters for medical evacuation support should the regiment be ordered to jump on these locations. The meeting ended; Mine was to work out the concept of operation for each target prior to a conference at 0730 the next day.[15]

Mine and his staff worked most of the evening. It was a restless night for all of the Paracommando Regiment. Though around 1,400 refugees had been evacuated by the close of air operations at 2100, some 200 refugees remained huddled in a hangar. Studying the mission requirements for Paulis, Mine decided that the 11th and 13th Companies would provide the airborne assault elements for the coming operation. He ordered the perimeter reduced to allow these units to rotate men into the hangar, while maintaining one-third of his men on the line. Sporadic firing continued all evening, particularly along the 12th Company's sector, where the young commandos, nervous and exhausted, were inclined to open fire at the smallest disturbance. Simba infiltrators harassed the paras, and Ledant's men maintained roving patrols inside the perimeter to maintain security. With all the activity and firing, no one in the Paracommando Regiment had a restful night.[16] For most, the night of 24 November was their third in a row without sleep.

The combined planning conference for Dragon Noir began at 0730 on 25 November. The principals attending the conference were Colonels Laurent, Isaacson, and Logiest. Mine's staff, in its overnight study, had come up with a recommendation to change the schedule of the operations:

> D Day: Stanleyville
> D + 2 at 0400Z: Paulis
> D + 3: Evacuation of Paracommandos from Paulis to Kamina
> D + 4: Evacuation of Paracommandos from Stanleyville to Kamina
> D + 5 at 0400Z: Bunia followed by overland movement to Watsa
> D + 9: Evacuation of Paracommandos from Bunia to Kamina for final withdrawal.[17]

The change was based on several salient facts. First, the condition of the Paracommandos was suspect. If Dragon Noir was executed on 26 November, it would mean that the paras would endure four consecutive nights without sleep. Laurent's men were tired; the 13th Company was 10 percent combat ineffective—mainly due to fatigue. Second, the rebels had proved to be tougher opponents than expected. In the fighting for Stanleyville, the rebels had stood fast. Indeed, Albert Wouters, a Belgian airman, had been killed that very morning. The earlier plan established in the second Brussels conferences—to simultaneously seize Bunia and Paulis, each with one company—was now perceived as unrealistic. Laurent and Mine wanted at least two companies on the ground at Paulis. Furthermore, with the latest shipment of parachutes, the regiment had only enough to execute one operation.[18]

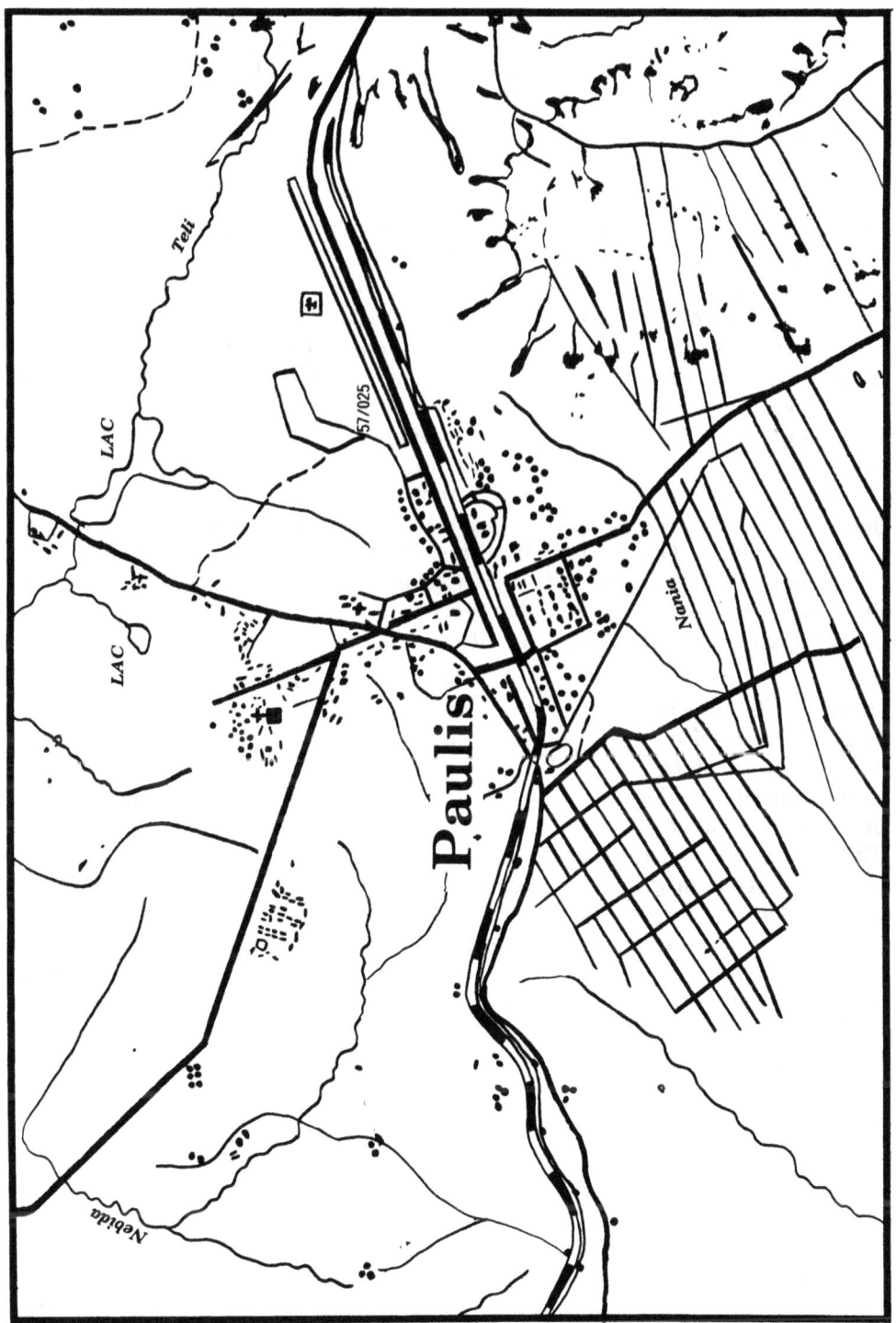

Map 14. Planning map of Paulis (simulation of tourist map used)

It was decided that the Paracommandos would assault Paulis the following morning. The 11th and 13th Companies would jump from four C-130s. Three C-130s, loaded with four armored jeeps, four radio jeeps, and seven AS-24s, would follow them and land on the field. Twelve C-130s would return the following day for their evacuation. With this agreement, the meeting broke up. While Mine prepared an operations order, Isaacson and Logiest returned to Leopoldville.[19]

Since Washington and Brussels were anxiously waiting for the results of this conference, Godley wasted no time in getting a cable on the wires. In outlining the major points of discussion, Godley's first paragraph was critical to the outcome of the decision-making process. It said, "Laurent wants limit next phase to DRAGON NOIR. Laurent's force is too small, tired, and has too few parachutes to attempt DRAGON BLANC at same time."[20] With both Washington and Brussels seeking to limit the number of subsequent operations, the decision makers seized on the opening phrase. In discussions between Johnson's Ranch and Washington, President Johnson made it plain that he did not intend to be drawn further into a Congolese civil war. He would approve one—and only one—additional operation. Across the Atlantic, Spaak was having serious doubts about even going to Paulis. Only when his chef de cabinet, Viscount Davignon, and the prime minister, Theo Lefévre, intervened in favor of a second operation, did Spaak reluctantly agree. As the execution order for Dragon Noir went out at 252309Z, it was clear that it was to be the final Dragon operation.[21]

The Paracommandos were ready when the order to execute came through. Again, however, it had taken a full day's work to prepare for Dragon Noir. Mine spent all morning studying the limited information on Paulis. The capital of Ulele province, Paulis lay some 280 miles to the northwest of Stanleyville. The city's major communication links consisted of its gravel-paved airport, some 4,199 feet long, and an east-west railway. The aerial photography from Running Bear had put to rest earlier fears that the strip might be unusable because of rain. Since heavy woods surrounded the city, the airstrip would have to serve as the single drop zone. Its short length, however, necessitated multiple passes to get the paras out. All of the field's facilities were located on its southern side, along with the town brewery. Unlike at Stanleyville, the airport at Paulis was immediately adjacent to the city; indeed, the strip was almost an extension of the main street. At the center of the city was a traffic circle that was critical to movement through its center. The European quarter was southwest of the traffic circle, but hotels and businesses were scattered throughout the town. There was one military camp northwest of the city on the road to Poko.[22]

Mine had little intelligence on the rebels or their hostages in Paulis other than that from Aketi. Though there were no indications of rebel reactions as yet to Dragon Rouge, Radio Stanleyville had broadcast the news of the assault. Estimates of the number of hostages inside Paulis generally cited figures of around 300. Though one report indicated the rebels expected Bunia to be the next drop, Mine had to assume that the rebels in

Paulis would also be prepared for a parachute assault—including plans to massacre their hostages. In contrast to Dragon Rouge, the sole responsibility for Dragon Noir would be the Paracommando Regiment. Vandewalle was fully occupied subduing Stanleyville, and the column at Aketi—Ops Nord under Lemercier—could not hope to reach the city before the paras abandoned it.[23]

Laurent and Mine had studied the operation in Stanleyville. Their first concern was the close air support. Both felt that the initial pass by the B-26s had done more to alert the Simbas than it had to suppress hostile fire. The American aircrews and Colonel Isaacson shared their thoughts.[24] Isaacson cabled Adams about the B-26s and bluntly stated: "Cannot overemphasize my lack of confidence in the ability of these aircraft to do more good than harm in this type operation. Further, I am not confident we can lash up another cooperative venture."[25] Adams, however, insisted on the inclusion of the B-26s in the plan for Dragon Noir. Faced with this decision, Mine and Laurent turned to matters solely under their control. Concerned over the slow movement his troops had effected into Stanleyville, Laurent ordered that all excess equipment, including personal equipment bags, be airlanded into Paulis. Laurent then instructed his battalion commander to send one company into the city as soon as it was on the ground. The armored jeeps would follow once the airlanding began.[26]

Unexplainably, Laurent decided to use only four armored jeeps, even though he had eight additional vehicles available. In keeping with the second Brussels planning conference, American C-124s had flown eight armored jeeps to Kamina to support simultaneous operations at Bunia and Paulis. Laurent had the manpower necessary to utilize the additional vehicles, and he certainly needed the additional firepower and mobility. With twenty C-130s in the Congo, Isaacson could have provided the airlift. It would seem, then, that the new plan for Dragon Noir, though it added additional troops, overlooked this opportunity for additional mobility.[27]

At 1700, Mine briefed his plan for Dragon Noir (see map 15). In 3 passes from 4 C-130s, 240 men would seize Paulis airfield by airborne assault at first light on the 26th. Out of this assault echelon, one company would clear the airfield for the airland element of vehicles and supplies, while the second company moved immediately into the city.[28]

Mine assigned each assault element its mission. The 11th Company, the same unit that had initially penetrated into Stanleyville, would land in the center and western portions of the drop zone. After assembly, it would immediately move into Paulis, from the east and south, to locate and liberate any hostages. The 11th Company also had to establish a roadblock northwest of the city to stop any rebel reinforcements coming from the military camp. The 13th Company (-) would land on the east and center of the airfield, clear its runway, and hold it for the remainder of the operation. The 13th Company's secondary missions included manning a roadblock between the airfield and the city and providing a reserve platoon for search operations. The reconnaissance section, along with Ledant's jumpmasters,

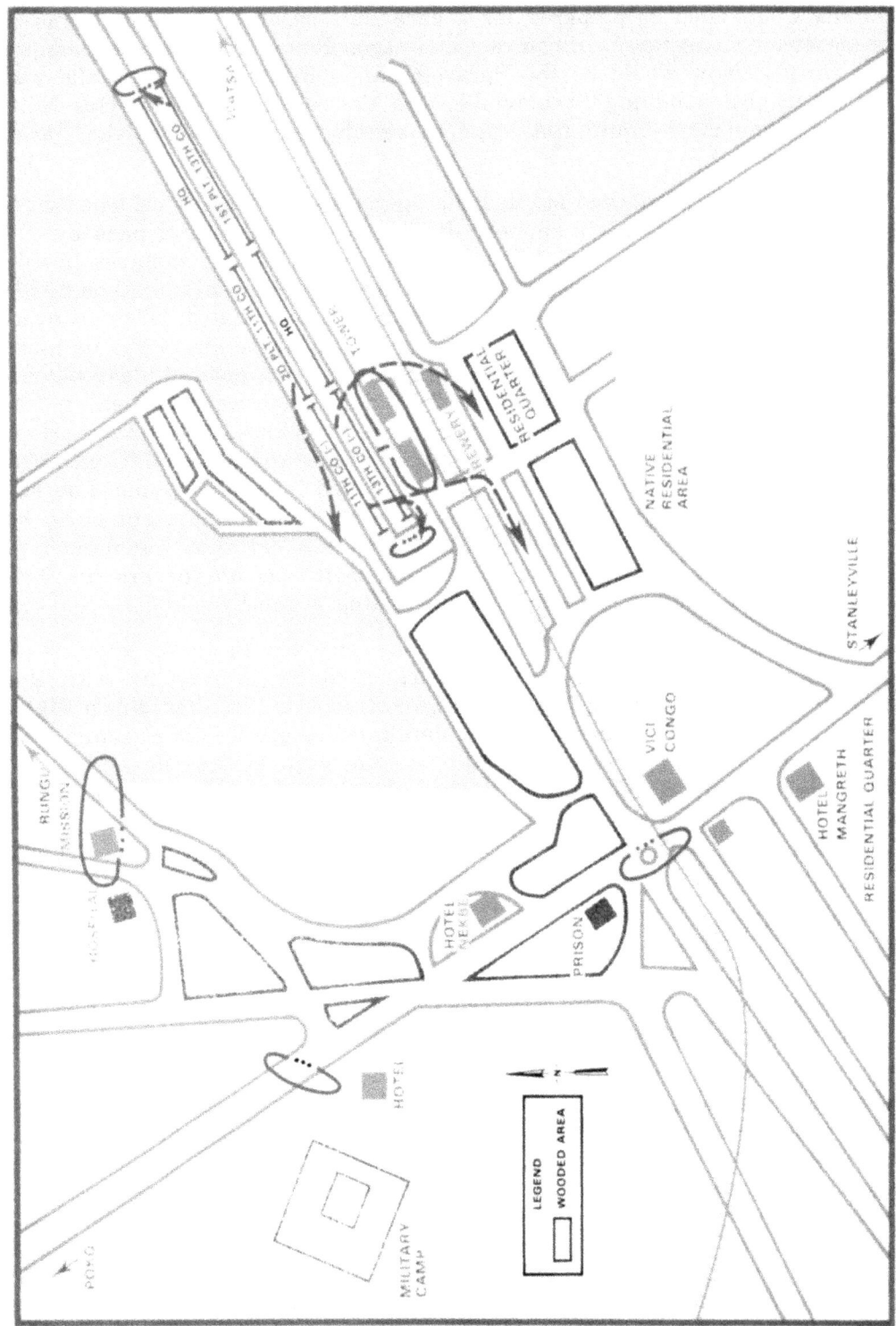

Map 15. Dragon Noir assault plan

would conduct independent search-and-rescue missions. The 12th Company and Headquarters Company (-) would remain in Stanleyville on standby reserve. With the briefing complete, the individual leaders went back to their units to issue their orders. By early evening, all that remained to be done was the loading of the C-130s after they arrived from Leopoldville.[29]

Following the airborne and airland assaults on 24 November, most of the aircraft under Gradwell's command had flown directly to Leopoldville. As mentioned earlier, three had gone to Kamina and from there had made refugee evacuation flights back to Stanleyville. By the close of the day, there were seventeen C-130s at Leopoldville.[30]

Out of those seventeen C-130s, at least five were in need of repair. Once it became clear that the aircraft would remain in Leopoldville, Gradwell's maintenance team had packed up and flown in from Kamina. With the assistance of Sabena Airlines' ground maintenance teams, they worked through the evening patching damaged fuel cells and repairing less-serious damage. By midday on the 25th, the aircraft for Dragon Noir were ready— if the crews were able to fly them.[31]

Gradwell's aircrews, like the Paracommandos, were tired, and most were sick. They had gone into crew rest at Leopoldville, trying to grab needed sleep inside their aircraft or in the military airfield hangars. Unfortunately, most of the pilots and crews had severe stomach problems. While they were at Kamina, they had been told to drink the locally brewed beer or soft drinks instead of the local water. As it turned out, the beer was equally infested with bacteria, and by the evening of 24 November, the crews were suffering from diarrhea and vomiting. Consequently, the aircrews received little actual rest during their sojourn at Leopoldville.[32]

Colonel Gradwell and his staff anxiously awaited Colonel Isaacson's return to Leopoldville after his coordination meeting with the Belgians. Perhaps in order to emphasize his role as the senior American, Isaacson had not included Gradwell or his staff in the consultations. In midafternoon, Isaacson returned and briefed Gradwell on the upcoming mission. Gradwell's target was Paulis, and in keeping with the earlier contingency planning, it would require seven C-130s to get the Paracommandos and their equipment onto the airfield. Isaacson told Gradwell that the Belgians wanted three passes on a west-to-east approach for the four assault aircraft. The three airland C-130s, following immediately behind the lead four aircraft, would land once the Belgians gave the signal. Based on Isaacson's briefing, Gradwell's staff went to work, though some doubted that Isaacson really understood airborne operations.[33]

In planning the airlift for the Paulis operation, Gradwell faced two major difficulties. First was the question of staging. When subsequent operations were first discussed, it had been envisioned that the Paracommando Regiment would first withdraw to Kamina to facilitate further operations. With the unexpectedly large refugee evacuation from Stanleyville, however, there had not been time to redeploy the troops designated for Paulis. Consequently, Gradwell's aircraft would have to fly to Stanleyville and pick up the Belgians before they flew to Paulis. By this time, Stanleyville Airport was crowded with aircraft: there were around ten tactical aircraft based on the field to support Vandewalle and several miscellaneous transports from Air Congo and the Belgian Air Force. Major James Poore, Gradwell's assistant operations officer, was worried whether the seven C-130s from Leopoldville would actually be able to land. Originally, planners had estimated that the field would only hold three C-130s at a time, but Poore thought he could get all seven Dragon Noir aircraft onto the field if he had time to prepare. Poore was also worried about Isaacson's briefing; Isaacson was a fighter pilot, not an airlift specialist, and he could not match Poore's expertise on airborne operations. With this in mind, Gradwell decided to launch his C-130s in reverse order for the flight to Stanleyville. Poore, in Chalk Seven, would launch four to five hours ahead of the others to coordinate the loading with the Belgians.[34]

The second problem associated with the Paulis operation involved navigation. Gradwell's navigators had been extremely accurate in planning and executing the drop on Stanleyville. But they had had several advantages in that operation. Situated on the Congo River, Stanleyville was easy to locate once the navigator spotted the Congo River. Furthermore, Gradwell's experience in the Congo and Isaacson's weather reconnaissance ahead of the Dragon Rouge flight had simplified the navigational problems. Paulis, in contrast, had a postage stamp for an airfield that was surrounded by trackless jungle; only careful navigation would put the task force over such a difficult target.[35] Nonetheless, by late afternoon, Gradwell's men were ready for the second of the Dragon operations.

At 2200, Chalk Seven, with Poore on board, landed at Stanleyville Airport. Major Roger Hardenne met him at the aircraft and escorted him to the Belgians' operations center. En route, Poore heard some moaning coming from one of the buildings along the ramp. Hardenne, sensing the American's curiosity, disgustedly explained that the ANC were slowly killing several wounded Simbas. Poore decided they should continue to the tower.[36]

There, Poore met with Colonel Laurent and his staff to discuss the coming operation. He explained the necessity of clearing the ramp area for the six incoming C-130s. Laurent directed that Major Josef Vaes and men from Headquarters Company help in the task. During the next several hours, Poore, Vaes, and Captain Strobaugh worked to clear the field. The Belgians manhandled the aircraft off the tarmac and soon had the airfield ready for Gradwell's arrival.[37]

With the execution signal at 2309Z, Gradwell prepared for immediate launch. Captain Long, his pilot, had the C-130 on the run-up pad and was preparing to take off when every light on the airport went out. Standing on the ramp beside Isaacson, Gradwell walked up the flight deck to Long and said, "Go ahead, we've got to go. There is no holding back now." It was a risky decision, and Gradwell knew the danger; if one of his aircraft had problems on takeoff, it would be extremely difficult to get back to the darkened field. Long took off into the blackness, as did the following two aircraft. Fate smiled; all planes launched without difficulty. During the flight, Gradwell made contact with Kamina to reconfirm the execution signal. He knew that once on the ground, he might be out of contact should the operation be canceled. About an hour out of Stanleyville, Kamina reconfirmed the execution signal: Dragon Noir was on![38]

At 0245, Gradwell's aircraft began landing at Kamina in fifteen-minute intervals. Long made the first landing; it was risky. Fog had settled on the field, and he had to make several passes over the strip before he could identify it. Once Long had the aircraft on the ground, Gradwell went to the tower to turn on its beacon. Each of the following aircraft made an initial low-visibility approach over the field, picked up the beacon, and circled back to land. Poore and Strobaugh greeted each ship, and the Belgians muscled them into the small ramp area. Vaes and his men immediately began loading the cargo on the airland chalks. By 0400, the last aircraft was on the ground at Kamina—less than an hour before they were to launch for Paulis.[39]

Laurent's staff had planned for a final coordination meeting with Gradwell and his pilots at 0405. The Belgians wanted a face-to-face meeting with Gradwell rather than Isaacson. With the rapidly approaching launch time, Gradwell's men remained with the aircraft, pouring over routes and checking instruments. Poore went to the meeting to represent the Americans and, in the last-minute discussions, made a startling discovery. Whereas Isaacson had reported the Belgians wanted a west-to-east approach into the drop zone, Laurent's staff was clearly planning on an east-to-west assault. Poore immediately recognized the potential for disaster: Laurent's men, oriented by their direction of flight, might go charging off in the wrong direction. Poore dashed out to the aircraft to pass on the new approach to the crews, but the pilots and navigators argued against the change. Tired and keyed up, the last thing they needed was a major alteration in the operation just as they prepared for takeoff.[40]

At 0500, the first aircraft rolled down the runway for Paulis, followed closely by the remainder. Now, an eighth aircraft joined the task force. All the time the seven primary aircraft were on the ground, Chalk Eight had orbited over the city as an emergency spare. If one of the principal aircraft had experienced difficulty on takeoff, this aircraft would have landed and taken on its cargo. Once all the primary aircraft were in the air, Chalk Eight had joined the formation to serve as an additional evacuation airplane. The next destination for the aircraft was Paulis.[41]

On the way to Paulis, Poore informed Gradwell about the approach problem. Poore went back to the troop bay and reconfirmed the Belgian plan with Colonel Laurent. Laurent grabbed a headset and excitedly told Gradwell, "This is a catastrophe. This is nearly an impossibility!" Gradwell replied, "We, therefore, will not drop that way. We will make it the other direction." Poore then passed the new approach on to Gradwell's navigator. As they approached Paulis, all the aircraft had the new heading worked out.[42]

Finding Paulis was a challenge. In accordance with General Adams' guidance, Isaacson had two B-26s out in front of the task force, but as the C-130s neared their target, it was clear that this time the Cubans were thoroughly lost. The weather had not helped; Gradwell's pilots had flown around and through thunderstorms along the way. Now as they came in on the target, the only thing visible to them was the area directly below their aircraft. Fog covered the ground, making lateral visibility virtually impossible. At 0535, based on radar and dead reckoning, the navigators turned on the red warning lights.[43]

As soon as the red standby signals went on, Ledant's jumpmasters began their prejump commands. This time, the paras stood up at the ten-minute warning and soon were hooked up. Laurent's men were dead tired; Poore, watching from the flight-deck hatch, saw two paras laughingly trying to wake up a comrade. This individual, once he had finished his prejump sequence, promptly went back to sleep. Every time his friends jostled him awake, he would doze, waiting for the green light.[44]

As in Dragon Rouge, Gradwell's pilots had dropped to low altitude for the approach into Paulis. This drop was to take place from 600 feet. At 0555, Captain Long spotted what he believed was the airstrip flashing below his aircraft. Simba gunners confirmed Long's suspicions, as they hit his aircraft four times before he cleared the field. Gradwell, not wanting to confuse the operation, called for no drop on the first pass and warned his pilots to avoid the buildings if at all possible. The aircraft swung in a circle for the second pass.[45]

Riding in the troop bay of Chalk One, Colonel Laurent had been standing up for fifteen minutes when he felt the aircraft shudder from hostile fire and begin a turn. Again, the Belgian commander grabbed a headset and asked Gradwell what was happening. Gradwell explained the situation and told him "OK Charlie, we'll try again!" True to his word, Gradwell brought the formation around, and the green light went on.[46]

Dragon Noir began at 0602. This time, there was no surprise, as the Simbas surrounding the airfield opened up with a vengeance on the low-flying C-130s. Gradwell's pilots bored in, and the paras began exiting the aircraft. The fog worked to the benefit of the crews by screening them from the Simba fire. Nevertheless, three out of the four initial aircraft took hits from the ground fire, and the paras suffered their initial casualty of Dragon Noir. Sergeant Rossinfosse, the last man in the starboard stick of Chalk One, was hit as he exited on the first pass. Fortunately, a loaded magazine in his shirt pocket deflected the round away from vital organs; seriously wounded, Rossinfosse provided the first name in red for Dragon Noir.[47]

Down on the ground, the Paracommandos swung into action even before the remainder of the 246 troops were delivered on the second and third passes. The fog, again, worked to the advantage of the descending paras: while they could not see the ground while swinging in the air, the Simbas could not see them either. Elements of the 13th Company, led by Major Mine, assaulted the control tower and silenced a machine gun that had

One of the second wave of Paracommandos at Paulis

been spraying the C-130s. The 2d Platoon, 13th Company, moved toward the western end of the strip, while the remainder of the company cleared the runway. At 0630, Major Hardenne, again acting as Dragon control, signaled Gradwell that the airfield was cleared for landing.[48]

Chalk Five came in to land at 0640. As the pilot crossed the western end of the field, his aircraft came under heavy fire but touched down safely. Hardenne suspended further landings until the enemy could be driven back. Fortunately, Chalk Five brought in two armored jeeps under Sergeant Goris. He soon had them in action.[49]

Goris raced down the strip to the western end of the field. Circling above, Gradwell could see the two armored jeeps attacking the Simbas west of the field. Captain Huyberechts, with five jumpmasters, accompanied the reconnaissance vehicles. At the end of the field, Huyberechts decided against penetrating the wood line with so few men. Instead, he ordered Goris to sweep the area with fire to force the Simbas back. The Simbas withdrew, and Hardenne called in the remainder of the airland element. Goris and Huyberechts returned to the tower to gather the remainder of their men for search operations.[50] Meanwhile, the 11th Company was already inside the city.

The 11th Company had assembled and proceeded directly into Paulis. Captain Pierlink's company split up by platoons for its missions inside the city: the 1st Platoon moved off for the mission; the 2d Platoon moved out to block off the military camp; and the 3d Platoon moved south through the residential quarter to the center of Paulis.

Lieutenant Witteman's 1st Platoon ran through the town encountering scattered resistance. On the way to the mission, they picked up several refugees, and the paras had them move with the formation, screening them from hostile fire. Witteman's platoon reached the mission at 0700 and rescued around fifty missionaries who had been held as hostages (see map 16).[51]

For many of the hostages, however, Witteman was about forty-eight hours too late. The intelligence reports had been correct; the rebel leadership in Paulis had been particularly brutal. The Simbas had gathered thirty-five to forty American and European hostages several weeks earlier. They had already massacred several thousand Congolese in the city; now, after Dragon Rouge, they were eager to kill their foreign hostages. When Stanleyville fell, the rebels gathered in another thirty to forty hostages at the mission. On the night of 24 November, they began killing them, taking the first group out for execution. As their initial victim, they selected Reverend Joseph Tucker, an American missionary. For the next forty-five minutes, the Simbas tortured Tucker, finally killing him by driving a stake through his skull. The rebels butchered the others and returned for more victims the next evening. By the time Witteman's platoon arrived, the Simbas had executed some twenty of the hostages.[52]

Soon after his arrival at the mission, Witteman had gathered most of the hostages. He found that all were men and boys, but they told him that

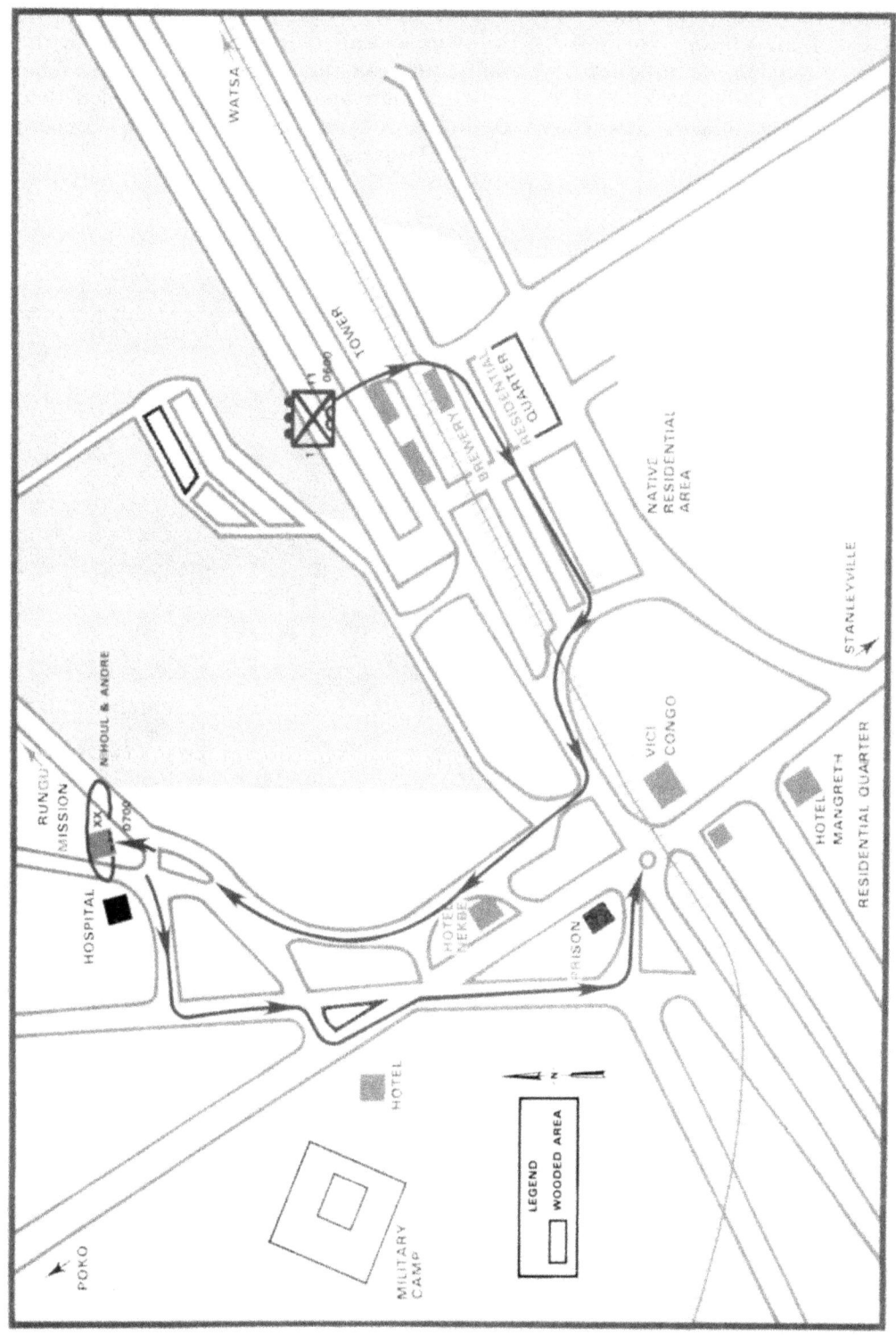

Map 16. Dragon Noir, movement of the 1st Platoon, 11th Company

their wives and families were nearby in a housing area. Witteman sent part of his platoon to look for the women and children. While this search was going on, an unidentified truck came roaring up to the mission. When the driver failed to halt, Witteman's platoon opened fire. It wounded three men: a Mr. Slegers, the Dutch consul and local brewery owner; Corporal Nihoul; and Trooper André, of the 1st Parachute Battalion.[53]

Paracommandos at the airfield, Paulis

Earlier, shortly after Witteman's departure from the airfield, Slegers had come to Major Mine at the airfield looking for assistance. Slegers had told Mine that there was a large group of hostages in the mission and that the Simbas would soon kill them. Slegers offered Mine the use of two trucks located at his brewery if Mine would enter the place and clear it of enemy resistance. Mine reacted quickly: he took a section from the 13th Company and the S2 section of his headquarters and secured the brewery. After clearing the brewery, Mine put Slegers in the lead vehicle to guide them to the mission. Before starting, Mine cautioned the excited Dutchman to approach the mission cautiously and to stop well short of it to identify himself. There had been no time to mark the trucks with yellow crosses, and Mine feared that if the 11th Company had already reached the mission, the troops might open fire on a suspicious vehicle. Mine's worst fears came true; when Slegers approached the mission, he ignored Mine's warning and drove straight up to his destination. This is why Witteman's platoon had opened fire on Slegers, wounding him and the two paras. Fortunately, their wounds were not mortal, and Mine soon had them and the hostages on the way back to the airport.[54]

While Witteman's platoon secured the mission, Lieutenant Hardy and the 2d Platoon moved to block off rebel movement from the military camp. Hardy's men assembled on the northern side of the airstrip and went through its wood line to reach the most direct route to the military camp. Like Witteman, Hardy had his men run through the city. They brushed off several skirmishes with the Simbas along the way and reached the military camp at 0712 (see map 17). Though Hardy established his blocking position without attacking the rebel base, his platoon attracted the rebels' attention. One of Hardy's men, Vandersteen, was wounded in one of the Simbas' periodic attacks. Hardy held this position until the 11th Company withdrew to the airport later in the day.[55]

Lieutenant Peirelinck, commanding 11th Company, reports to Colonel Laurent

Lieutenant Gustaaf Mertens' 3d Platoon, as in Stanleyville, had the search mission in the center of Paulis (see map 17). Mertens' first objective was the main hotel, where, according to Slegers, all the women were being held hostage. Running through the streets, Mertens' men hit stiff resistance at each intersection. They bypassed the residential area and continued on to the Hotel Mangreth. They discovered that Slegers' information was

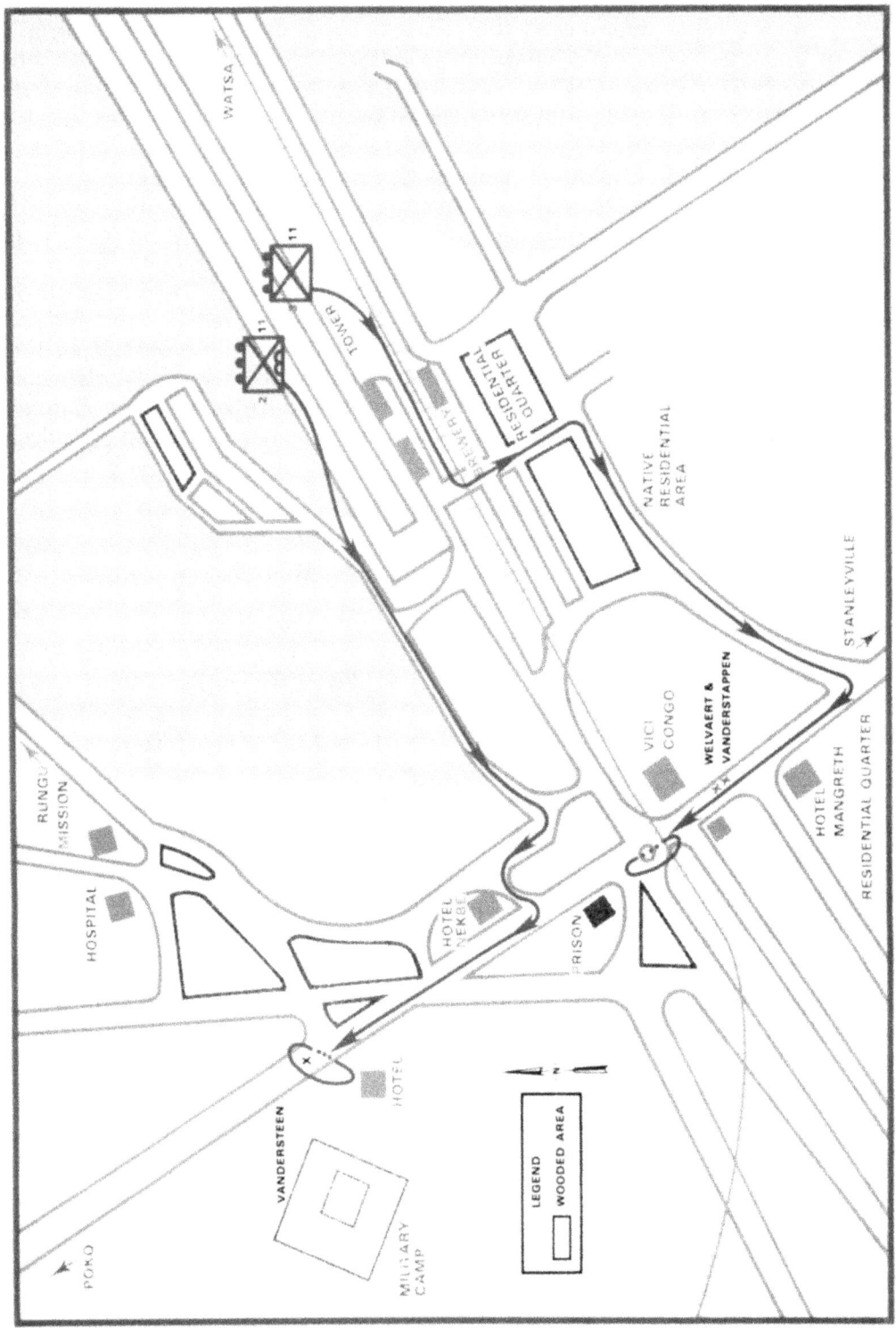

Map 17. Dragon Noir, movement of the 2d and 3d Platoons, 11th Company

wrong. Mertens found the hotel empty, and the 11th Company's executive officer, Lieutenant Mattens, ordered him to secure the area around the central traffic circle area.[56]

As the platoon moved forward, it encountered heavy resistance in the area of the Vici Congo. At 0745, Mertens' men were swept by hostile fire from the house of the local Simba leader. Sergeant Lucien Welvaert, a machine gunner, was hit in the stomach and died instantly. His assistant, Vanderstappen, was also wounded. Mertens designated a team to protect and evacuate the wounded Vanderstappen and Welvaert's body. These men found that Welvaert had followed Mine's guidance about leaving excess equipment behind to the letter; aside from eighty pounds of ammunition, Welvaert had nothing else on his body. He had left behind all rations and water in order to carry more ammunition. Meanwhile, Mertens succeeded in reaching the vital crossroads and established a perimeter defense. With the establishment of this position, the 11th Company secured the city. Captain Pierlinck's men remained in Paulis up to 1600 in order to search out hiding refugees and evacuate them to the airfield.[57]

At the airfield, further actions were under way to secure the perimeter. Between 0715 and 0945, on the orders of Colonel Laurent, Captains Vanderperre and Lauwers—along with jumpmasters Vermeuken, Gillet, Hassewer, Wouters, Pieters, and Decuyper—moved to clear out twenty houses along the border of the airfield. They drove out the rebels, killing two and capturing four wounded Simbas without suffering any casualties. At the same time, the 13th Company extended the perimeter to include the brewery (see map 18). Lieutenant Bourgeois took one section of his platoon to occupy the building. While Lieutenant Kovilic maintained defensive positions around the control tower and at both ends of the strip, Lieutenant Henrot took one section into the city to assist the 11th Company in searching for refugees.[58]

The refugee evacuation, with the benefit of the Stanleyville experience, was going smoothly. By the time that Chalk Seven landed, discharged its cargo, and prepared to take off, the Belgians had eighty-three refugees ready for evacuation. When Captain James Hunt, at the controls of Chalk Eight, saw Chalk Seven take off, he radioed Gradwell and asked for instructions. Gradwell contacted Dragon Control, now in the hands of Lieutenant Colonel Cailleau, and asked if there were further evacuees. When Cailleau answered in the affirmative, a new station broke in and told the astonished Gradwell that the spare aircraft could land only to extract Belgian wounded. After Gradwell confirmed with Cailleau the presence of Belgian wounded, Hunt landed. On the ground, Hunt confronted a group of hysterical civilians, and Gradwell told him to take them out. Later, Gradwell discovered that the unidentified control station on the radio net, which also was using Dragon Control as its call sign, was at Stanleyville. Nevertheless, Chalk Eight took out almost sixty refugees and the wounded paras.[59]

By 0850, the Paracommandos had located, rescued, and evacuated over 200 people. As in Stanleyville, Major Holvoet and his men carefully screened

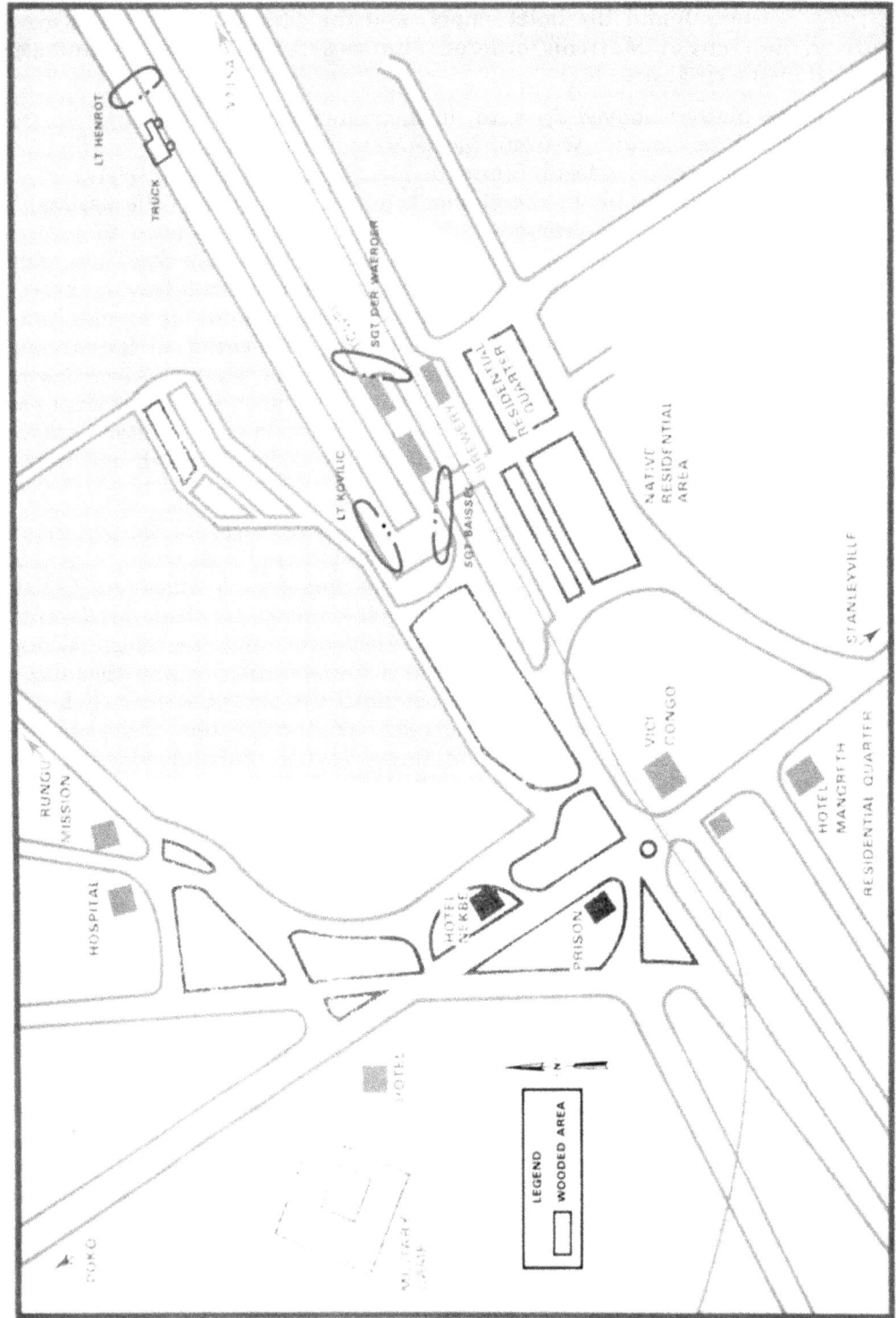

Map 18. Dragon Noir, the extraction

these refugees for information concerning the locations of other non-Congolese. This was particularly true of the male hostages rescued at the mission; they worked closely with Holvoet in pinpointing the probable hiding places of their families. Once the paras had the needed information, patrols were sent out to bring in the people. Colonel Laurent personally controlled these patrols, which relied heavily on Ledant's jumpmasters and Sergeant Goris' reconnaissance jeeps. Two officers stood out in these rescues: Major Hardenne and Captain Huyberechts.[60]

Laurent sent out the first patrol at 0830. Commanded by Major Hardenne, it was composed of Sergeant Goris (with two armored jeeps), four volunteers from Lieutenant Mertens' platoon, and a truck from the brewery. With one jeep in front, followed by the truck and second jeep, Hardenne pushed his convoy south of the town. Hardenne's men came under fire at the same location where Welvaert had been killed. This time, Goris' six machine guns made short work of the opposition. Shortly afterward, they succeeded in rescuing four Europeans. By 1000, Hardenne was back at the airfield asking for new orders.[61]

While Hardenne was out on his initial rescue, Captain Huyberechts and his jumpmasters were similarly engaged. Mounted on three of the AS-24s, Huyberechts made several trips into the European residential area to locate and evacuate isolated refugees. The overworked AS-24s started breaking down, so Huyberechts returned to the field and secured a Volkswagen and the other two armored jeeps. He made one last trip into the residential quarters to pick up a reportedly wounded woman. Huyberechts found the woman, but she was dead. Grimly, his team loaded the body and returned to the airport.[62]

When Huyberechts returned to the field, Hardenne's group had already been out on its second mission. In a villa on the southern outskirts of the city, Hardenne found eight women, two children, and one man. During this trip, Hardenne's men discovered the body of a young woman slain shortly before their arrival. Concerned with rescuing the living, Hardenne reported the location of the body before continuing his search; it was this corpse, mistakenly described as wounded, that Huyberechts recovered shortly afterward.[63]

After he had returned the dead and living to the airfield, Huyberechts went out on his second mission reinforced by a section of the 1st Parachute Battalion. This time, Huyberechts' flying column pushed nine kilometers south of Paulis along the road to Stanleyville. Again, the armored jeeps scattered sporadic Simba attacks along the way. By noon, Huyberechts had another eight refugees back at the control tower.[64]

At 1100, Hardenne set off on a third rescue. His objective now was the Societé Costituri, a farm eight kilometers west of the city. Once more, Goris led the column as it pushed through the native quarter destroying three Simba roadblocks. At the farm, Hardenne's men were surprised to find Congolese workers calmly toiling in the fields. They were more surprised when twenty-nine refugees came out of hiding to be loaded on the vehicles.

This group, which included six Americans, was safely at the airfield by 1300.⁶⁵

Similar patrols continued for the remainder of 26 November. Major Hardenne made another four trips, while Huyberechts engaged in two more. In the most distant patrol, Commandant Holvoet and Captain Vanderperre rescued seven refugees forty kilometers west of Paulis. This mission, the final of the day, did not return until well after sunset. All told, these patrols brought in at least seventy non-Congolese from the outlying areas around Paulis.⁶⁶

Meanwhile, elements of the 11th and 13th Companies had continued house-to-house searches inside the city. When Mine reported that Paulis was empty of non-Congolese at 1600, Laurent ordered the paras to withdraw from the city. As the afternoon sun disappeared, Mine established a reduced perimeter around the western end of the airfield with the 11th and 13th Companies. By that evening, the paras had around 150 refugees awaiting evacuation on the next day. While his troops and their civilian charges looked forward to another uneasy night, Colonel Laurent met with his staff to finalize their withdrawal plans.⁶⁷

C-130 Hercules landing at Paulis airstrip to remove hostages and withdrawing paratroops

Laurent faced some difficult decisions. The rescue missions conducted during the day had exhausted the hard intelligence on hostages in the area. As Simba reinforcements moved toward Paulis, further patrols ran an increasing risk of ambush with a decreasing probability of finding more refugees. Laurent had to consider his political and military guidance; he could not risk fruitless casualties. Dragon Noir had already cost one dead and five wounded—all but one due to Laurent's decision to use his troops in independent platoon actions. Laurent also had another factor to consider—time. Gradwell's aircraft were to return the next day with an expected arrival time of 1200. That would leave only six hours of daylight to finalize evacuation preparations. In discussing this dilemma with his staff, Laurent came to a decision: with the exception of one final patrol, the regiment would close in on the airport and stand by for evacuation.[68]

After Laurent's decision, Mine based his extraction plan on his attack order. In keeping with the assault plan, the 13th Company retained defensive responsibility for the airfield. The 11th Company would move the remaining refugees to the strip, and after they were gone, assist in loading materiel and vehicles. Pierlinck's company would then depart, followed in stages by Ledant's jumpmasters and headquarters elements. The 13th Company, along with key leadership personnel, would fly out on the last three aircraft. Lieutenant Henrot, the 13th Company's executive officer, would occupy the eastern end of the strip until the last C-130 landed, when he would retire to its western end for extraction. Mine and Laurent stressed one final point in briefing the extraction plan: each leader must have an accurate manifest of his men before that last aircraft took off. Laurent's nightmare was to abandon inadvertently a sleeping trooper, whose fate at the hands of the Simbas would be grim.[69]

After a relatively quiet evening, the next day began early for Laurent's men. At 0700, Majors Hardenne and Rousseaux took out the last patrol and returned at 0930 with five final refugees. Hardenne wanted to go again; this last group told him there were more hostages some forty kilometers away. He begged Laurent to authorize the mission, but the regimental commander reluctantly refused. Hardenne cried in frustration, a feeling that was felt by all the paras—especially Laurent.[70]

Right on schedule, Gradwell's aircraft began flying in at 1200. Based on their experience the previous day, the pilots came in with minimum fuel loads as an allowance for the short field. The extraction began immediately. Ten minutes later, Chalk One was on the way to Leopoldville with a load of refugees. Colonel Isaacson flew in with the second C-130 to discuss the final extraction. Isaacson brought in two strings of battle simulators for the Belgians to use in covering the last aircraft. Laurent was not too keen on the idea; he feared that his troops, particularly his machine gunner in the tower, might react to the sound of firing by shooting at it. After Isaacson's blunder on the airlift planning, Laurent was resentful and suspicious of him. Nevertheless, he agreed, and the simulators were given to Lieutenant Henrot to cover his withdrawal.[71]

Gradually, the evacuation continued, with each aircraft landing and taking off in less than twenty minutes. By 1427, only Henrot's men, with one section at either end of the field and one gunner in the tower, manned the perimeter. The Paracommandos waiting at the eastern end of the field knelt, facing north and south, with weapons ready until they boarded. Section leaders, platoon leaders, and commanders counted them aboard, and the aircraft ramp closed for takeoff. Each C-130 ran up to full power before rolling down the short strip, with each pilot becoming thoroughly acquainted with a particularly tall palm tree at the western end of the field. At 1600, Chalk Eleven came into land, and Lieutenant Henrot set off the simulators prior to chasing the aircraft down the runway.[72]

Major Hildebrand, at Chalk Eleven's controls, reported excitedly, "My God, they're firing at the other end of the runway!" Circling overhead with Laurent to ensure that everyone got off, Gradwell told Hildebrand (still on the ground) about the uncoordinated deception. The nervous pilot then lowered his ramp, and Henrot's men, accompanied by Majors Mine and Ledant, boarded. The C-130 then lifted off at 1610, signaling the end of Dragon Noir. In thirty-four hours, Dragon Noir succeeded in rescuing 375 refugees. Over twenty hostages had been killed since 24 November, and Laurent's troops suffered one dead and five wounded. While the Dragon operations were over, however, the Congolese turmoil continued.[73]

Though he knew Paulis was the last operation, Godley and the Leopoldville diplomatic community made one final attempt to delay the withdrawal of the Dragon force. But Godley was fighting an uphill battle: with all the Americans now accounted for, Washington considered the question of further rescues to be a purely Belgian question. Godley was not likely to get any support from Brussels either; Spaak had reluctantly supported Paulis but had clearly stated that further operations by the Paracommandos would risk the character of an occupation. Still, when faced with reports indicating another 1,000 hostages might still be in rebel hands, Godley felt compelled to dispute the withdrawal decision.[74]

Withdrawal of Paracommandos to the airfield, Paulis

On 26 November, Godley cabled Washington in a last-ditch effort to resurrect the operations planned for Bunia and Watsa. Godley conceded that there were reasons for canceling further operations, but he argued that abandonment of the remaining hostages would absolutely destroy the humanitarian nature of Dragon Rouge and Dragon Noir. Godley's concerns, clearly based on the need to save lives, did not carry sufficient weight to overrule the political considerations as viewed in Washington or Brussels.[75]

By 26 November, the backlash from Dragon Rouge was in full swing. Demonstrations had broken out in a number of African countries against the interventions. In Kenya, while crowds burned cars outside the American, Belgian, and British embassies, Kenyatta gave free reign to Kanza in the press. Cairo was the scene of further demonstrations, which climaxed with the burning of the USIA Library and the lambasting of President Johnson by the government press. The Eastern bloc also used the situation to its advantage: "spontaneous" demonstrations occurred in Moscow, Prague, and Peking. It was too much for President Johnson. He did not desire to "get tied in on the Congo and have another Korea or another Vietnam, just because of somebody wandering around searching for Jesus Christ." Averell Harriman, whose instincts made him want to execute Dragon operations Blanc and Vert, later admitted that he gave into peer-group "cold feet." Spaak's mind was also unchanged; efforts would be made to step up assistance to Vandewalle, but Laurent's regiment was coming home.[76]

The last plane before the takeoff to Kamina from Paulis

At 1506Z on 26 November 1964, Secretary of State Rusk cabled Leopoldville with the response to Godley's final plea: "Decision not rpt not undertake operations Bunia and Watsa or any other DR [Dragon Rouge] actions after Paulis was taken at highest levels U.S. and Belgian Governments."[77] This was a firm no. Rusk pointed out that the problem was now essentially Belgian, and since Spaak had concurred with the withdrawal, the Dragon operations were over. But the Simba Rebellion was not over; Congolese and non-Congolese continued to die. Godley and his fellow diplomats were the ones who had to greet the planes returning with the victims.[78] Everyone in the Congo knew that the killing would go on, and everyone was bitter, especially the Belgian Paracommandos.

With the decision to withdraw, Laurent's regiment regrouped at Kamina on 27 November. Major Vaes, the rear detachment commander in Stanleyville, worked closely with Captain Strobaugh to get the Belgian troops back to Kamina. That night, the officers of the Dragon force held a party to celebrate a job well, if only partially, done. Walking into the club, Jim Erdmann spotted several paras with a machine gun at the bar. As his companions laughingly filled the gun's cooling jacket with suitable refreshments, each para in turn drank the gun dry. Even as he watched this Bacchanalian ritual, Erdmann overheard two of the paras discussing the futility of the operation, which though it had removed most of the whites, had not solved anything. "Perhaps," one remarked, "then we should give them arms and let them kill each other off." That, as both Erdmann and the paras knew, was well underway in Stanleyville.[79]

The Stanleyville trials

Vandewalle's forces—at least Hoare's mercenaries and the Belgian advisers—had been relatively disciplined in securing Stanleyville. While Hoare's men were prone to looting, and Vandewalle did have to put security detachments on the city's banks, these troops did not engage in wholesale slaughter. The situation changed, however, when government troops began arriving.[80]

On the afternoon of 24 November, General Mobutu and Security Minister Nendaka arrived at Stanleyville. Accompanied by a bodyguard of Israeli-trained Congolese paratroops, Mobutu ordered a halt to the evacuation of all Congolese. Nendaka, with the assistance of a United States Agency for International Development (USAID) police adviser, set up a screening process. Despite the presence of the USAID adviser, the Congolese methods were brutal. Nendaka had nominated a Major Mahurubu as the city's new military commander. Governor Mahurubu, originally of Stanleyville, had lost his family when the rebels took the city. He returned seeking vengeance. Mobutu's paras questioned six prisoners captured by the Belgians that morning and decided one was a Simba. They put his eyes out with a bayonet; their fellow ANC troops slowly finished killing him the next day.[81]

November 25th saw the beginning of a long-standing Congolese tradition, the *ratissage* (a ritualistic revenge of the Congolese that can be accompanied by cannibalism); preoccupied with this pursuit, the Congolese were now not inclined to reconciliation. Just like the Simbas before them, the ANC moved in behind Vandewalle and Laurent and began the rape of Stanleyville. When the Simbas marched in on 4 August, the citizens of Stanleyville had adorned themselves with greenery as a sign of their sympathy. Now that the ANC was back, all the Congolese were sporting white headbands as a symbol of their loyalty. Nonetheless, Nendaka established a huge holding area in one of the local stadiums and began trials on 3 December. Those who were lucky were allowed to return to their homes; the unfortunate, like the hundreds of people annihilated during the Simbas' moment of glory, made a one-way trip to the Tshopo Bridge. Still, at least these people had a "trial." Others were not so fortunate. On 26 November, a new group of ANC arrived at the airfield. Finding a group of Congolese in the Sabena Guest House, they selected forty and drove them down to the river and killed them. This brutality so shocked Colonel Laurent that he demanded that the ANC remove all their prisoners from the airfield; at least his men would not be forced to listen to the prisoners' screams. It was madness, it was brutal, but it was the Congo, and it should not have surprised anyone.[82] In discussing the atrocities, Captain Strobaugh wrote:

> The Congolese National Army (ANC) is a different matter. Perhaps my four days experience and events that I witnessed at Stanleyville were not a true representation of the majority of the Congolese National forces, but I saw nothing to convince me otherwise. The senseless butchery and mutilation of civilians and military prisoners is unbelievable. There was absolutely no difference between the everyday acts of the ANC and the well-publicized atrocities committed by the rebels. Only the uniforms were different. Until you have seen a prisoner who has had his eyes put out and is then

bayoneted 12 hours later and left to bleed to death, or another prisoner who was killed by shooting his eyes out or any of the other examples of barbarism that I have already noted, it is impossible to imagine a free world-supported military unit with no apparent human feelings or sense of right and wrong. War against an armed enemy is one thing, but the senseless face to face killing of prisoners and unarmed civilians is the mark of animals, not civilized persons. I wonder if the people of the Congo might possibly find that the cure is as bad as the disease.[83]

The disease went on. Vandewalle found that he had all that he could handle in Stanleyville. As a barometer illustrating the intensity of his operations, Vandewalle's close air support aircraft made over thirty-seven sorties on 26 and 27 November. Furthermore, Vandewalle had reinforcements flown in from Kamina, Leopoldville, and Elisabethville. But the battle continued. On 28 November, Vandewalle reported that he would need at least another week to secure the city. He also reported that Punia, taken on the drive to Stanleyville, was now back in rebel hands. The day before, Vandewalle's men had pushed across the Congo River to the Rive Gauche and brought back twenty-eight bodies along with a handful of survivors. Elsewhere in the Congo, other government columns were stalled, or worse; some were forced to backtrack to repacify controlled areas.[84] It was this air of futility that burdened Laurent's forces as they boarded the C-130s for home.

Belgian paratroops awaiting withdrawal at Paulis airstrip

The parade at Kamina before the final move to Belgium

Paracommandos march before the Belgian people, 1 December 1964

Colonel Laurent accepting flowers from an appreciative Belgian during a march before the Belgians

On 28 November, the Belgian Paracommando Regiment loaded on to Gradwell's C-130s for the flight home. At the base, Laurent announced his withdrawal and paraded his troops. As a sign of their personal and professional respect, Ambassadors Godley and De Kerchove, accompanied by Colonels Williams and Monmaert, reviewed the formation and expressed their gratitude. By 1 December, the Paracommandos were back in Brussels, where *les gars* (the boys) received a hero's welcome. In addition, both Gradwell and Laurent were personally decorated by the Belgian king, and Laurent's men marched proudly through the streets of Brussels under the adoring eyes of the Belgian people. But even while the Belgian press took *les gars* to its heart, the Belgian government continued to agonize over the Congo: Belgians were still dying there.[85]

On 29 March 1965, Leopoldville announced that the Simba Rebellion was finished; on that day, Watsa had fallen to Hoare. He discovered that thirty-eight Belgians had been massacred in the four-month interim since State Department analysts had predicted the city could be taken in a "few days." But the swift strike into Stanleyville did not end the Simba Rebellion. Europeans and Congolese would continue to die, victims of continued Simba unrest and the Katanganese rebels. In the meantime, the pullout continued.[86]

Following the conquest of Stanleyville, Vandewalle's logistic advisers began their rotation back to Belgium. The intrepid Liegeois went back first. Unfortunately, on 29 November, the DC-6 flying him to Leopoldville for a meeting crashed on takeoff from Stanleyville. Liegeois was seriously injured, and he spent months recovering from the accident. By 22 December, the vast majority of Belgian military advisers had returned to their country.[87] None were confident that they had had any significant effect in quelling the Congolese strife. All of these men were tired. One of Lemercier's final entries, typical of their feelings, was

> Monday, 14 Dec 64
>
> Report to Lieutenant Colonel Goossens, concerning the mission to Bumba; see Dec 1: report completed on this mission, which describes how the 6th Kataganese Company was suprised at Lisala by 66 rebels (6th Kataganese Company has: 168 effectives, three machine guns and three mortars). The ANC without "logistic" advisors can't protect itself.
>
> Recommendation: Shoot Lieutenant Katinala, Commander of this company.[88]

On 24 December, Vandewalle followed his men. Greeted by his wife at the airport, he met privately with Davignon and Spaak. When asked, years afterward, what type of parade he received in Brussels, Vandewalle smiled and replied: *"Silence. Absolument* [absolutely] *Silence."*[89]

Fighting continued in the Congo. JTF LEO, originally intended as a short-term mission, remained in the country until August 1965. Hoare's men continued to fight for the ANC until his departure in November of the same year. On 25 November, Mobutu again seized power, and the political situation became relatively stable.[90]

Operational Postmortem

"Like Spanish moss, the present Congo Government has its roots in the air, not in the Congolese hinterland."[1] This comment, written in 1964 before the Simba Rebellion engulfed the country, stresses the Congo central government's lack of popular support. After Congolese independence, to strengthen the government's authority, the United Nations, the United States, and later, Belgium established a strategy of reconciliation and stabilization in the Congo.

But though these powers agreed on a common strategy, they disagreed on the underlying objectives of that strategy. Congolese leaders, such as Kasavubu, Adoula, or Tshombe—who had to be reckoned with in any settlement—were only concerned with the establishment of military control over the Congo, not with reconciling internal differences in the country. In attempting to bring order to the Congo, neither the United States nor Belgium seemed to grasp this fundamental premise of Congolese politics. Belgian goals in the country centered more on maintaining business interests in the face of the spreading chaos. This preoccupation explains Belgium's reluctance to encadre the ANC or to consider a direct military intervention. The United States, on its part, sought to forestall Communist influence in central Africa without becoming directly involved. Though Spaak discounted the Communist threat, the United States, nonetheless, wished to use Belgium as a front for containing Communist expansion in the Congo. Consequently, while the Belgian-American-Congolese coalition agreed on a common strategy, the entities within the coalition pursued disparate objectives within the framework of that strategy.

The Western nations and their Congolese associates were not only confused and uncoordinated in their overall approach to the Congo, but they were equally perplexed and disorganized in their appraisal and treatment of the Simba Rebellion. To the Congolese leaders, the Simbas were merely a political threat, represented by the leadership of Gbenye, Soumialot, or perhaps, Olenga. To the Belgians, the Simbas were just another example of Congolese internal unrest, which, like previous examples, would not seriously affect Belgian business interests. To the Americans, the Simbas were a Communist-inspired movement to gain control of the Congo. No one seemed to grasp the true nature of the rebel movement.

In many respects, the Simba Rebellion grew out of the Congo's colonial legacy. One hundred years of colonial domination, enforced by military suppression, had alienated the Congolese tribes from their national government. Congolese independence and the turmoil that followed had only increased that alienation. Since the Simba Rebellion was tribally motivated, Gbenye, Soumialot, and Olenga, as artificial political leaders, could only enforce allegiance on their immediate followers and, thus, possessed only minimal control over the rebellion at large. Therefore, eliminating these men would not have ended the revolt. Though Simba leaders assured Westerners of their safety, the instability of the Simba leaders' control over their tribal members made it highly unlikely that Belgian businesses would continue to operate unmolested inside rebel territory. Americans further complicated matters through their assumption that the rebellion was the product of Communist infiltration, a misguided notion, since the Communists had a minor role in the Congo prior to 1965. Ironically, the intervention in Stanleyville led to an increase in Communist and radical aid to the rebels.

The failure of Westerners and their Congolese associates to understand the nature of the Simba movement hampered the military campaign waged against the rebels. To deal with the Simbas, Congolese leaders—principally Tshombe and Mobutu—fixed on immediate military actions as the best means to defeat them. In contrast, the United States and Belgium endeavored to fight the Simbas on a nonoperational basis. The expansion of the CIA's air force and Vandewalle's peculiar charter reflected this attempt. When Tshombe recruited South Africans as mercenaries—after the United States and Belgium failed to provide an alternative—both Belgium and the United States attempted to distance themselves from Tshombe's campaign while continuing their support of him. With such an off-again, on-again approach to supporting Leopoldville, it is not surprising that Vandewalle's carefully contrived campaign plan resulted in a confused series of distinct military operations that ultimately forced the intervention in Stanleyville.

As an extension of the Belgian-American coalition in the Congo, the Dragon operations reflected the political confusion of its sponsors. Just as the United States and Belgium had believed that a low-key approach to the campaign against the Simbas would allow the two countries to avoid a direct intervention, so both countries hoped that an equally restrictive approach to Dragon Rouge would limit the political costs of the operation.

The planning for Dragon Rouge demonstrated the reluctance of both the United States and Belgium to commit themselves to a direct military intervention. On the American side, the CWG had considered and rejected three different unilateral rescue plans in favor of continued political initiatives. Once Belgium agreed to a combined planning conference, the CWG's exclusion of USSTRICOM from the planning signaled the CWG's intent that Dragon Rouge was to be a Belgian show. But like the coalition campaign against the Simbas, Dragon Rouge was a Belgian initiative subject to American manipulation. On the Belgian side, Spaak refused to consider an intervention until Belgian citizens were arrested. Once committed to the operation, however, Spaak's and Segers' guidance to Laurent paralleled that of the JCS to General Dougherty. Consequently, the Brussels planning conference developed the plan for Dragon Rouge on the basis of negative considerations.

At no time during the planning or execution of Dragon Rouge did those associated with it receive a clear mission statement. Confusion within the CWG over the intent of Dragon Rouge generated reams of material that skirted around the issue of purpose but never addressed it. Questions over the linkage with Vandewalle, the nature of Dragon Rouge (whether it was to be an intervention or a humanitarian rescue), and the political costs of the operation continued to dominate the thoughts of the CWG throughout the planning period. When the Americans failed to arrive at a clear mission statement, that task fell to the Belgians—specifically, to Colonel Laurent. Based on the guidance of Spaak and Segers, Laurent arrived at the rather hazy conclusion that his mission was not to "make war, but to conduct a humanitarian rescue."[2] Since the planners were confused about what they were trying to accomplish in the Congo, their task in planning the operation was formidable.

Influenced by political hesitancy and negative guidance, the ad hoc planning for Dragon Rouge had serious deficiencies. Nonetheless, considering that out of the 111 days between the fall of Stanleyville and the onset of Dragon Rouge that the planners at the Brussels conference had only forty-eight hours to plan an entirely new operation, their efforts were admirable. Since USSTRICOM was prohibited from participating in the conference, forty-eight hours was hardly sufficient time for those who did participate in the planning to sift through the available intelligence. Thus, the planners had to rely on what was placed before them; unfortunately, the Kindu reports (which accurately forecast the Stanleyville massacre) were not included. In any case, the Brussels conference suffered from a serious lack of operational intelligence. Much of the problem with the planning stemmed from the CWG's desultory interest in military plans. Partly due to the CWG's influence, Laurent's forces were too small for the mission (as the secretary of state realized on 22 November, when he asked for an American unit). Fortunately, the Brussels planners had overridden the CWG's earlier ideas on the size of the force. If the CWG had succeeded, Laurent would have had to take Stanleyville with only one company. On the other hand, the CWG did succeed in manipulating the planning conference in the matters of staging bases and, ultimately, in the use of a deception plan. Unfortunately, preoccupation with these issues allowed the equally important considerations of airlift, communications, and medical support to be neglected.

Members of the CWG never seemed to realize that as the Dragon force left Belgium on 17 November, the plan for the operation was incomplete. Since the members of the CWG had expected that the Dragon force would deploy directly to the Congo, their satisfaction with the overall plan demonstrated their ignorance of military affairs as pointed out by General Adams.

The deficiencies in OPLAN 319/64 were glaring, but considering the political constraints affecting the planners, the CWG's refusal to acknowledge those faults was inevitable.

Even had OPLAN 319/64 been a complete operations order, the Dragon force needed time to study it and resolve potential conflicts. Since the operation was a combined one, issues of interoperablity made the need for time even more important. As the Americans and Belgians had never conducted combined airborne operations—and OPLAN 319/64 was incomplete—the need for time became paramount.

By pushing for the initial deployment to Ascension Island, Spaak provided the time necessary for the Dragon force to become a team. Aided by Godley, MacArthur, Adams, and Lemnitzer, Spaak convinced the CWG that a deployment from Belgium to the Congo was unrealistic. Had he failed, Colonel Gradwell and Colonel Laurent would not have had those three days at Ascension Island to work out the problems of a combined operation.

Interoperability is the overriding issue in any combined operation. The Dragon force had to settle doctrinal issues before it boarded the aircraft for the assault on Stanleyville. With the aid of Major Poore, Gradwell convinced Laurent to use the American CARP (computed airborne release point) system and Close Look doctrine to control the operation. Poore further convinced Laurent that the airfield was a suitable drop zone. But while the Belgians' parachute equipment was suitable for use in C-130s, the Belgians had never jumped from Hercules transports. Again, Poore, along with Strobaugh, provided the critical assistance in training the Belgians. Working with Hardenne, in the area of communications, Strobaugh also trained the Belgians to use American radios, and when the need arose, he assumed control of the air operations net. By the time the Dragon force deployed to Kamina, these doctrinal and training issues of interoperability were resolved.

But interoperability hinges on more than just doctrine, training, or equipment. Successful interoperability depends also on common or sympathetic national objectives. Clearly, the United States and Belgium were not aligned on the overall issues involving the Congo. Fortunately, the Dragon force succeeded in overcoming these barriers to cooperation. Based on the rapport between Gradwell and Laurent, the American aircrews and Belgian paras soon developed a sense of mutual respect and trust that overrode many of the difficulties involved in the operation. Although Clingerman cited the confusion that existed between the two national forces over who would provide intelligence on Stanleyville, nonetheless, by the time the Dragon force launched from Kamina, the Belgians and Americans within the task force had become a team, thus providing clarity of purpose to the operation.

Though successful interoperability of forces was developed for the operation, the command and control of the intervention at Stanleyville was chaotic. Born out of confusion within the progovernment coalition, lines of authority were muddled and often in conflict. Though the operation was a cooperative venture, the United States and Belgium had difficulty in sustaining their association. A profound difference in views divided the Belgian-American coalition, witnessed by Spaak's surprise press release about the deployment to Ascension and his concurrent order for the Belgians to move to Kamina.

Unfortunately, the same differences that beset the Belgian-American coalition also affected the two countries' relationships with the Congolese. Tshombe and Mobutu never envisioned Dragon Rouge as a simple evacuation: they wanted to strike the rebels whenever and wherever possible. American and Belgian officials—military and diplomatic—spent as much time controlling the Congolese as they did in coordinating Dragon Rouge.

Even in coordinating the operation with the Congolese, the Belgian-American coalition was divided. The CWG saw the operation differently than Ambassadors Godley and MacArthur. The same gap existed between Spaak and his ambassador, De Kerchove. Moreover, the Belgian-American effort inside the Congo was also splintered. Godley; Williams, as head of COMISH; Isaacson, as head of JTF LEO; and the CIA were all working to support the operation. But though placed in charge, Godley could not control everything. The Belgian effort was similarly split between Marliere, Logiest, and Vandewalle. Once Vandewalle began his final drive, he was beyond anyone's control. With the Belgian-American effort in the Congo split externally by its national leaders and divided internally by its agents, the difficulties in supporting Dragon Rouge were predictable.

As lines of authority were already confused before the Dragon force staged forward, the force's arrival in the Congo added an additional layer of complexity to the already chaotic command and control. At the national level, the Big Punch procedures demonstrated the differences in the American and Belgian approaches to the operation: Spaak was willing to allow Vandewalle to initiate the system, but the CWG was then to retain that power. Within the intermediate command level, USSTRICOM assumed operational control of the Dragon force without the benefit of having participated in its planning.

For the Belgians, there really was no control headquarters, as the Belgian Joint Staff had to rely on American communications to pass on its instructions. At the tactical level, confusion erupted in both the Belgian and American camps. Colonel Isaacson's role as Dragon Chef was superfluous—and ultimately disruptive—serving only to extend command rivalry between USEUCOM and USSTRICOM into the American airlift. Similar problems arose between Laurent and Vandewalle when those two met at the last minute to coordinate their efforts. Laurent viewed L'Ommengang with deep-seated misgivings, and Vandewalle reciprocated with the feeling that Dragon Rouge was unnecessary and might cost more lives in the remainder of the Congo than it rescued in Stanleyville. The confusion came through in Lieutenant Colonel Erdmann's journal entry for 23 November:

> e. *Too many bosses.* 9 commanders in the operation by this time. 1) State Dept., 2) Hqs USAF, 3) EUCOM, 4) JTF Leo, 5) JTF Leo Advon, 6) Air Lift Commander (with 2 higher HQ—322 ADIV and

EUCOM/USAFE), 7) COMISH 8) Belgian Army at Kamina 9) CIA man and Cuban (B-26) pilots.[3]

That Erdmann, while running Gradwell's command post, did not bother to list USSTRICOM as another "boss" points to the mix-up over who was in control.

An effective communications system might have eased the already jumbled command-and-control situation. But the communications support for the Dragon operations remained inadequate. Emphasis on security led to many of the communications difficulties with Dragon Rouge by overloading the communications system with classified traffic. The enormous volume of classified message traffic overwhelmed the capacity of the Talking Bird and forced the task force to rely on open-channel voice communications via the Twilight Net. Even after the deployment of three joint communications support elements, the message traffic remained too heavy for the system to handle. When the debate was going on in Washington and Brussels over an order to execute on 23 November, the communications channels to Leopoldville were out. When the decision was finally made to postpone the operation, ordering the stand-down was impossible; Laurent made the decision on his own. Had Washington and Brussels wanted to execute the operation, Laurent's forces would have had to reassemble and reload for the mission. Once confirmation reached Leopoldville that the operation had been executed, Godley turned to commercial telephone circuits to pass reports on to Washington, since teletype traffic remained slow.

Even the Twilight Net, the mainstay of the operation, was inadequate. Had the United States and Belgium decided to abort Dragon Noir, the order could not have been passed to Gradwell and Laurent until they were en route to Paulis from Stanleyville. Moreover, the confusion on the Twilight Net almost disrupted the evacuation operations on the first day at Paulis. When one considers that these problems occurred during the staged deployment of the Dragon force, the potential for disaster entailed by a continuous deployment becomes clear. Had the Dragon force been ordered to deploy directly to Stanleyville, it would have been out of contact until it reached the target. With the exception of refueling stops at Morón, Ascension, and Kamina, the only channel open to the task force would have been the Twilight Net. Though the mission could have been aborted, it would have been difficult to pass coordination or intelligence information via the open communications channel. Consequently, the communications support for strategic control of the Dragon operations was underwhelming. Furthermore, similar problems arose at the tactical level.

Dragon Rouge ultimately changed from an independent operation into a coordinated assault with Vandewalle's L'Ommengang. Although Ambassador Godley pointed out the need for communications support for Vandewalle's advance, the CWG prohibited him from attaching any signals personnel to the column. After invoking that prohibition, the CWG directed that Godley maintain contact with the 5th Brigade. Without the necessary communications equipment, however, Vandewalle was unable to report his progress during the final drive on Stanleyville. Moreover, by the time of

L'Ommengang's arrival in Stanleyville, five different languages were in use by the friendly forces. Difficulty in communicating with the Spanish-speaking Cuban pilots had already caused problems in controlling the close air support. Further language difficulties led the Belgians to request that Strobaugh handle communications with the American pilots. Fortunately Strobaugh's close working relationship with the Belgians prevented the language barrier from disrupting operations. Overcrowding on the Twilight Net also disrupted communications within the task force in Stanleyville and Paulis. In addition, Strobaugh experienced extreme difficulty in passing vital traffic back to Leopoldville. Much of the problem rested on the absence of a communications annex to the operation order. As confusion mounted, net discipline broke down, and inessential traffic clogged the channel. The interference of Dragon control in Stanleyville with the air evacuation at Paulis was only one example of this problem.

Overall, the command, control, and communications system established for the Dragon operations increased difficulties rather than diminished them. The lines of command and control, from the executive level to the tactical leaders, ran to a host of players. Each of these agencies operated in a semi-independent fashion, with limited coordination between them. Furthermore, the communications support necessary to control these divergent actors and to coordinate among them was ineffective. Luckily for the Belgians and Americans, the Simbas' initial reluctance to slaughter their hostages gave the United States, Belgium, and the Congo the time necessary to work within this faulty system of command and control.

Dragon Rouge was one of the most difficult hostage rescues on record. The distance involved, the austere support, the use of combined forces, the number of hostages, and the lack of intelligence increased its difficulty. That Dragon Rouge took place in hostile territory in the middle of a civil war, and that it was as much an evacuation operation as a hostage rescue, further compounded the difficulties associated with it. Still, the operation was remarkably successful in its primary purpose of saving the hostages. Dragon Rouge rescued 1,600 hostages and refugees at a cost of 33 dead hostages (61, if those on the Rive Gauche are included). In addition, there were two dead and three wounded Belgian Paracommandos, as well as minimal rebel casualties from hostilities. The Third World reaction, while violent and unexpectedly vocal, did not have a lasting impact on the United States or Belgium. So while the results of Dragon Rouge were not ideal, they were better than might have been expected against such difficult odds.

However, if one applies the definition of success that was operative at the time of Dragon Rouge, an assessment of the operations' results will be less charitable. Looking back at that definition, as stated in the U.S. State Department's research memo, "DRAGON ROUGE: African Reactions and Other Estimates," illuminates the issue:

> A. *A Successful Drop*
>
> 'Success' should be measured in terms of the swiftness with which the troops go in and out, and the completeness of the salvage operation.

B. *An Unsuccessful Drop*

The problems created for the West would obviously be exaggerated if, 1) DRAGON ROUGE precedes Vandewalle to Stanleyville by some days, thus (notwithstanding the nonmilitary objectives of the operation) unilaterally ending the rebellion and leaving Belgian paratroopers in charge of an 'occupied' city, and/or 2) a number of hostages were killed despite the paradrop.[4]

By this definition of 18 November 1964, Dragon Rouge was neither a success nor a failure. While Laurent's troops were in Stanleyville only forty-eight hours, the salvage operation in the Congo was hardly a complete one. The operation did not end the rebellion, and hostages were killed. The CWG's serious reluctance to consider the need for greater forces to affect an outright intervention led to these inconclusive results, since it limited the options of those faced with ordering and executing the operations. Like the longstanding effort to reconcile and to stabilize the turbulent Congo, the Dragon operations yielded a brilliant success that was tarnished by other related failures.

Appendix A

Personalities, Code Names and Terms, and Acronyms

PERSONALITIES

Congolese Personalities

Cyrille Adoula	Congolese minister of security; political ally of Mobutu.
Christophe Gbenye	Minister of interior during Lumumba's tenure; self-styled successor to Lumumba's leadership role; founder of the CNL; president of the Republique Populaire du Congo, and as such, nominal leader of the Simba Rebellion.
Joseph Kasavubu	President of the Democratic Republic of the Congo since independence; political and tribal leader of the Bakongo.
Patrice Lumumba	First prime minister of the Democratic Republic of the Congo; leader of the MNC; killed in 1961; semi-deity of the Simba Rebellion.
Joseph Mobutu	Chief of staff and later commanding general of the ANC in 1964.
Leonard Mulamba	Lieutenant colonel commanding Stanleyville ANC garrison; an excellent military leader in an army of incompetents.
Pierre Mulélé	Political associate of Lumumba; former minister of education; leader of the Kwilu Rebellion 1963–64.
Victor Nendaka	Congolese minister of security; political ally of Mobutu.
Nicholas Olenga	Associate of Lumumba; military lieutenant of Soumialot; commanding general of the People's Army of Liberation.
Gaston Soumialot	Associate of Lumumba; nominal subordinate of Gbenye in the CNL; opened the eastern wing of the CNL to associate it with the 1964 uprisings; minister of defense of the rebel regime.

Moise Tshombe	President of Katanga province in 1960; leader of the Katangan secession 1960—63; prime minister of the Democratic Republic of the Congo during the Simba Rebellion.

Belgian Personalities

Viscount Davignon	Spaak's deputy.
Ambassador De Kerchove	Belgian ambassador to Leopoldville.
Colonel Charles Laurent	Commanding officer, Belgian Paracommando Regiment.
Colonel Guillame Logiest	Chief of CAMAC, the Belgian military assistance mission in the Congo.
Colonel Louis Marliere	Military adviser to Mobutu.
Paul-Henri Spaak	Belgian foreign minister since 1961, long-time associate to Averell Harriman; former NATO secretary general.
Colonel Frédéric J. L. A. Vandewalle	Former security chief in the Belgian Congo; Belgian consul in Katanga during Tshombe's secession; adviser to Tshombe during the Simba Rebellion; designed and executed the Vandewalle Plan.

American Personalities

General Paul D. Adams	Commander in chief, U.S. Strike Command; also, commander in chief, Middle East, Africa, South Asia; responsible for U.S. military operations in the Congo; a dominant personality in the crisis.
G. McMurtrie Godley	American ambassador to Leopoldville; a particularly strong-willed diplomat.
Colonel Burgess Gradwell	Commander of the USEUCOM airlift for Dragon Rouge.
Averell Harriman	Under secretary of state for political affairs; served as President Lyndon B. Johnson's front man during the crisis.
Colonel Clayton Isaacson	Commander of JTF LEO; assumed operational control of Gradwell's force.
General Lyman Lemnitzer	Commander in chief, U.S. Forces in Europe.
Douglas MacArthur II	American ambassador to Brussels.
G. Mennen Williams	Assistant secretary of state for Africa.
General Earl Wheeler	Chairman of the JCS.

CODE NAMES AND TERMS

United States

Close Look	Line astern, low-level airborne delivery doctrine.
Flag Pole	Embassy plan to rescue Hoyt.

OPLAN 515 Ready Move	Initial USSTRICOM plan to aid in evacuation operations.
OPLAN 515/I Ready Move II	Deployment of JTF LEO to the Congo.
OPLAN 514 Ready Move III	USSTRICOM plan for two-battalion operation to seize and hold Stanleyville.
OPLAN 519 High Beam	USSTRICOM plan (rewrite of 514) to use a brigade to conduct the operation.
Low Beam	*Version a.* U.S. military special warfare mission to conduct covert American rescue—rehearsed as Golden Hawk
	Version b. CIA covert mission attached to Vandewalle's column.

Belgian

Dragon Blanc	Proposed Bunia rescue.
Dragon Noir	Paulis rescue.
Dragon Rouge	Stanleyville rescue.
Dragon Vert	Proposed Watsa rescue.
Les Gars	"The Boys": the Paracommandos.
L'Ommengang	Vandewalle's ground column.

Congolese

jeunesse	Youth gangs associated with the rebellion.
ratissage	Congolese tradition of brutality toward the vanquished.
Simba	Swahili for lion; fully indoctrinated rebel soldier.

ACRONYMS

ANC	Armée Nationale Congolaise.
APL	Armée Populaire de Libération.
CAMAC	Belgian military assistance liaison to the Congo.
CARP	Computed airborne release point.
CNL	Conseil National de Libération.
COMISH	U.S. military assistance mission to the Congo.
CWG	Congo Working Group.
FATAC	Congolese tactical air force.
ICRC	International Committee of the Red Cross.
JCSE	Joint Communications Support Element.

Lima I	Vandewalle's lead column of L'Ommengang under Liegeois.
Lima II	Vandewalle's second column of L'Ommengang under Lamouline.
MNC	Mouvement Nationale Congolaise.
SENREPLEO	Senior representative to Leopoldville.
TACTA	Tactical commanders terrain analysis (maps).
UN	United Nations.
USAFE	U.S. Air Force Europe.
USAID	U.S. Agency for International Development.
USEUCOM	U.S. European Command.
USIA	U.S. Information Agency.
USCINCMEAFSA	U.S. commander in chief Middle East, Africa, South Asia
USSTRICOM	U.S. Strike Command

Appendix B

Order of Battle-Command Structure

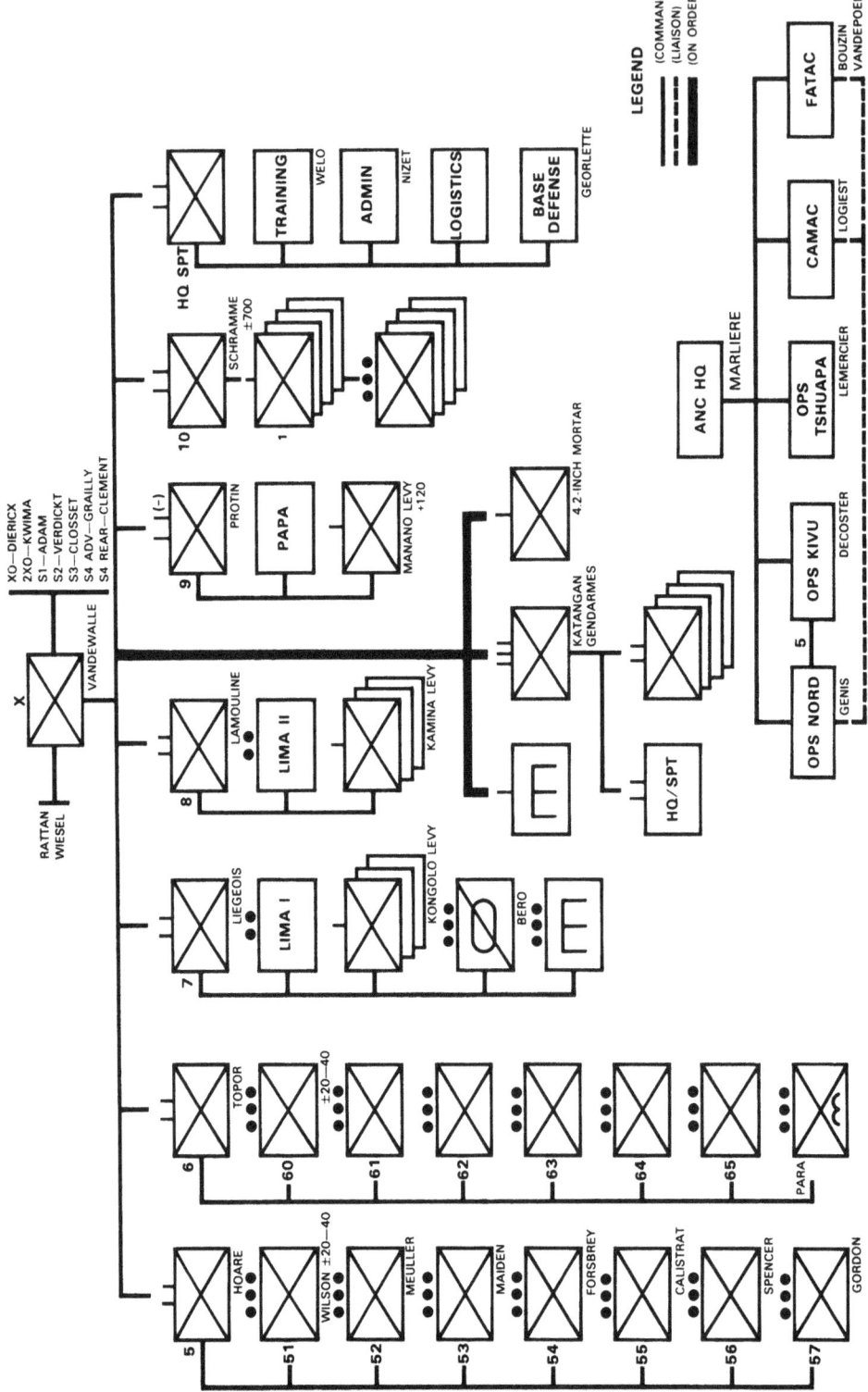

Figure 1. L'Ommengang table of organization

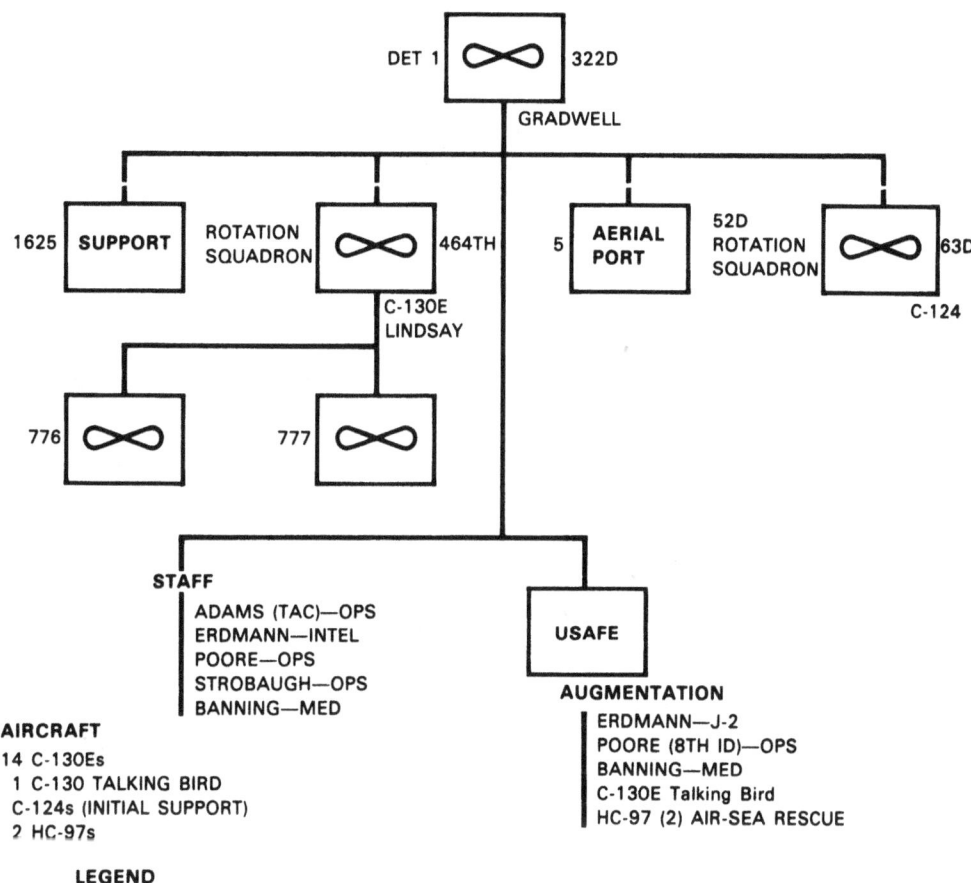

Figure 2. USEUCOM airlift

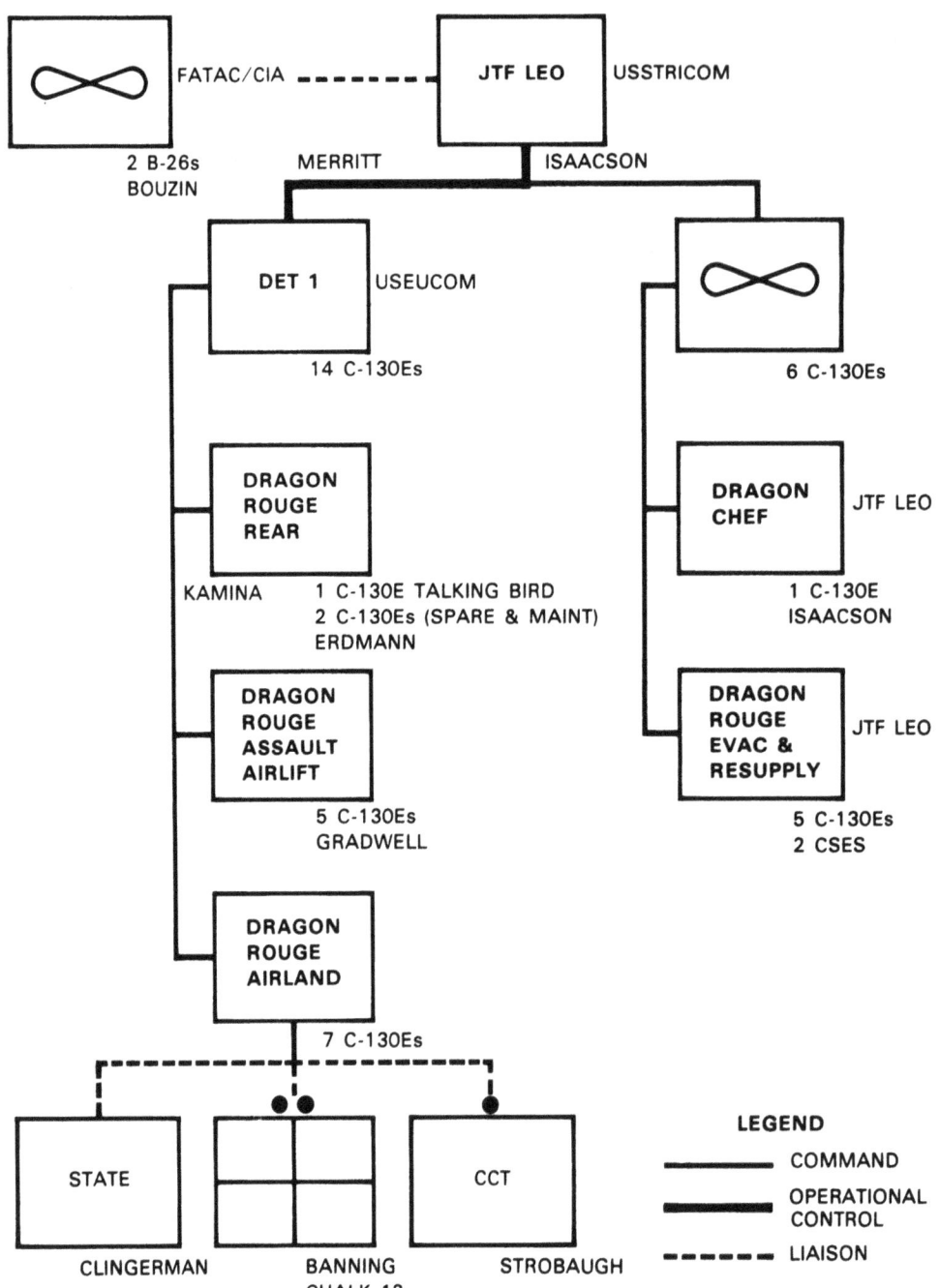

Figure 3. Dragon Rouge airlift

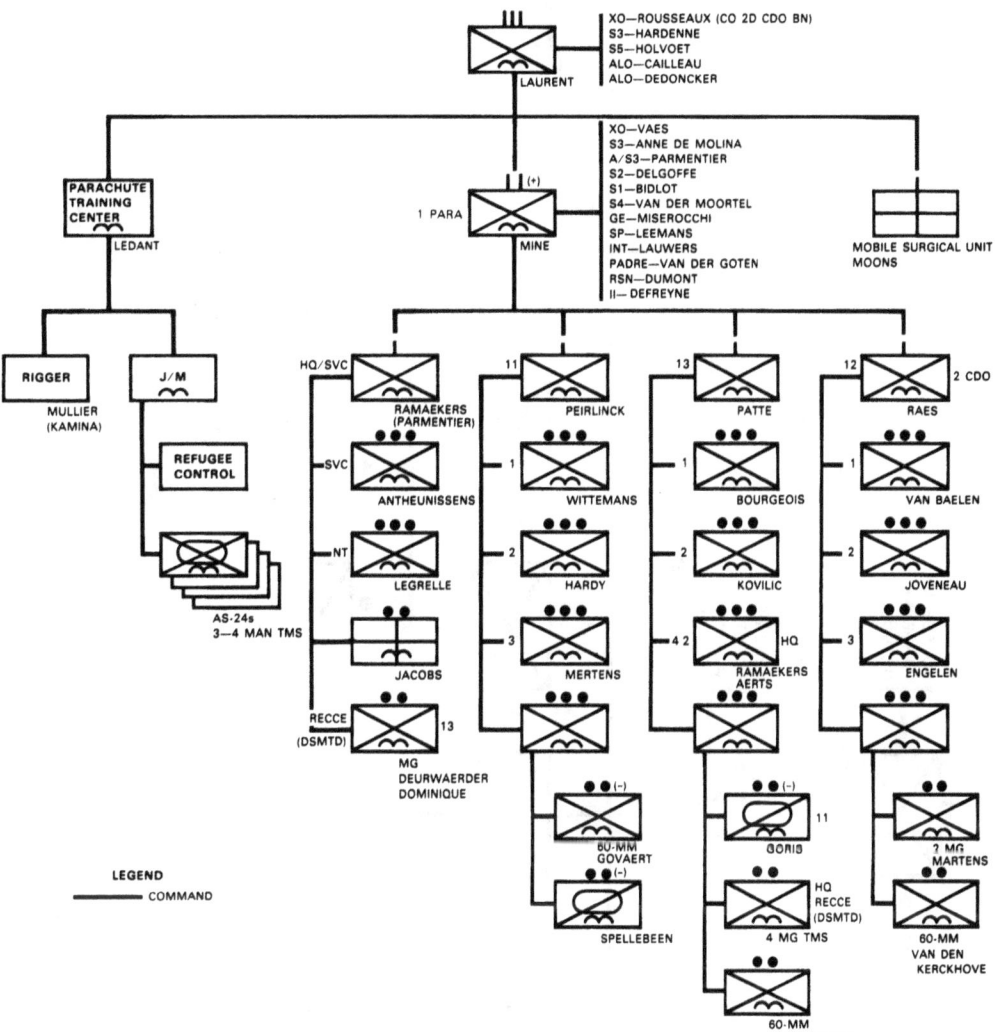

Figure 4. Dragon Rouge

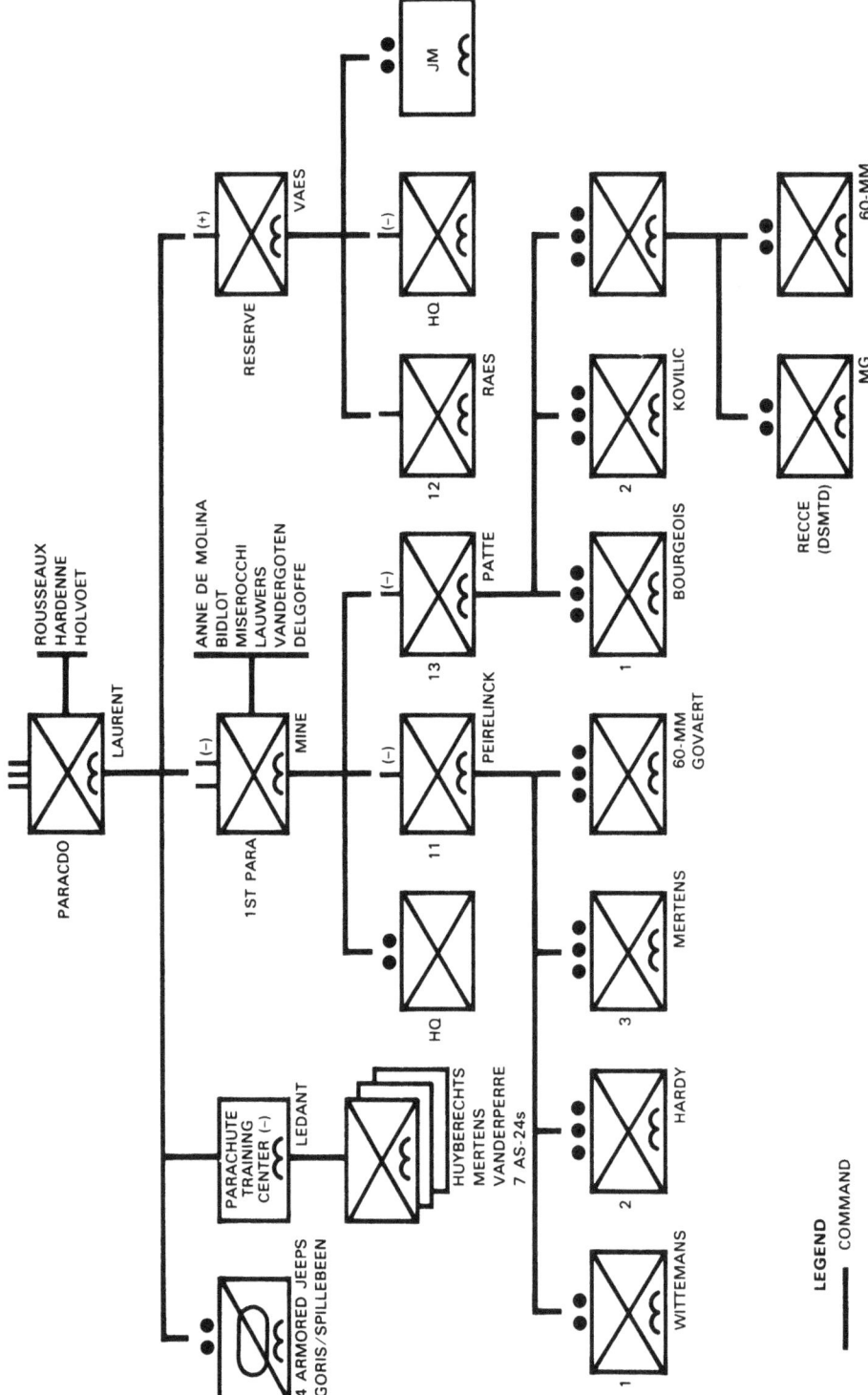

Figure 5. Dragon Noir

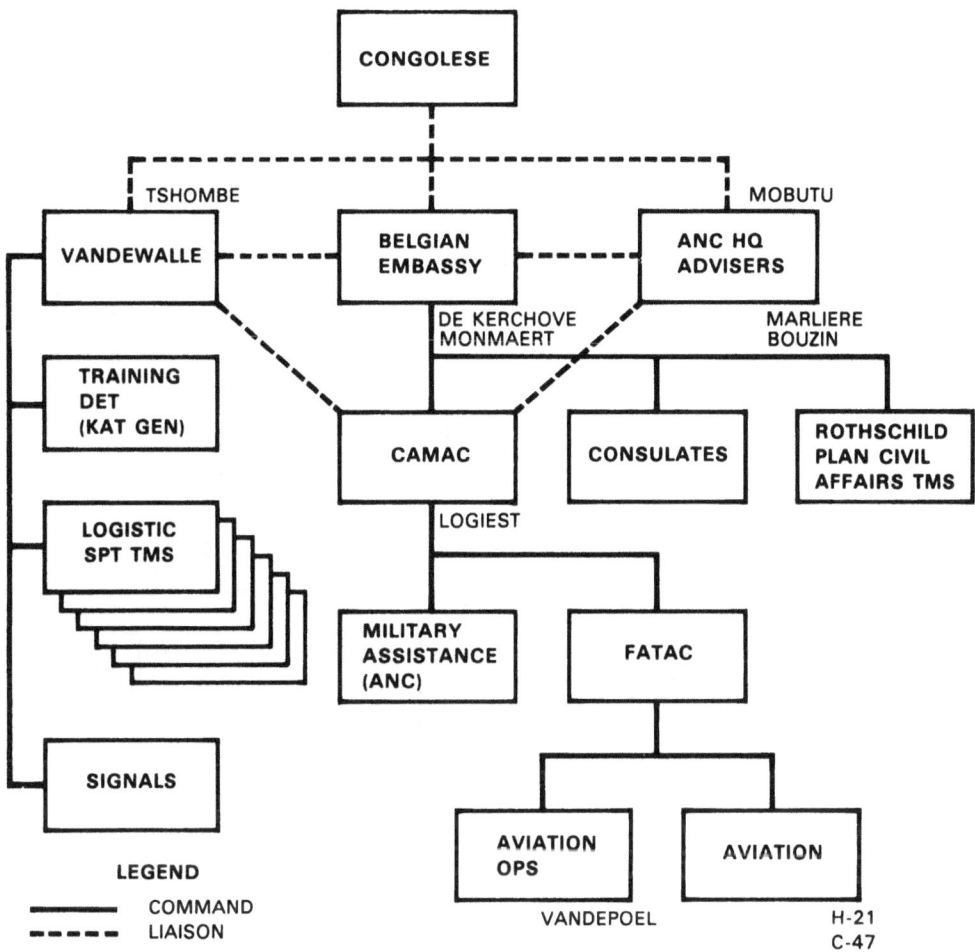

Figure 6. Belgian assets in the Congo, September 1964

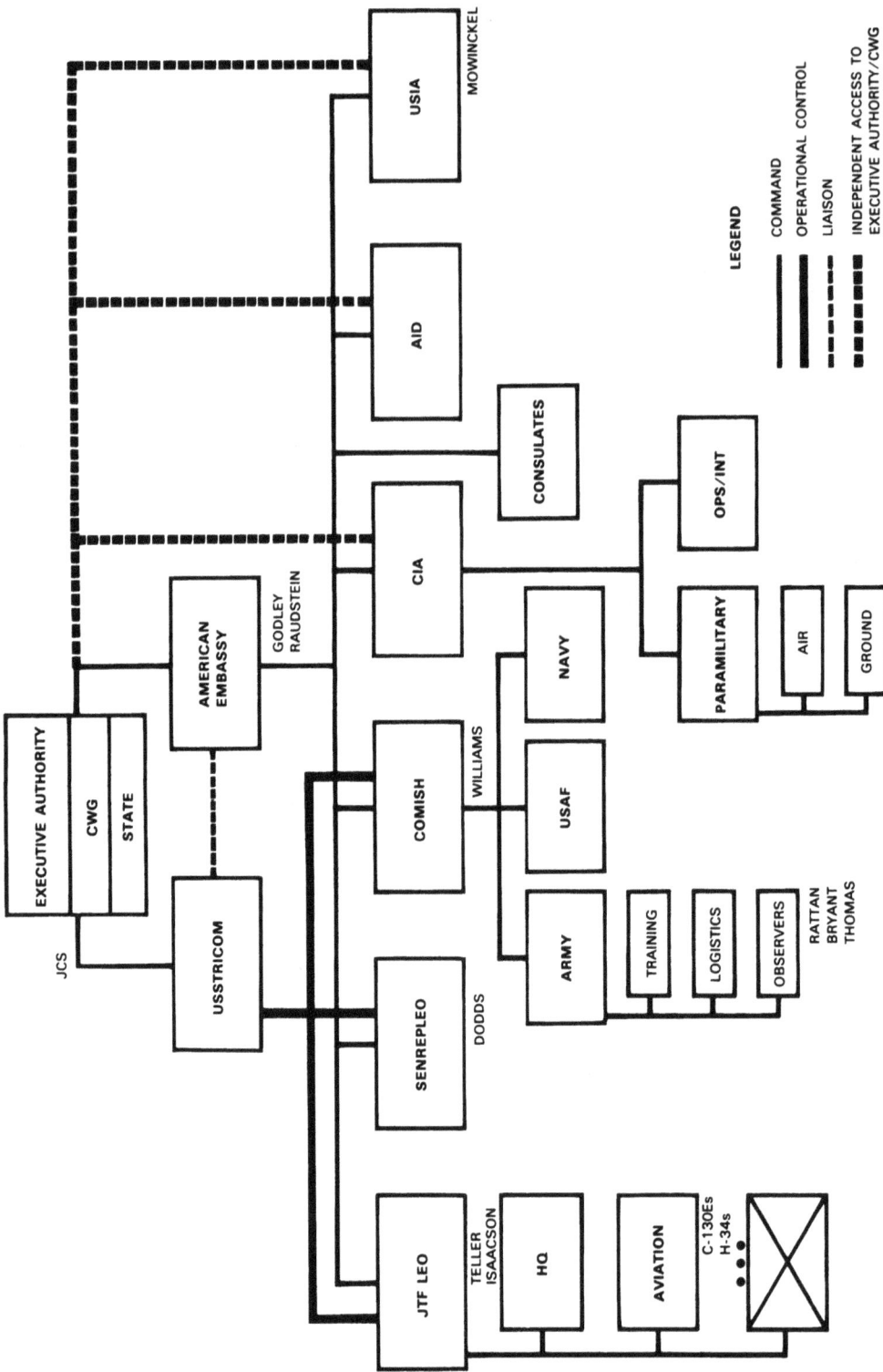

Figure 7. U.S. assets in the Congo, September 1964

Appendix C

Chronology

Date	Event
30 Jun 60	Independence of the Democratic Republic of the Congo.
6 Jul 60	Mutiny of the Force Publique.
9 Jul 60	Secession of Kasai and Katanga provinces.
9 Jul 60	Belgian intervention in the Congo.
10 Jul 60	Leopoldville requests UN troops to restore order and force Belgian withdrawal.
15 Jul 60	Arrival of first UN troops.
13 Nov 60	Creation of rival Stanleyville regime.
Jul 60 to May 63	UN operations turn from law and order mandate to open military campaign to restore Leopoldville's control over the entire Congo.
29 May 63	Tshombe surrenders Katanga and goes into exile.
Aug 63	Mulélé returns and begins limited guerrilla operations in Kwilu province.
Fall 63	Opening of Belgian and American security assistance missions in Leopoldville. Formation of the CNL.
21 Jan 64	State of emergency declared in Kwilu due to Mulélé's revolt.
Spring 64	CIA air force begins operations in support of the ANC.
Mar 64	CNL opens office in Bujumbura, Burundi.
Apr 64 to May 64	Limited uprisings in the eastern Congo, thanks to ANC brutality and incompetence, turn into open rebellion.
Jun 64	CNL, guided by Soumialot and Olenga, exploit the rebellion.
Jul 64	The rebellion, led by Olenga and his Popular Army of Simbas and *jeunesse*, marches north.
22 Jul 64	Kindu falls to the rebels.
Jul–Aug 64	Mercenaries arrive in the Congo.
5 Aug 64	Stanleyville falls to the rebels. Five American diplomats remain in rebel hands.

5–7 Aug 64	Embassy considers Operation Flagpole but cancels it.
6–7 Aug 64	Vandewalle called to foreign ministry in Brussels; departs for Leopoldville the next day.
6–8 Aug 64	Harriman-Spaak consultations in Brussels.
11 Aug 64	JTF LEO deploys to Leopoldville accompanied by G. Mennen Williams and William Lang.
19 Aug 64	Olenga marches on Bukavu and is defeated the next day; minicrisis over Dodd's escapade.
21 Aug 64	Olenga orders "trial without mercy" of the American diplomats.
22 Aug 64	State Department asks Godley for counterhostages.
24 Aug 64	Acting on Tshombe's instructions, Hoare stages Operation Watch Chain disaster; Vandewalle takes charge of campaign.
29 Aug 64	Formation of the Congo Working Group.
4 Sep 64	The CWG visits the JCS; asks for hostage rescue study.
5 Sep 64	Tshombe attends OAU convention, which ultimately places Kenyatta on rebel side.
5–7 Sep 64	Planning for Operation Golden Hawk.
12 Sep 64	Publication of JCSM-788-64, which presents covert and overt rescue options and suggests direct intervention.
Mid-Sep 64	Vandewalle has general agreement on his plan to retake the eastern Congo; begins operations with consequent loss of control.
Mid-Sep 64	All rebel leaders gathered in Stanleyville.
25 Sep 64	Red Cross mission into Stanleyville; Americans moved from prison to Sabena Guest House.
1 Oct 64	Separate military operations and air attacks turn Vandewalle plan into disjointed campaign.
1 & 7 Oct 64	Direct threats against Westerners as reprisals for government air attacks.
3 Oct 64	Tshombe activates 21st Squadron (mercenary).
	United States begins reduction of visibility effort.
7 Oct 64	United States threatens air suspension.
9 Oct 64	JCS orders USSTRICOM to plan for intervention.
14 Oct 64	New rebel threat; OPLAN 514 on alert.
15 Oct 64	Tshombe ignores threat; suspension of alert goes into effect.
19 Oct 64	Adams forwards OPLAN High Beam to JCS and CWG; CWG rejects the plan.
	Soumialot begins threatening Belgian lives in Stanleyville.
23 Oct 64	Tshombe places 21st Squadron under CIA control; air operations resume under tight restrictions.
24 Oct 64	Lemercier discovers dead hostages in Boende.
	Dr. Carlson arrested as CIA spy.

26 Oct 64	Palmer arrives in Brussels to reaffirm Harriman-Spaak strategy.
28 Oct 64	Rebels arrest all American and Belgians in Stanleyville.
	Bouzin proposes combined Belgian-American rescue.
1 Nov 64	Lima I begins drive on Kindu.
4 Nov 64	Lima I takes Kimbombo and finds dead hostages; night march on Kindu.
5 Nov 64	Lima I takes Kindu and prevents systematic massacre.
6–7 Nov 64	Kindu debriefing reports reach Washington and Brussels.
8 Nov 64	As a result of U.S. pressure, Spaak proposes combined operation; Spaak becomes the driving force behind the operation.
9 Nov 64	CWG proposes new diplomatic initiatives.
10 Nov 64	JCS orders USEUCOM to assemble planning team in Brussels; JCS excludes USSTRICOM.
11–13 Nov 64	Brussels planning conference.
12 Nov 64	British propose unilateral intervention with two battalions; offer is withdrawn after learning of Belgian-American planning.
14 Nov 64	USEUCOM publishes OPLAN 319/64 Dragon Rouge.
	Spaak recommends staging to Ascension Island; CWG balks at the suggestion; Vandewalle apprised of Dragon Rouge and Low Beam and suggests the need for other operations.
	Belgian and Americans begin active preparations for the operation.
15 Nov 64	Carlson tried and sentenced to death.
	JCS alerts airlift element for possible movement on 17 November.
16 Nov 64	Congolese reject CWG's 9 November suggestion for talks with rebel leaders.
	Belgians and Americans agree on second Brussels conference.
	JCS directs execution of Ascension move on 17 November.
	Clingerman dispatched to Brussels.
17 Nov 64	JCS-CWG-Belgian-USEUCOM debate over cover plan.
	JCS orders USEUCOM and USSTRICOM to send planners to Brussels; USSTRICOM to assume operational control of airlift for Dragon Rouge at Ascension.
	Big Punch procedures debate begins.
	CWG asks Vandewalle to advance his timetable.
	As the deception fiasco attracts media attention, first press speculations over mission.
18 Nov 64	The Dragon force closes at Ascension.
	Second Brussels planning conference begins.
	CWG begins diplomatic initiatives on Congolese request for rescue.
	Laurent and Gradwell work out operational problems.
19 Nov 64	Big Punch procedures established.

	Clingerman briefs Dragon force at Ascension.
	Rebels propose negotiations; CWG reacts and proposes full-scale cease-fire talks in Nairobi.
	Vandewalle resumes drive.
20 Nov 64	Second planning conference produces concepts for operations in Bunia, Paulis, and Watsa.
	Vandewalle reaches Aluta; plans to push for Stanleyville regardless of Dragon Rouge.
	Spaak rejects CWG initiative on negotiations.
	CWG insists on the negotiations to forestall Carlson's execution.
	Spaak announces presence of Dragon force on Ascension and alerts Belgians for move to Kamina.
	CWG announcement on Nairobi talks disrupts relations with Tshombe.
	American Embassy in Leopoldville asks for Clingerman to accompany Dragon force and for signals team to accompany Vandewalle. CWG accedes to first request, rejects second.
	CWG hesitates on move to Kamina.
21 Nov 64	Rebels threaten to eat their prisoners.
	CWG proposes UN Security Council meeting; Spaak rejects initiative.
	Tshombe authorizes intervention.
	JCS orders move to Kamina with possible direct move to Stanleyville.
	JTF LEO reports Vandewalle may be delayed at Aluta since the ferry is out.
	CWG considers operation on 22 November; rejected by Belgians.
22 Nov 64	Dragon force arrives at Kamina; remains on semialert.
	Debate over 23 November drop results in another sleepless night for the Dragon force.
	Nairobi talks begin.
	Vandewalle and others push for 24 November drop to facilitate linkup.
	Press inquiries on presence of Paracommandos at Kamina.
	Secretary of state suggests use of American battalion to reinforce Dragon Rouge; proposal rejected by secretary of defense; secretary of state then suggests British or French troops; JCS alerts second C-130 squadron for deployment to Spain in case a reinforcement is necessary.
	USSTRICOM, through JTF LEO, assumes operational control of airlift for Dragon Rouge.
23 Nov 64	Continued discussions over need to execute Dragon Rouge.
	Second C-130 squadron ordered to Morón.
	Vandewalle begins final drive.
	Big Punch given for Dragon Rouge.

23 Nov 64	0600:	Dragon Rouge begins with airborne assault.
	0700:	Rebels assemble hostages.
	0715:	Paracommandos move on city.
	0740:	Paracommandos reach city limits.
	0745:	Massacre begins.
	0750:	Paracommandos reach massacre site.
	1100:	Vandewalle links up with Dragon Rouge.
	1700:	Vandewalle assumes control of city; Dragon Rouge ends.
24—25 Nov 64		Planning for Dragon Noir.
25 Nov 64		Belgian-American concurrence develops for execution of Dragon Noir as final rescue.
26 Nov 64		Dragon Noir.
		Vandewalle crosses to Rive Gauche.
27 Nov 64		Dragon force extracted and assembled at Kamina.
28 Nov 64		Dragon force returned to Brussels.
1 Dec 64		Victory parade in Brussels for the Paracommandos.
29 Mar 65		Watsa, objective of Dragon Vert, falls to Hoare, who reports thirty-eight Belgian hostages killed by local rebels since 24 November.
		Leopoldville declares the Simba Rebellion is over.
Aug 65		JTF LEO withdrawn.
25 Nov 65		General Mobutu seizes power.

Appendix D

Results of the Dragon Operations
DRAGON ROUGE

Belgian Paracommandos

Injured in Airborne Operations:
  Corporal Daubercy, HQ Company, 1st Para.
  Private Vanaelten, 11th Company.
  Private Warschotte, HQ Company, 1st Para.
Killed in Action:
  Adjutant Wouters, Belgian Air Force.
Wounded in Action:
  Private Closset, 13th Company.
  Private De Waegeneer, 11th Company (died of wounds).
  Private Nobels, 12th Company.

5th Brigade (23—24 November)

Killed in Action:
  George Clay, South African NBC correspondent.
Wounded in Action:
  Bruce Harper (died of wounds).
  Hans von Lierde.
  Unknown number of Low Beam Cuban exiles.

Hostages

Killed at Avenue Sergeant Ketele:
  Americans—
    Paul Carlson.
    Phyllis Rhine.
  Belgians—
    Estimated twenty.
Wounded at Avenue Sergeant Ketele:
  Forty Belgians (five died of wounds).
Killed in other areas of Stanleyville:
  Robert Latham, UN mission representative.
  Hugh McMillan, Canadian, at Kilometer 8.
  Unidentified Belgian, Public Market.
  Twenty-eight priests, nuns, and missionaries, Rive Gauche.

Wounded in other areas of Stanleyville:
  Mary Harrison, Rive Gauche.
  Robert McAllister, Irish, Kilometer 8 mission.
  Kenneth and Paul McMillan, Canadians, Kilometer 8 mission.
  Charles Schuster, Rive Gauche.
  Colleen Taylor, Rive Gauche.
  Joy Taylor, Rive Gauche.
  Pauline Taylor, Rive Gauche.
Rescued:
  Sixteen hundred.

DRAGON NOIR

Belgian Paracommandos

Injured in Airborne Operation:
  Private Cuylaerts, 11th Company.
Killed in action:
  Corporal Welvaert, 11th Company
Wounded in Action:
  Private André, HQ Company, 1st Para.
  Corporal Nihoul, 13th Company.
  Sergeant Rossinfosse, 13th Company.
  Private Vanderstappen, 11th Company.
  Private Vandersteen, 11th Company.

Hostages/Refugees

Killed:
  Joseph Tucker, American.
  Twenty-one foreign missionaries and civilians.
Wounded:
  Mr. Slegers.
Rescued:
  Estimated 375 ± 25.

HOSTAGES/REFUGEES KILLED IN NORTHEASTERN CONGO AFTER THE DRAGON OPERATIONS

Bafwasende:

Fourteen Europeans.

Banalia:

Sixteen Europeans.

Bunia:

Four Europeans.

Isangi:

Six Europeans.

Wamba:

Twenty-six Americans and Europeans.
  William McChesney, American.
  James Rodger, British.
  Eight priests.
  Sixteen foreign civilians.

Watsa:
 Thirty-eight Belgians.

Notes

Introduction

1. The author wishes to emphasize the international aspects of the mission, such as long-range deployment and the use of multinational forces. The second point of emphasis is the use of hostages as a political-military bargaining tool. The author has been unable to find any other incident during the post-World War II era that meets these criteria and predates the Dragon operations.

2. U.S. Department of State, Foreign Area Research Documentation Center, External Research Staff, "The Congolese Rebellion of 1964," with subarticles: Keith Wheelock, "The Rise and Fall of the Rebel Movement," and M. Crawford Young, "Political Dynamics of the Rebellion" (Washington, DC, June 1965), iii, hereafter cited as State, "Congolese Rebellion of 1964." In a different view of the operational necessity of Dragon Rouge, Colonel Vandewalle points out that while twenty-five Belgians had been killed without justification by the rebels, only four or five had been murdered in the face of government ground attacks. Consequently, he concludes that Dragon Rouge could not be justified solely on the basis of preventing a massacre if Stanleyville had been taken through government ground action. See Colonel e.r. Frédéric J. L. A. Vandewalle, *L'Ommengang: Odyseé et Reconquête de Stanleyville, 1964* (Brussels, Belgium: Le Livre Africain, Collection Temoinage Africain, 1970), 122.

Chapter 1

1. King Leopold's intentions came through clearly when in reference to the Congo, he remarked, "I mean to miss no chance to get my share of this magnificent African cake." As quoted by Basil Davidson, *The Story of Africa* (London: Mitchell Beasley Publishers and Mitchell Beasley Television, 1984), 173.

   Leopold's, and later Belgium's, policies all aimed to assure colonial control over the Congolese. Under the Belgian administration, educational programs for the Congolese prepared them for labor and low-level management positions. To ensure that their exploitation of the Congolese did not unify the natives, the Belgians promoted tribal identification. The Force Publique, with its soldiers based outside their tribal lands, served as the ultimate sanction against Congolese resistance to Belgian control.

   These measures were so effective that the Belgians developed a paternalistic attitude toward their African charges. When other European colonies began to call for independence, the Belgians remained confident in their ability to control the Congo. In the late 1950s, shortly before the Congolese achieved their independence, the Belgians had rejected a proposal to free the Congo within thirty years as being too radical an idea. For a discussion of Leopold's and Belgium's control, see: American University, Washington, DC, Foreign Area Studies, *Zaire: A Country Study*, DA Pam 550-67 (Washington, DC: U.S. Government Printing Office, 1979), 28—45; M. Crawford Young, *Politics in the Congo: Decolonization and Independence* (Princeton, NJ: Princeton University Press, 1965); and M. Crawford Young and Thomas Turner, *The Rise and Decline of the Zairian State* (Madison: University of Wisconsin Press, 1985), 3—46.

2. The Belgians, after failing to prepare the Congolese educationally, left them with an equally flawed constitution. The Loi Fondamentale did not clarify the relationship between regional and central governmental authority. In a country torn by ethnic conflict, the regional versus central authority debate became another version of tribal dispute. To control the situation, the Belgians and the Congolese governments expected the Belgian cadred Force Publique to continue in its traditional role. Neither the Belgians nor the Congolese expected the Force Publique to disintegrate. Emile Janssens, Lieutenant General e.r. Belgian Army, interview with the author, Brussels, Belgium, 8 January 1986; and Ernest W. LeFever, *Crisis in the Congo: A United Nations Force in Action* (Washington, DC: Brookings Institution, 1965), 7—10.

3. As a controversial operation, the UN mission in the Congo was the subject of numerous studies. See: LeFever, *Crisis*; Conor Cruise O'Brien, *To Katanga and Back: A UN Case History* (New York: Simon and Schuster, 1962); Thomas M. Franck and John Carey, *The Legal Aspects of the United Nations Action in the Congo* (New York: Oceana Publications, 1963); Edward Hymof, *Stig Von Bayer: International Troubleshooter for Peace* (New York: James H. Heineman, 1965); Madeleine G. Kalb, *The Congo Cables: The Cold War in Africa—From Eisenhower to Kennedy* (New York: Macmillan Publishing Co., 1982); Ernest W. LeFever and Wynfred Joshua, *United Nations Peacekeeping in the Congo, 1960—1964: An Analysis of Political, Executive, and Military Control*, 4 vols. (Washington, DC: Brookings Institution, 1966); A. G. Mezerik, ed., *Congo and the United Nations*, 3 vols. (New York: United Nations International Review Service, 1960); Stephen R. Weissman, *American Foreign Policy in the Congo, 1960—1964* (Ithaca, NY: Cornell University, 1974); and U.S. Strike Command, Director of Intelligence, J2, "Historical Analysis of Insurgency in the Congo (L) Since 1960," 7 August 1960, Paul D. Adams Papers, File 17, U.S. Army Military History Institute (MHI), Carlisle Barracks, PA, hereafter cited as USSTRICOM, "Insurgency."

4. American U., *Zaire*, 41—42; and Kalb, *Congo Cables*, 276—80.

5. State, "Congolese Rebellion of 1964," pt. 1, 1—2.

6. Following the mutiny of the Force Publique, the Congolese expelled all of its Belgian officers. The new army, renamed the Armée Nationale Congolaise (ANC), was broken up into regional commands with little or no allegiance to the central government. In an effort to improve the army's loyalty, the government promoted Congolese sergeants to senior officer positions and drastically increased the army's pay, which by 1963 took 30 percent of the country's budget. General Mobutu resisted UN, and later Belgian-American, efforts to reduce the size of the ANC in favor of improving its quality. For Mobutu, such a reduction represented a reduction in his base of power; naturally, he resisted such a program. Consequently, the ANC, like the Force Publique, remained an instrument of oppression to the Congolese. See: Kalb, *Congo Cables*, 46—109; USSTRICOM, "Insurgency," 3; LeFever, *Crisis*, 125—26, 132—33; Young, *Politics*, 458—59, 471; Vandewalle, *L'Ommengang*, 55; and U.S. Commander in Chief Middle East, Africa, South Asia [CINCMEAFSA], Military Assistance Planning Reference Book: Congo 1 August 1964 (MacDill Air Force Base, FL: USCINCMEAFSA, 1964), table 2, C 1—3, hereafter cited as *MAP: Congo 1964*.

7. American U., *Zaire*, 47; Kalb, *Congo Cables*, 4—8, 151, 186, 289, 377; O'Brien, *To Katanga*, appx. 2; USSTRICOM, "Insurgency," 4—5; Vandewalle, *L'Ommengang*, 96, 97, 144; LeFever, *Crisis*, 79—81, 88—112; and Young, *Politics*, 379—80.

8. Vandewalle, *L'Ommengang*, 92—96; and Weissman, *Congo*, 210, 230—35.

9. Kalb and Weissman emphasize the cold war aspects of the United States actions in the Congo. As an overall goal, their emphasis is valid; with the mineral wealth of Katanga, particularly cobalt, the United States did not want to see a Soviet domination of the Congo. The strategy of reconciliation and stabilization supported that goal.

   Concerning the UN-American coalition, their cooperation was not always complete. Initially, the United States and the UN worked closely, but American complicity in Mobutu's seizure of power in late 1960 embarrassed the UN in the eyes of the Third

World. Lumumba's death, after the inauguration of the Kennedy administration, brought the two partners back together; Kennedy challenged Belgian support of Tshombe. Following Hammarskjöld's death, the UN and the United States pushed for and got a new mandate that allowed for the use of open military operations to crush the secession.

The American-Belgian coalition began with the change in government in Brussels in 1962. The new foreign minister, Paul-Henri Spaak, withdrew much of the Belgian support for Katanga, and when the UN announced its plan to withdraw by 1963, the United States approached Belgium with the Green Plan for bilateral military assistance to the Congo through the UN. After the UN rejected participation in such a plan, the United States and Belgium responded to General Mobutu's request for direct military assistance.

On Adoula's gamble, American observers expected him to continue to survive as prime minister—as he had done since 1961. When Tshombe returned with Belgian support, the American ambassador, G. McMurtrie Godley, was outraged. Godley had been acting ambassador during the Katangan secession and he detested Tshombe. Weissman, *Congo*, 61—63, 71, 115—51; Kalb, *Congo Cables*, 12—14, 24—25, 38, 46—212, 289, 371—72; O'Brien, *To Katanga*, 221; Frédéric J. L. A. Vandewalle, Colonel e.r. Belgian Army, interviews with the author, Brussels, Belgium, 11 and 14 January 1986; and LeFever, *Crisis*, 92, 127—33. Memorandum, Adlai E. Stevenson to the President, Subject: Extension of UN Force in the Congo, 22 February 1964; Memorandum for the President from Secretary of State Dean Rusk, Subject: Training of the Congolese Army (ANC), 15 February 1964; Memorandum for the President from Under Secretary of State for Political Affairs W. Averell Harriman, 20 April 1964; Memorandum for the President from William H. Brubeck, Executive Office of the President, 20 April 1964; and Memorandum for W. Averell Harriman from Deputy Secretary of Defense Cyrus Vance, 20 April 1964; all memorandums in National Security Files—Country Files: Congo, Container 81, Memos and Miscellaneous, vol. 1, 11/63—6/64, Lyndon Baines Johnson Library, Austin, TX. Further references to this collection of documents will be cited as LBJ-NSF-CF: Congo. *MAP: Congo 1964*, A.1; Message, AMEMBASSY Leopoldville 1492 to STATE, DTG 041905Z February 1964; Message, AMEMBASSY Leopoldville 1524 to STATE, DTG 071817Z February 1964; and Message, AMEMBASSY Leopoldville 2580 to STATE, DTG 131505Z June 1964; all messages in LBJ-NSF CF: Congo, Container 81, Congo Cables, vol. 1, 11/63—6/64.

10. The American military aid mission began in 1964 with a budget of 3.5 million dollars and focused on the logistic apparatus for the ANC. Parallel to COMISH, USAID worked closely with the Congolese police apparatus in an effort to relieve the ANC from police duty. After COMISH opened in 1963, it brought in an initial delivery of 183 vehicles for the ANC; they were inoperative by mid-1964.

    The Belgian mission, CAMAC, had an entirely different flavor. Belgian officers worked closely with the ANC leadership as advisers on training. While Logiest served as the chief of CAMAC, Colonel Louis Marliere acted as Mobutu's personal military counselor. Other Belgian officers served nominally under Logiest, but due to the vagaries of Congolese law, these officers were not under Belgian military authority. Consequently, Mobutu was able to manipulate the Belgian advisory effort when it suited him.

    With such an uncoordinated structure, the overall Belgian-American effort to restructure, reduce, and retrain the ANC moved too slowly. The United States took measures to improve its side of the coalition. Under the provisions of the Unified Command Plan, which assigns regional responsibilities to the major unified commands, U.S. Strike Command assumed responsibility for Africa in 1963. Designated as U.S. Commander in Chief Middle East, Africa, South Asia (USCINCMEAFSA), General Paul DeWitt Adams was the senior military officer responsible for the Congo security assistance program.

    General Adams had problems in coordinating the military training program with the U.S. State Department. Adams had met State's opposition when he asked to personally tour the area. The State Department did not want to advertise U.S. military interest in the troubled area; African nationalist sensitivities would have reacted strongly to such a signal.

Adams' break came in February 1964 when Adoula asked for an American military adviser. Though he asked for a brigadier general to act as a "Van Fleet" for the Congo, Adams ended up sending Colonel William A. Dodds as his senior representative in Leopoldville (SENREPLEO). Dodds' mission was twofold: he was to advise Mobutu on operations and training and at the same time serve as Adams' personal observer and spokesman. Dodds helped the ANC contain the Mulélé rebellion in Kwilu, and through him, Adams passed on some fairly blunt observations to Mobutu. On one occasion, when Mobutu kept pushing for increased American helicopter support, Adams directed Dodds "to inform Mobutu ... that the way to get guerrillas is to get in the field and to stay in the field keeping pressure on rebels unrelentingly," and to not "take any tripe from him."

Dodds' mission did not always meet with the approval of Ambassador Godley in Leopoldville. Like Adams, Godley was a man given to dominating those around him. With Dodds, COMISH, and later JTF LEO in his backyard as Adams' assets, Godley kept a close leash on their activities. This friction continued throughout the crisis and would complicate the American response to the fall of Stanleyville.

Nevertheless, it was Dodds' report in March 1964 that stimulated increased military support for the Congolese government. Dodds recommended, with Adams' concurrence, that the 1964 security assistance budget be increased to include combat air and airlift assets. The increase, $5.1 million, would provide the ANC with six T-28C fighter-bombers, six H-21 helicopters, ten C-47 transports, and maintenance support. Viewed as an emergency measure to prevent the collapse of the ANC in the field, the new program did not alter its predecessor's goal: the security assistance program remained oriented to reducing the ANC's size in favor of improving its quality. LeFever, *Crisis*, 127—31; Kalb, *Congo Cables*, 371—72; *MAP: Congo 1964*, A.1, S—1; Memorandum for the President from Secretary of State Dean Rusk, Subject: Training of the Congolese Army, 15 February 1964; Memorandum for the President from Under Secretary of State for Political Affairs W. Averell Harriman, 20 April 1964; Memorandum for the President from William H. Brubeck, Executive Office of the President, 20 April 1964; Memorandum for W. Averell Harriman from Deputy Secretary of Defense Cyrus Vance, 20 April 1964; Memorandum to the President from Adlai Stevenson, 22 February 1964; Vandewalle, *L'Ommengang*, 31—32, 44, 49; U.S. Agency for International Development, *Police Survey Mission to the Congo*, with annexes, June 1963 (Washington, DC: U.S. Government Printing Office, June 1963); Memorandum for the President from William H. Brubeck, Executive Office of the President, Subject: Congo, 25 February 1964, LBJ-NSF-CF: Congo, Container 81, Memos and Miscellaneous, vol. 1, 11/63—6/64; and U.S. Joint Chiefs of Staff, Joint Secretariat, Historical Division, *History of the Unified Command Plan* (Washington, DC, 20 December 1977), 23. Message, CINCSTRIKE to OSD/ISA, DTG 152000Z December 1963; Letter, CINCSTRIKE to Colonel William A. Dodds, USA, Subject: ANC Retraining, 14 February 1964; Message, CINCSTRIKE 1126 to JCS, DTG 071907Z February 1964; Message, CINCSTRIKE 1358 to JCS, DTG 131755Z February 1964; Message, CINCSTRIKE 3959 to SENREPLEO, DTG 191750Z April 1964; Message, CINCSTRIKE 2663 to JCS, DTG 202055Z March 1964; all messages and letter in File 17, Adams Papers. USSTRICOM, "Insurgency," 6.

11. Mulélé's association with the People's Republic of China seemed to be the stimulus for cold warrior fears over Communist influence over the rebels. Certainly, Gbenye and Soumialot's attempts to secure Chinese Communist funds and training added to those fears. Yet neither Mulélé nor the CNL ever arrived at a unified political platform. The tribal foundations of Mulélé's revolt limited its appeal. While the ANC, with the guiding hand of Colonel Dodds, succeeded in checking the rebellion in Kwilu, the ANC disintegrated in the eastern Congo.

In the eastern Congo, the ANC's brutality in suppressing local uprisings spread rebellion across tribal boundaries. Bufalero discontent in central Kivu province exploded in April, and the ANC fled to Bukavu, begging for evacuation. Like the Mulélé rebellion, the Bufalero tribesmen limited their campaign to tribal boundaries. Since Bukavu was in Bashi tribal lands, the Bufalero made no attempt to take Bukavu, an easy prize had they wanted it. In contrast, when Baluba dissidents overturned the Albertville government on 27 May, the ANC rallied against the small rebel force and conducted punitive actions against Babembe tribesmen. These atrocities so enraged the Babembe that they joined forces with the Baluba and overturned the Albertville government a second time on 17 June. This time, the ANC fled, and the rebels executed the government officials left at their mercy.

In attempting to forestall a complete ANC collapse, the CIA established a covert air force. Using front organizations—the Western International Ground Maintenance Organization in Lichenstein and the Caribbean Marine Aero Corporation in Miami, Florida—the agency hired ground maintenance personnel and Cuban exiles to pilot the force. American officials were careful to disassociate the United States government from these operations by maintaining that the Cubans were hired by the Leopoldville government. This policy collapsed in June when the news media documented that American pilots had been flying combat missions. Faced with this embarrassment, the State Department was forced to promise to prohibit such future activities. Ironically, the American officials on the scene, who shortly afterward became distressed by Tshombe's use of white mercenary troops, never considered these contract pilots in the same light. Regardless of such fine distinctions, the instant air force was soon in full operation using T-6s against Mulélé's rebels. These aircraft provided air cover sorties for UN evacuation operations around Kikwit during early 1964; UN pilots, glad to have the T-6s around, turned a blind eye to the nature of the pilots. As the year progressed, the CIA continued to expand this operation and others to meet rising demands. By one account, the agency had a Cuban force of 200 infantry, around 30 pilots, and 60 ground personnel in the Congo by 1965. Some of these infantry were to have a critical role in support of Dragon Rouge. Still, this covert support was not intended to secure the Congo; the only way to accomplish that objective was to retrain the ANC. State, "Congolese Rebellion of 1964," pt. 1, 2–5; LBJ-NSF-CF: Congo, Container 81, Memos and Miscellaneous, vol. 1, 11/63–6/64; U.S. Department of State, Memorandum for Governor Harriman, Subject: Chinese Communist Involvement in Congolese Involvement in Congolese Insurrections, 11 August 1964, LBJ-NSF-CF: Congo, Container 81, Memos and Miscellaneous, vol. 3, 8/64; Vandewalle, *L'Ommengang*, 63–64; Victor Marchetti and John D. Marks, *The CIA and the Cult of Intelligence* (New York: Alfred A. Knopf, 1974), 136; Message, STATE 335 to AMEMBASSY Leopoldville, transmitted 4:09 p.m., 15 August 1964, LBJ-NSF-CF: Congo, Container 81, Congo Cables, vol. 3, 8/64; Fred E. Wagoner, *DRAGON ROUGE: The Rescue of Hostages in the Congo* (Washington, DC: National Defense University, 1980), 29; and Barbara A. Wilson, "The Congo (Republic of the Congo—Leopoldville) Since January 1964," in *Research Notes on Insurgency Potential in Africa South of the Sahara* (Washington, DC: American University, August 1965), 77–78.

12. The *jeunesse* developed out of the discontent of the early 1960s. Taking Lumumba's promise of prosperity and development literally, they broke from tribal associations and sought political power. By the height of UN operations, the *jeunesse* had become teenage soldiers of fortune who allied themselves against any form of authority. Difficult to control, the *jeunesse* were responsible for much of the savagery in the turbulent 1960s. State, "Congolese Rebellion of 1964," pt. 1, 4.

13. The foundation of the Simbas' *dawa* was the belief that their magic would turn bullets into water. This belief was readily accepted by the ANC, whose troops at times used countermagic to offset the Simbas' magic. Certainly, the ANC's generally poor marksmanship gave credence to the Simbas' dogma. Once the Simbas ran into close air support, they learned that their *dawa* was less effective against .50-caliber machine guns and rockets. Their surprise at this failure soon turned into terror and ultimately rage against the Westerners still in rebel territory. Ibid., pt. 1, 5.

14. All officers interviewed by the author agreed that Colonel Mulamba was one of the few bright stars in the ANC's otherwise dismal officer corps. Mulamba's ability as an officer led to his downfall: though he rose to prime minister, Mobutu dismissed him as a political threat shortly after assuming dictatorial powers. Ibid., pt. 1, 5–6; Donald V. Rattan, Major

General USA Ret., interview with the author, San Antonio, TX, 14 October 1985; Jean Mine, Jacques Rousseaux, and Luc Raes, Colonels e.r. Belgian Army, interview with the author, Bouge, Belgium, 13 January 1986; Charles Laurent, Major General e.r. Belgian Army, and Georges Ledant, Colonel e.r. Belgian Army, interviews with the author, Ville Franche, France, 9 January 1986; Vandewalle interviews; and Janssens interview.

15. As quoted by State, "Congolese Rebellion of 1964," abstract, i.

16. Michael P. E. Hoyt and David K. Grinwis, "A Journal of the Experiences of the Staff of the American Consulate in Stanleyville from 1 August through 29 November 1964," May 1966, unpublished manuscript, 5, Dr. James M. Erdmann Papers, Department of History, University of Denver, Denver, CO. Hoyt and Grinwis maintained detailed notes on scraps of paper in order to assemble this journal of their captivity.

17. Grinwis' position as a CIA operative in Stanleyville is postulated in Ellen Ray, et al., eds., *Dirty Work 2: The CIA in Africa* (Secaucus, NJ: Lyle Stuart, 1980), 371. This supposition is further supported by certain messages that lend it credence. First, when the Red Cross mission flew to Stanleyville, its representative was to pass instructions to Hoyt that Grinwis had first priority for evacuation. Second, when Godley sent his proposal to State concerning restaffing the consulate, he discussed all the positions except that of the vice consul, a position that he indicated would be discussed through other agency channels. Message, STATE 692 to USMISSION Geneva, transmitted 12:07 p.m., 20 September 1964, LBJ-NSF-CF: Congo, Container 82, Congo Cables, vol. 5, 9/64—10/64; and Message, AMEMBASSY Leopoldville 1811 to STATE, received 7:13 p.m., 9 November 1964, LBJ-NSF-CF: Congo, Container 83, Congo Cables, vol. 6, 10/64—11/64. Some authors state that there were four CIA members on the consulate staff. The author has found no evidence to support this figure, a figure that seems to be an unreasonably large percentage of CIA personnel for an American consulate in central Africa. See Thomas Powers, *The Man Who Kept the Secrets* (New York: Alfred A. Knopf, 1979), 122; and Kalb, *Congo Cables*, 379.

18. David Reed, *111 Days in Stanleyville* (New York: Harper & Row, 1965), 8.

19. Ibid., 69—72, 220—22. For the best work on the missionaries, see Homer E. Dowdy, *Out of the Jaws of the Lion* (New York: Harper and Row, 1965).

20. Wagoner, *DRAGON ROUGE*, 73; and Richard Hamilton, Colonel USAF Ret., telephonic interview with the author, 21 August 1986.

21. Message, AMEMBASSY Leopoldville 357 to STATE, DTG 060102Z August 1964; and Message, AMEMBASSY Leopoldville 358 to STATE, received 12:54 a.m., 6 August 1964; both in LBJ-NSF-CF: Congo, Container 81, Congo Cables, vol. 3, 8/64.

22. Message, STATE 168 to AMEMBASSY Leopoldville, transmitted 1:26 a.m., 6 August 1964, LBJ-NSF-CF: Congo, Container 81, Congo Cables, vol. 3, 8/64.

23. Message, AMEMBASSY Leopoldville 364 to STATE, DTG 061255Z August 1964, LBJ-NSF-CF: Congo, Container 81, Congo Cables, vol. 3, 8/64.

24. Message, AMEMBASSY Leopoldville 372 to STATE, DTG 061603Z August 1964, LBJ-NSF-CF: Congo, Container 81, Congo Cables, vol. 3, 8/64.

25. Wagoner states that the U.S. State Department "encouraged" Godley in his planning. Considering the temerity of its initial response to the proposal and its later reluctance to accept unilateral intervention, its support for Flagpole was lukewarm at best. Wagoner, *DRAGON ROUGE*, 20—21; and Hoyt and Grinwis, "Journal," 7—9. Message, STATE 172 to AMEMBASSY Leopoldville, transmitted 12:47 p.m., 6 August 1964; and Message, AMEMBASSY 366 to STATE, DTG 061315Z November 1964; both in LBJ-NSF-CF: Congo, Container 81, Congo Cables, vol. 3, 8/64.

26. Message, AMEMBASSY Leopoldville 390 to STATE, DTG 070943Z August 1964, LBJ-NSF-CF: Congo, Container 81, Congo Cables, vol. 3, 8/64.

27. The American consul in Bukavu, Richard Matheron, was not spreading undue alarm. Matheron's counterpart, Kivu Central Province President Malago, was so shaken by the

security situation that he was calling for NATO troops. Matheron suggested that 600 of Tshombe's Katanganese might give Bukavu "at least [a] short lease on life." Message, AMCONSULATE Bukavu 97 to STATE, received 3:58 p.m., 3 August 1964, LBJ-NSF-CF: Congo, Container 81, Congo Cables, vol. 2, 7/64—8/64.

28. U.S. Strike Command, "JTF Leo Historical Report," (MacDill Air Force Base, FL, 30 December 1965), annex J, 16—17, in author's possession, hereafter cited as "JTF Leo Historical Report." Message, AMEMBASSY Leopoldville 413 to STATE, DTG 081540Z August 1964; Message, AMEMBASSY Leopoldville 431 to STATE, DTG 101228Z August 1964; and Message, AMEMBASSY Leopoldville 441 to STATE, DTG 101700Z August 1964; all messages in LBJ-NSF-CF: Congo, Container 81, Congo Cables, vol. 3, 8/64.

29. The JCS placed USSTRICOM transport aircraft in Ethiopia on alert in response to Godley's early appeals, but Secretary of State Dean Rusk thought the United States "should hang back and see what the Europeans will do." In communicating Rusk's comments to the White House, William Brubeck wrote that he thought "they will do nothing." Message, JCS 7711 to CINCSTRIKE, DTG 041928Z August 1964, LBJ-NSF-CF: Congo, Container 81, Congo Cables, vol. 2, 7/64—8/64. Memorandum from Bill Brubeck for Mr. Bundy, 4 August 1964; and Memorandum for the Honorable McGeorge Bundy from W. Averell Harriman, Subject: The Congo, 4 August 1964; memorandums in LBJ-NSF-CF: Congo, Container 81, Memos and Miscellaneous, vol. 2, 7/64—8/64; and Wagoner, *DRAGON ROUGE*, 12, 23.

30. Harriman was well aware of Spaak's stand on the Congo. U.S. Ambassador to Belgium Douglas MacArthur II had reported that Spaak, in reviewing Belgian domestic support for the Congo, had bluntly stated that he was not interested in "another Vietnam." In another message, MacArthur pointed out that the Belgian business community recognized that any Belgian military involvement would rebound against the "4 to 5 thousand Belgians now in [the] eastern Congo." Message, AMEMBASSY Brussels 177 to STATE, DTG 061638Z August 1964, LBJ-NSF-CF: Congo, Container 81, Congo Cables, vol. 3, 8/64; and Message, AMEMBASSY Brussels 181 to STATE, DTG 061843Z August 1964, LBJ-NSF-CF: Congo, Container 81, Memos and Miscellaneous, vol. 3, 8/64.

31. Message, STATE 179 to AMEMBASSY Brussels, transmitted 11:42 a.m., 7 August 1964, LBJ-NSF-CF: Congo, Container 81, Memos and Miscellaneous, vol. 3, 8/64.

32. Message, AMEMBASSY Brussels 193 to STATE, received 6:21 a.m., 8 August 1964; Message, STATE 223 to AMEMBASSY Leopoldville, transmitted 1:13 a.m., 10 August 1964; and Message, AMEMBASSY Brussels 200 to STATE, DTG 081117Z August 1964; all in LBJ-NSF-CF: Congo, Container 81, Memos and Miscellaneous, vol. 3, 8/64. Memorandum for the Honorable McGeorge Bundy from W. Averell Harriman, subject: The Congo, 11 August 1964, LBJ-NSF-CF: Congo, Container 81, Memos and Miscellaneous, vol. 3, 8/64; and Wagoner, *DRAGON ROUGE*, 24.

33. "JTF Leo Historical Report," 3—4; Wagoner, *DRAGON ROUGE*, 30—34.

34. Wagoner, *DRAGON ROUGE*, 72.

35. JCS, *Unified Command Plan*, 23; and U.S. Air Forces Europe, Office of Information, Historical Division, *The Congo Airlift—1960* (Frankfurt, Germany: 1 March 1961).

36. "JTF Leo Historical Report," 3—4; and Wagoner, *DRAGON ROUGE*, 30—34.

37. On 11 August, Governor Williams received a visit from the South African ambassador to the United States, Dr. William C. Naude. Naude wanted to discuss an urgent Tshombe request for two South African fighter squadrons. Looking for indications of American reaction to such assistance, Naude was told to "do as you like." Later, Godley pressed Kasavubu on the issue and demanded that he "pull all cards on [the] table." Williams, a strong Africanist, was distressed by Tshombe's South African contacts. He became even more distressed when the South African government followed his flippant guidance and did as it wished. Memorandum of Conversation, Subject: Tshombe Request for South African Assistance, 11 August 1964; and Message, AMEMBASSY Leopoldville 563 to STATE, DTG 171012Z August 1964; both in LBJ-NSF-CF: Congo, Container 81, Memos

and Miscellaneous, vol. 3, 8/64. Message, AMEMBASSY Leopoldville 472 to STATE, DTG 121428Z August 1964; and Message, AMEMBASSY Leopoldville 572 to STATE, DTG 171550Z August 1964; both in LBJ-NSF-CF: Congo, Container 81, Congo Cables, vol. 3, 8/64.

38. Vandewalle, *L'Ommengang*, 131—34.

39. Ibid., 1—12, 148—49.

40. The Vandewalle plan grew out of an extremely confused situation. When original ideas about using African, Belgian, or even Korean and Philippine troops failed, Tshombe's Katangan exiles became the only alternative.

Once Tshombe's army was selected, American observers feared he might use it for political gain. Thus, Ambassador Godley wanted the Katangans to hit Stanleyville as their first target, so they would be fully embroiled in the war rather than be available for use by Tshombe.

As Vandewalle evolved his plan, one of the thorniest issues was command and control. Mobutu wanted the Katangans integrated into the ANC. With Tshombe's support, Munango, the minister of interior, wanted them as a separate organization. To keep Mobutu and other Congolese from disrupting the operation, the solution was to blend the ANC with the Katangans. "Strawman" leadership would come from ANC officers, while the Belgian logistic teams, as "stiffeners," would provide the real leadership.

Command of the campaign was tripartite. As de facto defense minister, Tshombe supposedly directed the overall effort. As his adviser, Vandewalle directed the Katangans. General Mobutu retained control of the ANC, while his adviser, Colonel Marliere, would direct it. As overall head of the Belgian advisory effort, Colonel Logiest was to coordinate between Vandewalle and Marliere. In the field, however, Vandewalle retained control of his mixed columns—until Logiest or someone else removed them from his immediate direction.

The Belgians set up a separate planning staff that worked under joint Tshombe-Mobutu control. This staff was to ensure that the Congolese adhered to the campaign strategy based on cutting off rebel supply routes; retaining control of strategic cities by holding actions; and finally, rolling back the rebels in a coordinated campaign using six separate columns.

The principal assumption in Vandewalle's plan was the Congolese, the Americans, and the Belgians would cooperate The diverse political objectives of the involved parties, however, militated against cooperative efforts. For example, the original belief was that as the columns progressed, they would remain in place long enough to pacify and stabilize the newly regained areas. But as pressure built up on the Congolese to defeat the rebels, the opposite occurred: Tshombe and Mobutu fixed on destroying the rebellion, and the campaign turned into a series of uncoordinated military operations. Ibid., 279—82; and Vandewalle interviews. Message, USARMA Leopoldville CX-150 to DA, DTG 21152Z [sic] July 1964; Message, AMEMBASSY Leopoldville 292 to STATE, DTG 011955Z August 1964; and Message, AMEMBASSY Leopoldville 294 to STATE, DTG 012030Z August 1964; all in LBJ-NSF-CF: Congo, Container 81, Congo Cables, vol. 2, 7/64—8/64. Message, AMEMBASSY Leopoldville 414 to STATE, DTG 081637Z August 1964; and Message, USARMA Leopoldville CX-181 to DIA, DTG 11164Z [sic] August 1964; both in LBJ-NSF-CF: Congo, Container 81, Congo Cables, vol. 3, 8/64. Message, CINCSTRIKE/USCINCMEAFSA 8640 to JCS 192118Z August 1964, LBJ-NSF-CF: Congo, Container 82, Congo Cables, vol. 4, 8/64. Message (C), COMISH Leopoldville 9098 to CINCMEAFSA, DTG 131045Z August 1964 (U); and Message (C), USARMA CX163 to DA, DTG 030730Z August 1964 (U); both messages reviewed by the Defense Intelligence Agency, 5 March 1986, information as cited unclassified; both in LBJ-NSF-CF: Congo, classified holdings. Message, AMEMBASSY Leopoldville 559 to STATE, transmitted 7:00 a.m., 17 August 1964; and Message, AMEMBASSY Brussels 282 to STATE, DTG 181805Z August 1964; both reviewed and sanitized by STATE, 12 December 1985; both in U.S. Department of State, Historical Records, File POL 23-9 THE CONGO (Washington, DC), hereafter cited as State HF,

POL 23-9 THE CONGO. Message, STATE 223 to AMEMBASSY Leopoldville, transmitted 1:13 a.m., 10 August 1964; Message, AMEMBASSY Leopoldville 537 to STATE, DTG 150945Z August 1964; Message, AMEMBASSY Leopoldville 555 to STATE, DTG 161738Z August 1964; and Message, AMEMBASSY Leopoldville 572 to STATE, DTG 171550Z August 1964; all reviewed and sanitized by STATE, 30 April 1986; all in LBJ-NSF-CF: Congo, classified holdings.

41. State, "Congolese Rebellion of 1964," pt. 1, 12—13; Reed, *111 Days,* 41—42.

42. Reed. *111 Days,* 75—77; State, "Congolese Rebellion of 1964," pt. 1, 15—16.

43. Hoyt and Grinwis, "Journal," 12—14.

44. Ibid., 15—22, 23.

45. Donald V. Rattan, Major General USA Ret. (then a lieutenant colonel), "The Congo, 9 August—9 December, Bukavu to Stanleyville," unpublished and undated manuscript, Rattan Papers, San Antonio, TX, 2—27. Message, CINCSTRIKE/USCINCMEAFSA 8624 to COMUSJTFLEO, DTG 191656Z August 1964; and Message, CINCSTRIKE/USCINCMEAFSA 8627 to JCS, Personal for General Wheeler, DTG 191958Z August 1964; both in Adams Papers. Message, CINCSTRIKE/USCINCMEAFSA 8653 to COMUSJTFLEO, DTG 200257Z August 1964; and Message, STATE 390 to AMEMBASSY Leopoldville, for Ambassador from Secretary, transmitted 11:05 a.m., 20 August 1964; both in LBJ-NSF-CF: Congo, Container 82, Congo Cables, vol. 4, 8/64. Wagoner, *DRAGON ROUGE,* 36—40.

46. Hoyt and Grinwis, "Journal," 26.

47. Ibid., app. 4.

48. Message, STATE 418 to AMEMBASSY Leopoldville, transmitted 4:30 p.m., 22 August 1964, declassified by STATE, 30 April 1986, LBJ-NSF-CF: Congo, Container 82, Congo Cables, vol. 4, 78/64.

Chapter 2

1. Statement by the secretary of state, dated 29 August 1964, LBJ-NSF-CF: Congo, Container 82, Congo Cables, vol. 4, 8/64. During this same time, two rather cryptic memos crossed McGeorge Bundy's desk. On 18 August, a memo for Bundy contained the following: "Who penetrates the penetrators? or James Bond in blackface." The second memo, dated 24 August and also to Bundy, contained two notes. The first said, "Congolese security killer group in action." The second said, "Mercenary Commander Michael Hoare is ready to get on with the job." Both memos were initialed by a "P. L.," and while the author has been unable to decipher their meaning, they do indicate that covert operations were being initiated. The second memo ties the United States directly to the recruitment of Hoare for operations in the Congo. Both memos are in LBJ-NSF-CF: Congo, Container 82, Congo Cables, vol. 4, 8/64.

2. Wagoner fully examines the relation of President Johnson's election campaign to the American approach to the Congo. He draws the conclusion that Johnson and his staff, in particular McGeorge Bundy, deliberately limited American involvement in the Congo to avoid complicating the campaign. Though I agree with Wagoner's analysis in this matter, I believe that even after Johnson's election that the CWG continued to push the Harriman-Spaak strategy well beyond its useful life. In balancing my analysis against Wagoner's, I contend that there was an absence of leadership on the part of Johnson during the crisis.

3. If one uses the material in the National Security Files of the Lyndon Baines Johnson Library as a sample, this conclusion is inevitable. Aside from several intelligence reports from JTF LEO and the Defense Intelligence Agency, the vast majority of the intelligence

reporting, whether completed by the CIA or the State Department, concerned the political or strategic implications of the crisis. General Dougherty's comments to Wagoner on the intelligence available at the Brussels planning conference also support this conclusion. Russell E. Dougherty, General USAF, transcript of interview with Fred E. Wagoner, Offut Air Force Base, NE, 12 June 1976, Papers of Fred E. Wagoner, Columbia, SC.

4. U.S. Department of Defense, Director of Research and Engineering, Weapons Systems Evaluation Group, "The Congo Rescue Mission of November 1964" (Washington, DC, 8 April 1965), 4, in author's possession, hereafter cited as DOD, *Congo Rescue*.

5. Wagoner, *DRAGON ROUGE*, 55—56.

6. Message, COMUSJTFLEO 0122 to CINCSTRIKE/USCINCMEAFSA, DTG 061800Z September 1964, LBJ-NSF-CF: Congo, Container 82, Congo Cables, vol. 5, 9/64—10/64.

7. Wagoner, *DRAGON ROUGE*, 55.

8. Message, COMUSJTFLEO 0122 to CINCSTRIKE/USCINCMEAFSA, DTG 061800Z September 1964; and DOD, *Congo Rescue*, 5.

9. U.S. Joint Chiefs of Staff, Memorandum for the Secretary of Defense, Enclosure A to JCSM-788-64, Subject: Evacuation of U.S. Personnel, 12 September 1964, Wagoner Papers. The entire memorandum hereafter cited as JCSM-788-64.

10. Ibid., annex to appendix to enclosure A, 10.

11. Ibid., annex to appendix to enclosure A, 11—12.

12. Ibid., 6.

13. Ibid.

14. The JCS was an information addressee on Message, COMUSJTFLEO 0122 to CINCSTRIKE/USCINCMEAFSA, DTG 061800Z September 1964.

15. JCSM-788-64, annex to appendix to enclosure A, 10—11.

16. DOD, *Congo Rescue*, 5.

17. Wagoner, *DRAGON ROUGE*, 56. For an example of a terrain study, see U.S. Strike Command, STRAC Country Study: Congo Republic, XVIII Airborne Corps, November 1961, Combined Arms Research Library (CARL), U.S. Army Command and General Staff College, hereafter cited as "STRAC Area Analysis: Congo."

18. Colonel Vandewalle, a prolific writer who published a multivolume work on the Katangan secession, maintains a sense of humor that usually conceals his bitterness over this episode. Vandewalle's bitterness stems from his pride in his men, who risked life and limb to serve on these nonoperational logistic teams, and the lack of recognition granted them upon their return to Belgium.

   Just before he departed for the Congo, Vandewalle received a farewell message from Defense Minister Segers that ended with: "I thank you for having accepted this difficult mission charged with heavy responsibilities. I do not doubt that with your experience and qualities that you have already proved in the Congo, that you will fulfill it with success." Vandewalle, writing on the subject, commented "that this large splash of holy water was comforting." Vandewalle, *L'Ommengang*, 149—50, 160—64; and Vandewalle interviews.

19. Message, AMEMBASSY Leopoldville 222 to STATE, received 6:47 p.m., 27 July 1964, LBJ-NSF-CF: Congo, Container 81, Congo Cables, vol. 2, 7/64—8/64.

20. Vandewalle, *L'Ommengang*, 96, 97, 144.

21. In a report on the operation, CIA analysts began with, "This is included as an example of a military operation conceived and executed by the ANC and the mercenaries. The assault on Albertsville—hastily planned, poorly coordinated, and sloppily executed—may presage things to come." CIA, The Congo Situation, SC no. 10632/64, 4 September 1964; Mike Hoare, *Mercenary* (New York: Bantam Books, 1979), 13—19, 30, 35—37, 39—52; Vandewalle, *L'Ommengang*, 180—88; and Wagoner, *DRAGON ROUGE*, 44.

22. Vandewalle, *L'Ommengang*, 96, 164—247; Vandewalle interviews; Hoare, *Mercenary*, 58—59; Rattan interview.

23. State, "Congolese Rebellion of 1964," pt. 1, 12—15.

24. Ibid., 8—10.

25. Hoyt and Grinwis, "Journal," 34—38.

26. Message, STATE 600 to AMEMBASSY Leopoldville, transmitted 5:14 p.m., 4 September 1964, LBJ-NSF-CF: Congo, Container 82, Congo Cables, vol. 5, 9/64—10/64.

27. Wagoner, *DRAGON ROUGE*, 59—62; and William Attwood, *The Reds and the Blacks: A Personal Adventure* (New York: Harper and Row, 1967), 195—205.

28. State, "Congolese Rebellion of 1964," pt. 1, 21—22. Message, STATE 692 to USMISSION Geneva, transmitted 12:07 p.m., 20 September 1964; Message, AMEMBASSY Bangui 147 to STATE, received 5:28 a.m., 27 September 1964; and Message, AMEMBASSY Leopoldville 1255 to STATE, DTG 271233Z September 1964; all messages in LBJ-NSF-CF: Congo, Container 82, vol. 5, 9/64—10/64.

29. Message, AMEMBASSY Bangui 151 to STATE, received 12:13 p.m., 27 September 1964, LBJ-NSF-CF: Congo, Container 82, Congo Cables, vol. 5, 9/64—10/64.

30. Message, AMEMBASSY Khartoum 118 to STATE, received 9:51 a.m., 28 September 1964, reviewed by STATE, 30 April 1986, LBJ-NSF-CF: Congo, Container 82, Congo Cables, vol. 5, 9/64—10/64. The use of "reviewed" or "released" in references to other messages cited in these notes indicates that the agency named provided a sanitized or unclassified version of the message for use in research for this paper.

31. Republique Democratique du Congo, L'Armée Nationale Congolaise, 5th Brigade Mecanisée, Ordre D'Operation No. 1; and Republique Democratique du Congo, L'Armée Nationale Congolaise, 5th Brigade Mecanisée, Ordre D'Operation No. 2, 14 October 1964; both in Frédéric J. L. A. Vandewalle Papers, in author's possession. Vandewalle, *L'Ommengang*, 238—39, 244—47; and Hoare, *Mercenary*, 71—81.

32. Major Pierre Lemercier, "Journal de Campagne (extraits) Missions An Congo du 20 Septembre 1964 au 20 Décembre 1964," 2—36, Centre d'Instruction No. 1, S-3, Caserne Marie-Henritte, Namur, 26 February 1965, Centre de Documentation Historique des Forces Armées, Brussels. The Centre is hereafter cited as CDH.

33. Wagoner, *DRAGON ROUGE*, 67.

34. Lemercier, "Journal," 22, 25.

35. Wagoner, *DRAGON ROUGE*, 76; and Message, AMEMBASSY Leopoldville 225 to STATE, received 7:39 a.m., 28 July 1964, LBJ-NSF-CF: Congo, Container 81, Congo Cables, vol. 2, 7/64—8/64.

36. Message, STATE 922 to AMEMBASSY Leopoldville, transmitted 1:15 p.m., 11 October 1964, LBJ-NSF-CF: Congo, Container 82, Congo Cables, vol. 5, 9/64—10/64. Message, AMEMBASSY Leopoldville 1497 to STATE, received 3:57 a.m., 16 October 1964, reviewed by STATE, 30 April 1986, LBJ-NSF-CF: Congo, Container 83, Congo Cables, vol. 6, 10/64—11/64. Wagoner, *DRAGON ROUGE*, 77—80.

37. Message, CINCSTRIKE/USCINCMEAFSA 614/64 to JCS, DTG 191901Z September 1964; Message, JCS 8401 to CINCSTRIKE/USCINCMEAFSA, DTG 051947Z September 1964; Message, AMEMBASSY Leopoldville 1133 to STATE, DTG 181900Z September 1964, reviewed by STATE, 30 April 1986; Message, AMEMBASSY Leopoldville 1206 to STATE, received 7:27 a.m., 24 September 1964; Message, AMEMBASSY Leopoldville 1226 to STATE, received 3:04 p.m., 25 September 1964; Message, STATE 854 to AMEMBASSY Leopoldville, transmitted 7:21 p.m., 3 October 1964; Message, STATE 879 to AMEMBASSY Leopoldville, transmitted 8:24 p.m., 7 October 1964; and Message, AMEMBASSY Leopoldville 1468 to STATE, transmitted 12:50 p.m., 13 October 1964, all messages in LBJ-NSF-CF: Congo, Container 82, Congo Cables, vol. 5, 10/64—11/64. Vandewalle, *L'Ommengang*, 241.

38. Message, STATE 958 to AMEMBASSY Leopoldville, transmitted 2:59 p.m., 15 October 1964, LBJ-NSF-CF: Congo, Container 82, Congo Cables, vol. 5, 9/64—10/64; Draft telegram for Godley from Ball, 19 October 1964, LBJ-NSF-CF: Congo, Container 83, Memos and Miscellaneous, vol. 6, 10/64—11/64; and Wagoner, *DRAGON ROUGE*, 80.

39. Author's italics.

40. Message, JCS 9807 to CINCSTRIKE/USCINCMEAFSA, DTG 142147Z October 1964, LBJ-NSF-CF: Congo, Container 82, Memos and Miscellaneous, vol. 5, 9/64—10/64; and DOD, *Congo Rescue*, 6.

41. Message, USCINCSTRIKE 677/64 to JCS, DTG 150610Z October 1964, LBJ-NSF-CF: Congo, Container 82, Memos and Miscellaneous, vol. 5, 9/64—10/64; and DOD, *Congo Rescue*, 7.

42. DOD, *Congo Rescue*, 6—8; and Message, USCINCSTRIKE 677/64 to JCS, DTG 150610Z October 1964.

43. A T-29 reconnaissance aircraft had deployed to the Congo from USAFE in late September. Message (C), USAFE 40709 to USAIRA Leopoldville, DTG 220820Z September (U), information on T-29 declassified by DIA on 5 March 1986, LBJ-NSF-CF: Congo, Classified holdings; and Message, USCINCSTRIKE 678/64 to JCS, DTG 150720Z October 1964, LBJ-NSF-CF: Congo, Container 82, Memos and Miscellaneous, vol. 5, 9/64—10/64.

44. DOD, *Congo Rescue*, 9; and Memorandum to Mac from RWK, Congo Recon, 14 October 1964, LBJ-NSF-CF: Congo, Container 82, Memos and Miscellaneous, vol. 5, 9/64—10/64.

45. DOD, *Congo Rescue*, 10—11.

46. Ibid., 11.

47. Vandewalle, *L'Ommengang*, 255—56.

48. CIA Cable, TDCSDB-315/01019-64, 14 October 1964.

49. Message, JANAF Attaches Leopoldville CX-96 to DIA, DTG 171300Z October 1964, released by DOD on 25 May 1976, LBJ-NSF-CF: Congo, Container 83, Memos and Miscellaneous, vol. 6, 10/64—11/64.

50. Vandewalle, *L'Ommengang*, 256.

51. DOD, *Congo Rescue*, 11—12.

52. Extract of Message, CINCSTRIKE 735/64 to JCS, DTG 190725Z October 1964, declassified by OJCS, 1975, Erdmann Papers.

53. Ibid.

54. Wagoner, *DRAGON ROUGE*, 68—69; and Message, AMEMBASSY Leopoldville 1590 to STATE, received 5:46 p.m., 22 October 1964, LBJ-NSF-CF: Congo, Container 83, Congo Cables, vol. 6, 10/64—11/64.

55. Wagoner, *DRAGON ROUGE*, 84—86; Message, AMEMBASSY Leopoldville 1650 to STATE, DTG 271847Z October 1964, released by STATE, 23 December 1977, LBJ-NSF-CF: Congo, Container 83, Congo Cables, vol. 6, 10/64—11/64; and Message, CINCSTRIKE 841/64 to JCS, DTG 300045Z October 1964, LBJ-NSF-CF: Congo, Container 83, Memos and Miscellaneous, vol. 6, 10/64—11/64.

56. State, "Congolese Rebellion of 1964," pt. 1, 23; Message, AMEMBASSY Bujumbura 408 to STATE, received noon, 25 October 1964, reviewed by STATE, 30 April 1986, LBJ-NSF-CF: Congo, Container 83, Memos and Miscellaneous, vol. 6, 10/64—11/64; and Wagoner, *DRAGON ROUGE*, 82—83.

57. Message, COMUSJTFLEO 0412 to CINCSTRIKE/USCINCMEAFSA, DTG 011050Z November 1964, LBJ-NSF-CF: Congo, Container 83, Memos and Miscellaneous, vol. 6, 10/64—11/64; Vandewalle, *L'Ommengang*, 305—6; and Message, AMEMBASSY Bujumbura 477 to STATE, transmitted 6 p.m., 5 November 1964, LBJ-NSF-CF: Congo, Container 83, Congo Cables, vol. 6, 10/64—11/64.

58. Wagoner, *DRAGON ROUGE*, 87, 127; Memorandum to MAC from Sam Belk, 29 October attached to Message, AMEMBASSY Leopoldville 1667 to STATE, DTG 291708Z October 1964, LBJ-NSF-CF: Congo, Container 83, Congo Cables, vol. 6, 10/64—11/64; and U.S. Department of State, Director of Intelligence and Research, Research Memorandum, The Rebels and the Hostages: An Assessment, 6 November 1964, LBJ-NSF-CF: Congo, Container 83, Memos and Miscellaneous, vol. 6, 10/64—11/64.

59. Rattan, "Bukavu to Stanleyville," 49—54; and Vandewalle, *L'Ommengang*, 291.

60. Message, STATE 1132 to AMEMBASSY Leopoldville, transmitted 5:40 p.m., 3 November 1964, reviewed by STATE, 23 December 1977; Message, AMEMBASSY 1801 to STATE, DTG 071725Z November 1964, released by STATE, 23 December 1977; and Message, AMCONSULATE Bukavu 410 to AMEMBASSY Leopoldville, received at STATE, 1:24 p.m., 8 November, reviewed by STATE, 30 April 1986; all in LBJ-NSF-CF: Congo, Container 83, Congo Cables, vol. 6, 10/64—11/64.

61. Message, AMEMBASSY Leopoldville 1801 to STATE, DTG 071725Z November 1964.

62. Message, AMEMBASSY Brussels 945 to STATE, received 4:30 p.m., 14 November 1964, LBJ-NSF-CF: Congo, Container 83, Congo Cables, vol. 6, 10/64—11/64; and DOD, *Congo Rescue*, 15—16.

63. Kanza, one of the Congo's university graduates upon independence, was a political opportunist who had associated himself with the CNL. On 7 November, he met the Belgian Chargé in Dar es Salaam, Tanzania, to push for a negotiated settlement. His stance on the hostages convinced Spaak that Congolese offers to negotiate were nothing more than stall tactics in the hope of receiving aid from Communist China. DOD, *Congo Rescue*, 62.

64. DOD, *Congo Rescue*, 16; and Vandewalle, *L'Ommengang*, 306—7.

65. Adams and Godley both pushed for increased military pressure on the rebels as the best way to save the hostages. Adams, however, argued against the delay in mounting a combined operation. When he heard of Bouzin's proposal, he argued against it and asked that his command be immediately included in any combined planning. Ambassador Dumont, in Bujumbura, also pushed for action. He volunteered to go to Stanleyville and deliver an ultimatum in person to the rebels.

    On 3 November, the CIA pointed out that the rebel leadership was beginning to panic. Reports out of Boende, Kibomba, and later, Kindu supported this assessment. Unfortunately, the State Department and the CWG chose to place undue emphasis on the rebels' proclamation that the hostages were prisoners of war. Wagoner, *DRAGON ROUGE*, 87, 122. Message, AMEMBASSY Leopoldville 1756 to STATE, DTG 041757Z November 1964; Memorandum to MAC from Sam Belk, 29 October 1964, attached to Message, AMEMBASSY Leopoldville 1667 to STATE, DTG 291708Z October 1964; Message, AMEMBASSY Bujumbura 442 to STATE, received 4:52 p.m., 4 November 1964; and Message, STATE 291 to AMEMBASSY Bujumbura, transmitted 8:50 p.m., 6 November 1964; all in LBJ-NSF-CF: Congo, Container 83, Congo Cables, vol. 6, 10/64—11/64. U.S. Department of State, Director of Intelligence and Research, Research Memorandum RAF-51, The Rebels and the Hostage: An Assessment, 6 November 1964; Message, CINCSTRIKE/USCINCMEAFSA 882/64 to JCS, DTG 070006Z November 1964; Message, USCINCSTRIKE ADV 883/64 to JCS, DTG 070439Z November 1964; and Message, USSTRICOM 858/64 to JCS, DTG 021120Z November 1964; all in LBJ-NSF-CF: Congo, Container 83, Memos and Miscellaneous, vol. 6, 10/64—11/64. Message USCINCSTRIKE 1930 to JCS, DTG 050505Z November 1964, Adams Papers.

66. Message, CJCS 001745 to USCINCEUR, DTG 110051Z November 1964, LBJ-NSF-CF: Congo, Container 83, Memos and Miscellaneous, vol. 6, 10/64—11/64.

Chapter 3

1. Russell E. Dougherty, General USAF Ret., transcript of interview with Fred E. Wagoner, 16 March 1978, Wagoner Papers, in author's possession; James L. Gray, Lieutenant

Colonel USAF, interview with *Reader's Digest*, 1—3, in the *Reed Collection*, oral histories on Dragon Rouge in the collection compiled by David Reed (microfilm ed., Library, Hoover Institution on War, Revolution, and Peace, Stanford, CA); Bobby F. Brashears, Brigadier General USA, interview with the author, Fort Leavenworth, KS, 12 July 1985; and Message, JCS 001745 to USCINCEUR, DTG 110051Z November 1964.

2. DOD, *Congo Rescue*, 16; Wagoner, *DRAGON ROUGE*, 135; and Message, USSTRICOM 858/64 to JCS, DTG 021120Z November 1964, LBJ-NSF-CF: Congo, Container 83, Memos and Miscellaneous, vol. 6, 10/64—11/64.

3. Wagoner, *DRAGON ROUGE*, 131—32; and DOD, *Congo Rescue*, 17.

4. "Rapport JS-3," [Report on Dragon Rouge], CDH; Agence Militaire de Presse, Brussels, "Note: Biographique Du Colonel Laurent, Charles Felix Joseph," *Nouvelles Des Forces Armées*, Erdmann Papers; and Dougherty interview, 12 June 1976.

5. After the Dragon operations, Colonel Laurent became the Belgian military attaché in Paris, where he met Ambassador Harriman at a diplomatic function. Harriman complimented Laurent on the Paracommandos' ability to accomplish their mission with a much smaller force than the United States had considered necessary. Laurent interview.

6. James M. Erdmann, "Dragon Rouge: The United States-Belgian Decision to Intervene in the Congo," 24—26 November 1964, 7, unpublished manuscript, Erdmann Papers.

7. Message, AMEMBASSY Brussels 902 to STATE, received 10:21 a.m., 12 November 1964; Message, AMEMBASSY Leopoldville 1855 to STATE, received 9:10 a.m., 12 November 1964; Message, AMEMBASSY Brussels 916 to STATE, received 7:24 a.m., 13 November 1964; and Message, STATE 3184 to AMEMBASSY London, transmitted 4:34 p.m., 13 November 1964; all in LBJ-NSF-CF: Congo, Container 83, Congo Cables, vol. 6, 10/64—11/64. Message, JCS 001793 to USCINCEUR, DTG 121844Z November 1964, LBJ-NSF-CF: Congo, Container 83, Memos and Miscellaneous, vol. 6, 10/64—11/64.

8. James Erdmann, "Laurent Briefing Notes" (Heidelberg, Germany, 15 December 1975), unpublished notes, Erdmann Papers. Message, AMEMBASSY Brussels 912 to STATE, received 1:30 p.m., 12 November 1964; and Message, STATE 972 to AMEMBASSY Brussels, transmitted 8:41 p.m., 12 November 1964; both in LBJ-NSF-CF: Congo, Container 83, Congo Cables, vol. 6, 10/64—11/64. DOD, *Congo Rescue*, 17.

9. Message, AMEMBASSY Brussels 912 to STATE, received 1:30 p.m., 12 November 1964; Message, STATE 972 to AMEMBASSY Brussels, transmitted 8:41 p.m., 12 November 1964; and DOD, *Congo Rescue*, 19.

10. DOD, *Congo Rescue*, 19, 39; and Message, AMEMBASSY Brussels 912 to STATE, received 1:30 p.m., 12 November 1964. Message, AMEMBASSY Brussels 937 to STATE, received 7:01 p.m., 13 November 1964, LBJ-NSF-CF: Congo, Container 83, Congo Cables, vol. 6, 10/64—11/64.

11. Dougherty interview, 12 June 1976. Message, AMEMBASSY Brussels 938 to STATE, received 6:28 p.m., 13 November 1964; and Memorandum to the President, Subject: Congo Situation from McG. B. [McGeorge Bundy], 16 November 1964; both in LBJ-NSF-CF: Congo, Container 83, Memos and Miscellaneous, vol. 7, 11/64. Memorandum to Mac, Congo Recon., 14 October 1964.

12. Brashears interview; Laurent and Ledant interview; and James E. Poore, Colonel USAF Ret., interview with author, Charleston, SC, 10 April 1986.

13. Forces Armée Belge, "STAN-PAULIS, 24—27 Novembre 64: Intervention Humanitaire Belge-American Au Congo," June 1965, 5, Wagoner Papers, hereafter cited as "STAN-PAULIS."

14. Dougherty interviews, 12 June 1976 and 16 March 1978.

15. "STAN-PAULIS," 39—42; and Regiment Para Commando Centre Medical, "Objet: Mission DRAGON ROUGE et NOIR—Service de Santé," 24 December 1964, CDH.

16. Dougherty interviews, 12 June 1976 and 16 March 1978. "STAN-PAULIS," 39—42; and Commandement Maritime Ostende, Escadrille des Services, Centre des transmissions, A

L'Officier N 5/COMAR OST (2ex), Objet: Liaison Evere-Baka, "Evenements Congo Nov. 64," 14 January 1965, CDH.

17. James B. Avery, Colonel USAF, interview *Reader's Digest, Reed Collection*, 1—24; "STAN-PAULIS," 39—42; and Laurent and Ledant interview.

18. DOD, *Congo Rescue*, 20—21, 24—28.

19. Erdmann, "Dragon Rouge," 6.

20. Extract of Message, USCINCEUR ECJA 19978, 14 November 1964, USCINCEUR OPERATIONS PLAN 319/64, USEUCOM ASSAULT/EVACUATION SUPPORT—CONGO DRAGON ROUGE, "Concept of Operations," declassified by OJCS, 1975, Erdmann Papers, hereafter cited as OPLAN 319/64.

21. DOD, *Congo Rescue*, 19, 24.

22. Ibid., 22, 25—26.

23. Ibid., 24.

24. "STAN-PAULIS," 13.

25. OPLAN 319/64.

26. Ibid.

27. DOD, *Congo Rescue*, 24—25.

28. Message, STATE 972 to AMEMBASSY Brussels, transmitted 8:41 p.m., 12 November 1964; DOD, *Congo Rescue*, 21; Message, AMEMBASSY Brussels 960 to STATE, received 8:32 a.m., 17 November 1964, released by STATE, 4 March 1986, LBJ-NSF-CF: Congo, Container 83, Congo Cables, vol. 7, 11/64; and Memorandum for General Wheeler, Joint Chiefs of Staff, from W. Averell Harriman, 16 November 1964, Wagoner Papers.

29. Message, USCINCEUR ECJC-L 19981 to AMEMBASSY Brussels, DTG 151835Z November 1964, LBJ-NSF-CF: Congo, Container 83, Memos and Miscellaneous, vol. 6, 10/64—11/64. Message, STATE 1017 to AMEMBASSY Brussels, transmitted 8:38 p.m., 16 November 1964; and Message, AMEMBASSY Brussels to USCINCEUR, received STATE (953), 12:37 p.m., 16 November 1964; both in LBJ-NSF-CF: Congo, Container 83, Congo Cables, vol. 7, 11/64.

30. Message, CINCSTRIKE/USCINCMEAFSA 911/64 to JCS, DTG 160206Z November 1964, LBJ-NSF-CF: Congo, Container 83, Memos and Miscellaneous, vol. 7, 11/64.

31. Ibid.; and DOD, *Congo Rescue*, 27.

32. Message, CINCSTRIKE/USCINCMEAFSA 911/64 to JCS, DTG 160206Z November 1964.

33. Ibid.

34. Ibid.

35. Message, USCINCEUR ECJC-A00039 to JCS, DTG 161914Z November 1964; and Message, CINCSTRIKE/USCINCMEAFSA 967/64 to COMUSJTFLEO, DTG 172245Z November 1964; both in LBJ-NSF-CF: Congo, Container 83, Memos and Miscellaneous, vol. 7, 11/64. Message, CINCSTRIKE/USCINCMEAFSA 970/64 to JCS, DTG 180036Z November 1964; Message, CINCSTRIKE/USCINCMEAFSA 12359 to COMUSJTFLEO, DTG 172400Z November 1964; and Message, CINCSTRIKE/USCINCMEAFSA 964/64 to USCINCEUR, DTG 172200Z November 1964; all in State HF, POL 23-9 THE CONGO. DOD, *Congo Rescue*, 146.

36. Agence Militaire de Presse, "Notice D'Information Sur Les Para-Commandos," *Nouvelles Des Forces Armées*, Brussels, Erdmann Papers.

37. Ibid.

38. "STAN-PAULIS," 5; and Laurent and Ledant interview.

39. Laurent interview.

40. Reed, *111 Days*, 189; and Laurent interview.
41. Laurent interview.
42. Ibid.
43. "STAN-PAULIS," annex no. 21.
44. Laurent and Ledant interview.
45. "STAN-PAULIS," 7.
46. Reed, *111 Days*, 189.
47. Mine, Rousseaux, and Raes interview.
48. Regiment Para Commando, Etat Major Caserne Terre-Neuve, Namur, "Operation Dragon Rouge (Stanleyville)," 1, CDH, hereafter cited as "Paracommando Regt. Rept: Dragon Rouge."
49. U.S. Air Force, 839th Air Division, "History of the 464th Troop Carrier Wing (Medium) and Pope Air Base, North Carolina, 1 July—31 December 1964," (Pope Air Force Base, NC, 1965), 27.
50. Burgess Gradwell, Colonel USAF, interview with *Reader's Digest*, *Reed Collection*, 8—25.
51. Ibid., 25—26.
52. John Robinson, Major USAF, Interview with *Reader's Digest*, 4—5; and George Banning, Lieutenant Colonel USAF, interview with *Reader's Digest*, 5—7; both in *Reed Collection*.
53. James M. Erdmann, Lieutenant Colonel USAF, "Journal—DRAGON ROUGE," Erdmann Papers.
54. Erdmann, "Dragon Rouge," 20.
55. Message, USCINCEUR 00040 to JCS, DTG 162055Z November 1964; Message, JCS 001945 to USCINCEUR, DTG 171545Z November 1964; and Message, JCS 001955 to USCINCEUR, DTG 171749Z November 1964; all in LBJ-NSF-CF: Congo, Container 83, Memos and Miscellaneous, vol. 7, 11/64. Message, STATE 1006 to AMEMBASSY Brussels, transmitted 1:58 p.m., 16 November 1964, released by STATE, 20 December 1985; and Message, STATE 1014 to AMEMBASSY Brussels, transmitted 7:35 p.m., 16 November 1964, released by STATE, 12 December 1985; both in State HF, POL 23-9 THE CONGO. Message, AMEMBASSY Brussels 957 to STATE, received 5:27 a.m., 17 November 1969; and Message, AMEMBASSY Brussels 959 to STATE, received 9:34 a.m., 17 November 1964; both released by STATE, 30 April 1986, and both in LBJ-NSF-CF: Congo, Container 83, Congo Cables, vol. 7, 11/64.
56. DOD, *Congo Rescue*, 45—46.
57. Message, AMEMBASSY Leopoldville 1961 to STATE, DTG 181715Z November 1964; Message, AMEMBASSY Leopoldville 1962 to STATE, DTG 181720Z November 1964; and Message, AMEMBASSY London 2409 to STATE, DTG 181208Z November 1964; all in State HF, POL 23-9 THE CONGO. Message, USCINCEUR 00150 to JCS, DTG 181559Z November 1964, LBJ-NSF-CF: Congo, Container 83, Memos and Miscellaneous, vol. 7, 11/64.

Chapter 4

1. Message, AMEMBASSY 945 Brussels to STATE, received 4:30 p.m., 14 November 1964.
2. Ibid.; DOD, *Congo Rescue*, 36—37, 40, 47—48. Message, AMEMBASSY Leopoldville 1846 to STATE, received 11:38 p.m., 11 November 1964; Message, STATE 1000 to AMEMBASSY Brussels, transmitted 3:38 p.m., 15 November 1964; and Message, AMEMBASSY Leopoldville 1895 to STATE, received 8:42 p.m., 14 November 1964; all in LBJ-NSF-CF: Congo, Container 83, Congo Cables, vol. 6, 10/64—11/64. Message, STATE 1006 to AMEMBASSY Brussels, transmitted 1:58 p.m., 16 November 1964, released by STATE, 20 December 1985; and Message, AMEMBASSY Leopoldville 1078 to AMEMBASSY Brussels, received

STATE, 11:56 p.m., 15 November 1964; both in State HF, POL 23-9 THE CONGO. Message, JCS 001944 to CINCSTRIKE/USCINCMEAFSA and USCINCEUR, DTG 171536Z November 1964, LBJ-NSF-CF: Congo, Container 83, Memos and Miscellaneous, vol. 7, 11/64.

3. Remarkably, the CWG focused on Gbenye's classification of the hostages as prisoners of war as a sign of good faith. Since the September mission of the Red Cross had left Stanleyville, the CWG, the UN, and the OAU had been seeking further entrance into the rebel stronghold, but without success. Gbenye played this card well by using Thomas Kanza as spokesman for the rebellion. As spokesman for the rebellion, Kanza had succeeded in convincing Kenyatta that the rebels were sincere in their desire to negotiate an end to the rebellion. Gbenye's announcement that Dr. Carlson had been tried and condemned as a spy acted as a catalyst in convincing the CWG that further negotiations were necessary.

The irony of the situation was that no one in the CWG actually believed that the rebel leaders were secure enough to negotiate a release of the hostages without invoking a general cease-fire. Spaak had made the Belgian position clear, as had Kasavubu and Tshombe for the Congolese. No one believed that rebel offers to negotiate were more than simple stall tactics. Nor did the Belgians or the Congolese support reconciliation as an answer to the hostage situation; with Vandewalle poised for the final drive on Stanleyville, both Spaak and Tshombe knew that the end of the rebel regime was near. The only doubt in their minds dealt with the hostages' safety, particularly in regard to the notoriously unstable *jeunesse*. Even though the CWG had similar concerns, it proceeded with the negotiations.

On 16 November, the CWG asked Kasavubu to accept a new diplomatic initiative to secure a reconciliation in the Congo. Though Kasavubu responded negatively, the CWG appealed to Kenyatta for help in sparing Carlson's life. As Kenyatta had stated earlier, he assumed that such an appeal indicated a willingness to negotiate a cease-fire. Gbenye sweetened the possibilities for negotiation on 19 November by offering a prisoner exchange. This offer sparked new hope within the CWG and led to its proposal for a new round of negotiations.

By this time, the CWG had moved well beyond simple maneuvers to save Carlson by delaying his execution. In the CWG's proposal to Brussels, it suggested that reconciliation was possible if both the United States and Belgium were willing to impose it on Leopoldville. The Belgians, in particular Spaak and Davignon, were aghast. Spaak dismissed the maneuver as a mistake and refused to support it. Spaak warned that it would disrupt relations with Leopoldville. When Washington pressed on with the idea, Spaak announced the presence of the Dragon force at Ascension on 20 November and suggested it be moved to Kamina.

Spaak's announcement and the expectedly harsh Leopoldville reaction to the negotiations narrowed the CWG's intentions. Charged with handling the talks in Nairobi, Attwood went into them with a charter to negotiate a hostage release or to buy time for Vandewalle or Dragon Rouge. His charter forbade the discussion of any form of cease-fire. The CWG's attempt to expand the hostage negotiations into a strategic settlement had failed. Message, AMEMBASSY Bujumbura 447 to STATE, received 6:00 p.m., 5 November 1964, LBJ-NSF-CF: Congo, Container 83, Congo Cables, vol. 6, 10/64—11/64; and State, "Congolese Rebellion of 1964," pt. 1, 24. U.S. Department of State, Director Intelligence and Research, Research Memorandum RAF-57, Subject: Dragon Rouge: African Reactions and Other Estimates, 18 November 1964; William Brubeck, Memorandum for Mr. Bundy, 19 November 1964, with two papers: "The Congo—Problems for Decision," undated, and "The Price of Dragon Rouge," 19 November 1964; and Memorandum, Rationale for a New Political Initiative in the Congo; all in LBJ-NSF-CF: Congo, Container 83, Memos and Miscellaneous, vol. 7, 11/64. Wagoner, *DRAGON ROUGE*, 128—29, 156. Message, AMEMBASSY Bujumbura 483 to STATE, received 11:35 a.m., 18 November 1964, released by STATE, 30 April 1986; Message, AMEMBASSY Brussels 1002 to STATE, DTG 201110Z November 1964, released by STATE, 30 April 1986; Message, AMEMBASSY

Brussels 1011 to STATE, DTG 201702Z November 1964, released by STATE, 30 April 1986; Message, AMEMBASSY Leopoldville 2004 to STATE, DTG 201520Z November 1964; and Message, AMEMBASSY Bujumbura 494 to STATE, received 6 p.m., 20 November 1964; all in LBJ-NSF-CF: Congo, Container 83, Congo Cables, vol. 7, 11/64. DOD, *Congo Rescue*, 59, 62—63, 65, 126, 130. Message, STATE 1077 to AMEMBASSY Brussels, transmitted 8:15 p.m., 19 November 1964; Message, AMEMBASSY, Leopoldville 2008 to STATE, DTG 201804Z November 1964; Message, AMEMBASSY, Leopoldville 2007 to STATE, DTG 201705Z November 1964; Message, STATE 1922 to AMEMBASSY Nairobi, transmitted 3:32 p.m., 20 November 1964; and Message, AMEMBASSY Leopoldville 2021 to STATE, DTG 210055Z November 1964; all in State HF, POL 23-9 THE CONGO. Message, USARMA Leopoldville to DIA, DTG 142325Z November 1964, LBJ-NSF-CF: Congo, Container 83, Memos and Miscellaneous, vol. 6, 10/64—11/64.

4. Though JCSM-788-64 correctly stated that any operation to rescue all non-Congolese would constitute an intervention, the CWG could not bring itself to accept the truth of that statement. Much of this reluctance was attributable to the CWG's equally strong aversion to using the Dragon force. Clearly, the CWG hoped that Vandewalle would render Dragon Rouge unnecessary; at the same time, Vandewalle's pressure on the city made the execution of Dragon Rouge more likely. At times, the CWG grasped this relationship: at different times, it requested that Vandewalle slow or speed up his movement to allow for coordinated pressure on the city.

Even after the Dragon force began to move, the CWG could not come to terms with the rescue mission. After deciding that Dragon Rouge was humanitarian, the CWG struggled with ramifications of that term. Its struggle dealt with the question of the Congolese civilians left behind if Dragon Rouge removed all non-Congolese and then left before Vandewalle arrived. Africanists pointed out that such a lily white operation would hardly be humanitarian, and Mennen Williams suggested airlifting in ANC troops. Though opposed to Williams' suggestion, the CWG finally decided that Dragon Rouge could evacuate "up to 200 Congolese nationals." Tshombe canceled out this ruling when he forbade the evacuation of Congolese. Perhaps in order to clarify the objectives of Dragon Rouge, analysts attempted to define success or failure. That attempt resulted in a definition that ultimately proved inconclusive. These bouts of soul-searching did produce one positive result. In the discussions over Dragon Rouge, the need for follow-on operations soon surfaced. Once this need became apparent, then the need to coordinate Dragon Rouge with Vandewalle became paramount.

The link with Vandewalle, initiated by a CWG request to speed up the ground column in order to support Dragon Rouge, grew rapidly. Yet though the CWG established the Big Punch command and control system to facilitate a joint assault, it forbade the establishment of a communications link with Vandewalle's column. Once Vandewalle began to move, he was out of contact with Leopoldville or Kamina. This deficiency was symptomatic of the overall situation: the CWG wanted a humanitarian rescue, but was unwilling to extend it beyond Stanleyville; the CWG wanted to support Tshombe, but without political costs; the CWG wanted Laurent to rescue all non-Congolese, but restricted the size of his force; the CWG wanted an in-and-out rescue, but did not want to leave the city unoccupied; and in this last instance, the CWG wanted a joint assault, but did not allow adequate communications support for it. DOD, *Congo Rescue*, 38, 68—73. Memorandum to the President, Subject: The Congo Situation, initialed by McG. B., 16 November 1964; U.S. Department of State, Director of Intelligence and Research, Research Memorandum RAF-57, Subject: Dragon Rouge: African Reactions and Other Estimates, 18 November 1964; and William Brubeck, Memorandum for Mr. Bundy, 19 November 1964, with two papers: "The Congo—Problems for Decision," undated, and "The Price of Dragon Rouge," 19 November 1964; all in LBJ-NSF-CF: Congo, Container 83, Memos and Miscellaneous, vol. 7, 11/64. Message, AMEMBASSY Leopoldville 1970 to STATE, DTG 190015Z November 1964; Message, STATE 1334 to AMEMBASSY Leopoldville, transmitted 10:35 p.m., 20 November 1964; Message, STATE 1089 to AMEMBASSY Leopoldville, transmitted 2:17 p.m., 20 November 1964; and Message, STATE 1063 to AMEMBASSY Brussels, transmitted 1:41 a.m., 19 November 1964; all in State HF, POL 23-9 THE CONGO. Message,

STATE 988 to AMEMBASSY Brussels, transmitted 8:40 p.m., 13 November 1964, released by STATE, 30 April 1986, LBJ-NSF-CF: Congo, Container 83, Congo Cables, vol. 6, 10/64—11/64. Message, AMEMBASSY Leopoldville 2003 to STATE, DTG 201309Z November 1964; Message, STATE 1336 to AMEMBASSY Leopoldville, transmitted 10:37 p.m., 20 November 1964; and Message, STATE 1337 to AMEMBASSY Leopoldville, transmitted 10:43 p.m., 20 November 1964; all in LBJ-NSF-CF: Congo, Container 83, Congo Cables, vol. 7, 11/64. Wagoner, *DRAGON ROUGE*, 146—48, 168.

5. Aside from the abortive CWG attempt to expand the objective of negotiations to a strategic settlement, both the United States and Belgium engaged in efforts to justify the intervention. Unfortunately, the joint effort was not always a cooperative effort, as the CWG insisted on using them to keep Belgium out front.

    The first initiative dealt with obtaining Congolese permission for the operation. Spaak began the process when he tasked his ambassador to obtain written permission from the Congolese for the operation. As soon as the CWG learned of the proposal, it stepped in and expanded the demarche. Instructing Godley to "not rpt [repeat] not give consent to De Kerchove for approach by him to Tshombe," the CWG sought Belgian concurrence in a five-point program: obtain from Kasavubu undated signed letters to the Belgian and American presidents requesting the rescue operation; obtain Kasavubu's agreement to a public statement confirming the text of the two letters; obtain Kasavubu's agreement to pre-position contingency instructions to the Congolese UN delegation concerning the requested letters (the letters were to be held by the U.S. delegation); obtain Kasavubu's agreement to provide an ANC liaison officer to the Dragon force; and warn Kasavubu about the need for security to prevent leaks.

    The Belgians responded that the scenario put forth in the CWG proposal was too complex and, as yet, unnecessary. Still the CWG insisted, and the Belgians reluctantly agreed. Once the CWG had secured Belgian concurrence, it manipulated the original demarche and changed the letter to the American president into a letter to the American ambassador. The CWG explained this change to Ambassador MacArthur in an aside: it saw it as a "desirable implication of U.S. subsidiary role in having addressee letter to Belgians at higher level than U.S. addressee."

    When Ambassador Godley presented the proposal to the Congolese, the CWG's handiwork backfired. De Kerchove, the Belgian ambassador, went along but did not ask for a letter to the Belgian government. Though the CWG wanted letters signed by Kasavubu, rather than Tshombe—since Kasavubu was politically preferable—Tshombe presented the letter to Godley, a letter that authorized rather than requested the rescue operation. Consequently, the demarche had the reverse effect intended by the CWG. The letter made it appear that the United States had forced the issue and that the Congo and Belgium had merely agreed to the operation.

    This manipulation was occurring at the same time that the CWG was pursuing negotiations with the rebels. Combined with that effort, the CWG's pursuit of political objectives at Belgian and Congolese expense led to Spaak's announcement of the DRAGON force's presence at Ascension Island. The announcement by Spaak, coupled with Washington's announcements on the Nairobi talks, angered the Congolese. Tshombe was outraged and felt he was being openly maneuvered by the United States and Belgium. The timing could not have been worse; just as Godley was attempting to assuage Tshombe, he learned that the Dragon force was en route to Kamina without formal Congolese approval. Fortunately, Tshombe had already suggested the move, and Godley was able to agree to it without saying it was already in the process of fulfillment.

    Further complicating the situation, the CWG decided that another diplomatic initiative was needed. Following Spaak's announcement on Ascension, the UN General Assembly reacted hastily. U Thant, the secretary general, made an announcement that suggested Security Council involvement—a suggestion he soon dismissed. But the CWG had already reacted by proposing that the United States and Belgium call for a Security Council meeting to endorse Dragon Rouge. The CWG hoped that such a maneuver would block any Soviet attempt to secure a Congolese cease-fire; no one in the CWG seemed to realize that the Soviets stood more to gain by allowing Dragon Rouge to occur—and then capitalizing on its propaganda value—than by blocking it in the Security Council. In any case, the Belgians and Ambassador Godley opposed the demarche, and their opposition, along with U Thant's dismissal of the need for Security Council involvement, ended this latest spate of CWG creativity.

Unfortunately, the CWG's concentration on the political costs of Dragon Rouge—and diplomatic maneuvers to avert those costs—had drastic consequences for the hostages. The CWG's absorption in political affairs blinded it to the military aspects of Dragon Rouge. For instance, no one in the CWG studied the military requirements for securing the city until it was too late. DOD, *Congo Rescue*, 55—57, 66—69, 124, 127. Message, STATE 1275 to AMEMBASSY Leopoldville, transmitted 6:05 p.m., 17 November 1964; Message, STATE 1044 to AMEMBASSY Brussels, transmitted 12:48 a.m., 18 November 1964; Message, STATE 1045 to AMEMBASSY Brussels, transmitted 1:05 a.m., 18 November 1964; Message, STATE 1062 to AMEMBASSY Brussels, transmitted 1:20 a.m., 19 November 1964; Message, STATE 1056 to AMEMBASSY Brussels, transmitted 7:31 a.m., 18 November 1964; Message, AMEMBASSY Leopoldville 1974 to STATE, received 5:39 a.m., 19 November 1964; Message, AMEMBASSY Leopoldville 2022 to STATE, DTG 210110Z November 1964; Message, AMEMBASSY Leopoldville 2023 to STATE, DTG 210130Z November 1964; Message, AMEMBASSY Leopoldville 2024 to STATE, DTG 211025Z November 1964; Message, AMEMBASSY Leopoldville 2026 to STATE, DTG 211124Z November 1964; Message, AMEMBASSY Leopoldville 2036 to STATE, DTG 211045Z November 1964; Message, STATE 1313 to AMEMBASSY Leopoldville, transmitted 5:55 p.m., 19 November 1964; Message, AMEMBASSY Brussels 1012 to STATE, DTG 201740Z November 1964; Message, STATE 1077 to AMEMBASSY Brussels, transmitted 8:15 p.m., 19 November 1964; Message, STATE 1063 to AMEMBASSY Brussels, transmitted 1:41 a.m., 19 November 1964; Message, STATE 1099 to AMEMBASSY Brussels, transmitted 7:23 p.m., 20 November 1964; and Message, AMEMBASSY Leopoldville 2027 to STATE, DTG 211300Z November 1964; all in State HF, POL 23-9 THE CONGO. Wagoner, *DRAGON ROUGE*, 146—48, 155.

6. The question of other hostages was always a Belgian issue. Their safety generated Belgian reluctance to act on Stanleyville until the Simbas arrested all Belgians on 28 October. Once planning began for Dragon Rouge, the idea of follow-on operations came from Vandewalle. When he learned of the Stanleyville rescue, Vandewalle suggested on 14 November that the paras might be better employed on Bunia, Watsa, and Paulis. His suggestion, passed by Godley to the CWG, was raised by Washington with Brussels during the debate over moving the Dragon force to Ascension Island. Though accepted by Spaak as the basis for the second Brussels planning conference, the CWG was distressed over the prospect for further operations. Their concerns, as stated in "The Price of Dragon Rouge," were stated thusly: "Possibly the greatest risk [is] that following a jump on Stanleyville, it may seem prudent to extend DRAGON ROUGE to towns like Paulis, Watsa, and Bunia—thus considerably lengthening the operation."

With such deep-felt concerns before the execution of the first rescue, the American support of Spaak's decision to withdraw after the Paulis rescue was preordained. Message, AMEMBASSY Brussels 177 to STATE, DTG 061638Z August 1964; and Message, STATE 1000 to AMEMBASSY Brussels, transmitted 3:38 p.m., 15 November 1964. Message, AMEMBASSY Leopoldville 1895 to STATE, received 8:42 p.m., 14 November 1964, LBJ-NSF-CF: Congo, Container 83, Congo Cables, vol. 6, 10/64—11/64; DOD, *Congo Rescue*, 47—48; and "The Price of Dragon Rouge," 19 November 1964. For a discussion of withdrawal, see chapter 6.

7. A debate between the CWG and Ambassador Godley over the Big Punch procedure reflected the difference between the Belgian and the American approaches to the situation. Spaak granted Vandewalle, indirectly through De Kerchove, the power to initiate the process. In contrast, the CWG refused Godley's request for similar authority, as it wished to retain control of the operation. Since the process had to be passed over American communications channels, the CWG had direct control over the Belgian half of the process. When Spaak pushed to move the force to Kamina on 21 November, the Belgian

Defense Ministry passed a message to the American embassy for Laurent, placing his unit on alert. Before the Belgian message went to Ascension, the American embassy cabled Washington for permission to transmit it. Only after receiving Washington's concurrence did the embassy pass the alert.

The debate over the Big Punch procedure ultimately led to the deployment to Kamina. After reviewing the process, CINCEUR cabled the JCS to point out its ramifications. If Dragon Rouge were to be launched from Ascension Island, the JCS order had to arrive "no later than 0230Z on D minus 1" to meet the agreed-on drop time of 0400Z. Matching this time delay with the anticipated delay inherent in the Big Punch procedure, CINCEUR pointed out that "in broad terms, a drop can be made two days after [a] national decision is reached." Decision makers were faced with this problem and also were confronted with an increasing threat to the hostages. Word had come that the rebels might be moving the hostages, and that Vandewalle's advance had been halted due to ferry problems at Aluta. For these reasons, the CWG agreed to the move to Kamina. DOD, *Congo Rescue*, 68—69, 77; and Wagoner, *DRAGON ROUGE*, 146—48. Message, STATE 1063 to AMEMBASSY Brussels, transmitted 1:41 a.m., 19 November 1964; Message, AMEMBASSY Brussels 1017 to STATE, DTG 201915Z November 1964; and Message, STATE 1093 to AMEMBASSY Brussels, transmitted 5:20 p.m., 20 November 1964. Message, USCINCEUR 00623 to JCS, DTG 201335Z November 1964; and Message, COMUSJTFLEO to CINC STRIKE/USCINCMEAFSA, DTG 212030Z November 1964; both in State HF, POL 23-9 THE CONGO.

8. The CWG's doubts about Belgian priorities came through in the JCS instructions to General Dougherty for the second planning conferences. They stated, "every effort should be made to insure that Belgian planning provides for an expeditious rescue and evacuation of U.S. personnel." Clingerman was to "assist in planning specific measures to be taken to rescue Americans." Message, STATE 1013 to AMEMBASSY Brussels, transmitted 5:53 p.m., 16 November 1964; and Message, JCS 001984 to AMEMBASSY Brussels, DTG 172359Z November 1964; both in State HF, POL 23-9 THE CONGO.

9. Powers, *Man Who Kept the Secrets*, 122—23.

10. Message, STATE 1235 to AMEMBASSY Leopoldville, transmitted 8:49 p.m., 13 November 1964, LBJ-NSF-CF: Congo, Container 183, Memos and Miscellaneous, vol. 7, 11/64; Message, AMEMBASSY Leopoldville 1869 to STATE, received 8:34 a.m., 13 November 1964, released by STATE, 30 April 1986, LBJ-NSF-CF: Congo, Container 83, Congo Cables, vol. 7, 11/64; and Message, STATE 1241 to AMEMBASSY Leopoldville, transmitted 4:01 p.m., 14 November 1964, released by STATE, 12 December 1985, State HF, POL 23-9 THE CONGO.

11. Message, STATE 1235 to AMEMBASSY Leopoldville, transmitted 8:49 p.m., 13 November 1964; Message, AMEMBASSY Leopoldville 1869 to STATE, received 8:34 a.m., 13 November 1964; and Message, STATE 1241 to AMEMBASSY Leopoldville, transmitted 4:01 p.m., 14 November 1964.

12. Message, STATE 1235 to AMEMBASSY Leopoldville, transmitted 8:49 p.m., 13 November 1964; Message, AMEMBASSY Leopoldville 1869 to STATE, received 8:34 a.m., 13 November 1964; and Message, STATE 1241 to AMEMBASSY Leopoldville, transmitted 4:01 p.m., 14 November 1964.

13. Message, AMEMBASSY Leopoldville 1895 to STATE, received 8:42 p.m., 14 November 1964. Message, AMEMBASSY Leopoldville 1900 to STATE, received 8:00 a.m., 15 November 1964, LBJ-NSF-CF: Congo, Container 83, Congo Cables, vol. 6, 10/64—11/64.

14. Dr. James Erdmann, Lieutenant Colonel USAF Ret., interviews with the author, Denver, CO, October 1985; Poore interview; and Laurent interview.

15. "STRAC Area Analysis: Congo," annex F, app. 1, tab A.

16. Poore interview.

17. Ibid.

18. Ibid.; Gradwell interview, 50—58; and Laurent interview.

19. Erdmann, "Journal—DRAGON ROUGE"; and Gradwell interview, 41.

20. Erdmann, "Journal—DRAGON ROUGE."

21. Ibid. Message, BALDWIN CP to USCINCEUR, DTG 200001Z November 1964; and Message, CINCSTRIKE/USCINCMEAFSA 983/64 to COMUSJTFLEO, DTG 182010Z November 1964; both in State HF, POL 23-9 THE CONGO. Message, STATE 1337 to AMEMBASSY Leopoldville, transmitted 10:43 p.m., 20 November 1964; DOD, *Congo Rescue*, 143—44, 160—63, 175; and Burgess Gradwell, Colonel USAF, JTF Command Structure at Ascension, Erdmann Papers.

22. Charles Laurent, Colonel, "Journal De Campagne," [17—27 November 1964], unpublished diary, CDH.

23. "Paracommando Regt. Rept: Dragon Rouge," 2—4.

24. Ibid.

25. Vandewalle points out that Spaak would have had major political problems—domestic and international—had Gbenye been captured. Vandewalle, *L'Ommengang*, 357; Jean Mine, Major, Belgian Army, interview with *Reader's Digest*, *Reed Collection*, 46; Laurent and Ledant interview; and Mine, Rousseaux, and Raes interview.

26. Andre Anne de Molina, Major, "Notes on Ascension Island Intelligence Briefing by Mr. Clingerman," CDH.

27. Ibid.

28. Ibid.

29. Ibid.

30. Clingerman's briefing came almost a full day after Mine's formal orders group. It is not clear how much input the former consul had into the planning process before Laurent's or Mine's tactical briefing. The Belgians maintain that he provided the mission for the 13th Company, while the message traffic indicates that Clingerman pushed for movement into the city rather than tactical-political sideshows. Anne de Molina, "Notes"; Laurent and Ledant interview; Mine, Rousseaux, and Raes interview; and Mine interview, 46.

31. Erdmann, "Dragon Rouge," 31.

32. The author has one of the requested maps that the embassy provided Lieutenant Colonel Rattan at Kamina. Rattan Papers; Message, STATE 1347 to AMEMBASSY Leopoldville, transmitted 1:50 p.m., 21 November 1964; and Message, BALDWIN CP Msg Nr 2 to AMEMBASSY Leopoldville, DTG 191325Z November 1964; both in State HF, POL 23-9 THE CONGO.

33. Message, AMEMBASSY Leopoldville 2011 to STATE, DTG 201855Z November 1964; Message, STATE 1308 to AMEMBASSY Leopoldville, transmitted 4:11 p.m., 19 November 1964; Message, AMEMBASSY Leopoldville 2031 to STATE, DTG 211530Z November 1964; and Message, STATE 1366 to AMEMBASSY Leopoldville, transmitted 8:56 a.m., 22 November 1964; all in State HF, POL 23-9 THE CONGO. Wagoner, *DRAGON ROUGE*, 161—62.

34. Poore interview.

35. Erdmann, "Journal—DRAGON ROUGE"; "JTF LEO Historical Report," B-3; Message, STATE 1261 to AMEMBASSY Leopoldville, transmitted 5:36 p.m., 16 November 1964, released by STATE, 12 December 1985, State HF, POL 23-9 THE CONGO; and Erdmann "Dragon Rouge," 40.

36. Gradwell interview, 61, 84—99; Donald R. Strobaugh, Captain USAF, "Journal: Operation Dragon Rouge, Stanleyville, Republic of the Congo, 24—27 November 1964," (Wiesbaden, Germany: Det. 1, 5th Aerial Port Squadron, 322d Air Division," 3 December 1964), in Erdmann Papers and in author's possession; and Erdmann, "Journal—DRAGON ROUGE."

37. Centre d'Entrainement de Parachutage, "Journal De Campagne: Dragon Rouge," CDH; and Erdmann interview.

38. Centre d'Entrainement de Parachutage, "Journal De Campagne: Dragon Rouge," CDH; and Erdmann interview.

39. See notes 3 and 4 in this chapter.

40. Ibid.; see notes 5 and 7 in this chapter.

41. Message, AMEMBASSY Leopoldville 2004 to STATE, DTG 201520Z November 1964; and Message, STATE to WHITE HOUSE, DTG 201739Z November 1964; both in LBJ-NSF-CF: Congo, Container 83, Congo Cables, vol. 7, 11/64. Message, AMEMBASSY Leopoldville 2029 to STATE, DTG 211420Z November 1964; and Message, AMEMBASSY Leopoldville 2030 to STATE, DTG 211525Z November 1964; both in State HF, POL 23-9 THE CONGO. Wagoner, *DRAGON ROUGE*, 149.

42. Erdmann interview; Erdmann, "Journal—DRAGON ROUGE"; Erdmann, "Dragon Rouge," 39; and Message, BALDWIN CP 61012 to JCS, DTG 211255Z November 1964, State HF, POL 23-9 THE CONGO.

43. William Attwood, Ambassador, interview with *Reader's Digest, Reed Collection*, 82—107; DOD, *Congo Rescue*, 76—79, 83—84, 95—96. Message, STATE 1372 to AMEMBASSY Leopoldville, transmitted 8:38 p.m., 22 November 1964; Message, STATE 1148 to AMEMBASSY Brussels, transmitted 11:04 a.m., 23 November 1964; Message, AMEMBASSY Leopoldville 2038 to STATE, received 8:39 p.m., 21 November 1964; and Message, CINCSTRIKE/USCINCMEAFSA 1075/64 to JCS, DTG 212221Z November 1964; all in State HF, POL 23-9 THE CONGO. Message, JCS 2174 to CINCSTRIKE/USCINCMEAFSA, DTG 220515Z November 1964, LBJ-NSF-CF: Congo, Container 84, Memos and Miscellaneous, vol. 8, 11/64.

44. Richard Strauss, Transcript of interview with Fred E. Wagoner, Washington, DC, 5 September 1975, Wagoner Papers, copy in author's possession.

45. DOD, *Congo Rescue*, 49, 84—86; Message, CINCAFSTRIKE DOCC-OC28310 to JCS, DTG 221009Z November 1964, LBJ-NSF-CF: Congo, Container 84, Memos and Miscellaneous, vol. 8, 11/64; and Message, USAFE OCP21791 to USCINCEUR, DTG 230105Z November 1964, State HF, POL 23-9 TIIE CONGO.

46. DOD, *Congo Rescue*, 87.

47. As the American nearest Spaak, MacArthur was the first to see his sudden shift to hesitancy. Consequently, MacArthur waited till the operation was in effect before deciding not to give the message to Spaak. Ibid., 89.

48. Ibid.

49. Attwood interview, 82—107.

50. DOD, *Congo Rescue*, 89; Message, AMEMBASSY Leopoldville 2057 to STATE, DTG 221911Z November 1964, State HF, POL 23-9 THE CONGO. Message, JCS 2174 to CINCSTRIKE/USCINCMEAFSA, DTG 200515Z November 1964; and Message JCS 002183 to CINCSTRIKE/USCINCMEAFSA DTG 222310Z November 1964; both in LBJ-NSF-CF: Congo, Container 84, Memos and Miscellaneous, vol. 8, 11/64.

51. DOD, *Congo Rescue*, 90—91.

52. Message, AMEMBASSY Leopoldville 2076 to STATE, DTG 231655Z November 1964, State HF, POL 23-9 THE CONGO.

53. Ibid.

54. Ibid. Message, AMEMBASSY Leopoldville 2058 to STATE, DTG 222147Z November 1964, State HF, POL 23-9 THE CONGO.

55. MacArthur passed the information by phone followed by a message at 231920Z November 1974. Message, AMEMBASSY Brussels 1057 to STATE, DTG 231920Z November 1964, LBJ-NSF-CF: Congo, Classified Holdings, declassified 30 April 1986; and DOD, *Congo Rescue*, 92—93.

56. Message, AMEMBASSY Brussels 1057 to STATE, DTG 231920Z November 1964; and DOD, *Congo Rescue*, 92—93.
57. Rattan interview; and Vandewalle, *L'Ommengang*, 313.
58. Hoyt and Grinwis, "Journal," 65—67.
59. Dowdy, *Jaws of the Lion*, 146—47.
60. Strobaugh, "Journal"; Gradwell interview, 100—113; "Paracommando Regt. Rept.: Dragon Rouge," 9; and DOD, *Congo Rescue*, 148—50.
61. Isaacson did have one choice, but it was not a realistic option. After consultation with the JCS, Adams had offered him the option of adjusting H hour to a night drop without air support. For obvious reasons, Laurent was against any suggestion of a night airborne operation. Erdmann interview; Laurent and Ledant interview; Poore interview; Mine, Rousseaux, and Raes interview; and DOD, *Congo Rescue*, 29—31. Message, JCS 002104 to CINCSTRIKE/USCINCMEAFSA, DTG 201637Z November 1964; Message, CINCSTRIKE/USCINCMEAFSA 1074/64 to JCS, DTG 212155Z November 1964; and Message, CINC STRIKE/USCINCMEAFSA 1075/64 to JCS, DTG 212221Z November 1964; all in State HF, POL 23-9 THE CONGO.
62. Poore interview; Erdmann interview; and Laurent interview.
63. Vandewalle interview; and Laurent interview.
64. Message, J-2 USJTFLEO to DRAGON ROUGE, DTG 230850Z November 1964, CDH; Message, USARMA Leopoldville CX-322 to DIA, DTG 231930Z November 1964, LBJ-NSF-CF: Congo, Container 84, Memos and Miscellaneous, vol. 8, 11/64; Laurent, "Journal"; Message, AMEMBASSY Leopoldville 2076 to STATE, DTG 231655Z November 1964; and Erdmann, "Dragon Rouge," 39.

Chapter 5

1. Vandewalle, *L'Ommengang*, 349—51; and Vandewalle interviews.
2. Robin Mannock, interview with *Reader's Digest, Reed Collection*, 49—50; and Reed, *111 Days*, 234—36.
3. Vandewalle, *L'Ommengang*, 351—53; Rattan, "Bukavu to Stanleyville," 64—65; and Mannock interview, 49—63.
4. Colonel Clayton Isaacson, interview with *Reader's Digest, Reed Collection*, 10—15.
5. Erdmann, "Journal—DRAGON ROUGE"; and Gradwell interview, 125—28.
6. Gradwell interview, 128—33.
7. Laurent interview; Mine, Rousseaux, and Raes interview; Regiment Para Commando, CM, "DRAGON ROUGE et NOIR"; and "STAN-PAULIS," 17.
8. Mine interview, 29; "Paracommando Regt. Rept.: Dragon Rouge," 9; and Erdmann, "Journal—DRAGON ROUGE."
9. Mine interview, 29; "Paracommando Regt. Rept.: Dragon Rouge," 9; and The Men of 1st Para, interviews with *Reader's Digest, Reed Collection*, unnumbered pages, hereafter cited as 1st Para interviews. The transcription of the 1st Para group interview contains both numbered and unnumbered pages.
10. Mine interview, 29; "Paracommando Regt. Rept.: Dragon Rouge," 9—10; 1st Para interviews; and Captain Huyberechts, "Rapport des Operations: Stanleyville, 24 et 25 Nov 64, Paulis, 26 et 27 Nov 64," CDH, hereafter cited as Huyberechts, "Stanleyville, Paulis."
11. 1st Para interviews; and "Paracommando Regt. Rept.: Dragon Rouge," 10.
12. Reed, *111 Days*, 246; 1st Para interviews, 171—72; and Strobaugh, "Journal."
13. 1st Para interviews; and Mine interview, 31—32.
14. 1st Para interviews, 41—42.

15. Ibid., 178—85.
16. 1st Para interviews; Reed, *111 Days*, 247; "Paracommando Regt. Rept.: Dragon Rouge," 10; and Strobaugh, "Journal."
17. Erdmann, "Journal—DRAGON ROUGE"; Robert A. Lindsay, Colonel USAF Ret., "McKay Trophy Speech," Erdmann Papers; and Gradwell interview, 133—35.
18. Erdmann, "Journal—DRAGON ROUGE"; Lindsay, "McKay Trophy Speech"; and Gradwell interview, 133—35.
19. Walter Mertens, Lieutenant, Belgian Army, "Declaration Du 1LT Mertens, Objet—Mitrailleuse chenoise récupérée a Stanleyville lors de l'OPS 'DRAGON ROUGE,' " CDH; and Mine interview, page unnumbered.
20. Strobaugh, "Journal"; and Gradwell interview, 136—37. U.S. Air Force, untitled silent film, 16-mm B/W, taken at Stanleyville, 17—27 November 1964, Erdmann Papers. "Paracommando Regt. Rept.: Dragon Rouge," 11—12; and "STAN-PAULIS," 18—19.
21. 1st Para interviews; USAF film; and Laurent interview.
22. 1st Para interviews; and Mine interview, 25—26.
23. Hoyt and Grinwis, "Journal," 67—68.
24. James E. Stauffer, interview with *Reader's Digest, Reed Collection,* 104; Donald L. Parkes, interview with *Reader's Digest, Reed Collection,* 29—35; Gene Bergman and Jon Snyder, interview with *Reader's Digest, Reed Collection,* 110—41; Andre and Theo Papasoglakis, interview with *Reader's Digest, Reed Collection,* 4—5; and Alexander Barlovatz, interview with *Reader's Digest, Reed Collection,* 37.
25. As quoted by Reed, *111 Days*, 259.
26. Bergman and Snyder interview, 125; and Banning interview, 32—34, 54—61.
27. 1st Para interviews; and Regt. Para Commando, CM, "DRAGON ROUGE et NOIR."
28. 1st Para interviews, 49—50; and Pierre Vandergoten, "Journal de L'Intervention Belge a Stanleyville," 11, CDH.
29. 1st Para interviews, 49—50; and Vandergoten, "Journal," 11.
30. 1st Para interviews.
31. Ibid.; and Centre d'Entrainement de Parachutage, "DRAGON ROUGE."
32. "Paracommando Regt. Rept.: Dragon Rouge," 13; and "STAN-PAULIS," 19—23.
33. 1st Para interviews; and "Paracommando Regt. Rept.: Dragon Rouge," 13.
34. 1st Para interviews; "Paracommando Regt. Rept.: Dragon Rouge," 13; Grinwis interview, 408; and USAF film.
35. 1st Para interviews; "Paracommando Regt. Rept.: Dragon Rouge," 13; Grinwis interview, 408; and USAF film.
36. 1st Para interviews.
37. Colonel Laurent's sensitivity to losses among his men are graphically displayed in his campaign journal. In each instance of a loss or wounded trooper, Laurent wrote the soldier's name in red. Laurent, "Journal"; and 1st Para interviews.
38. 1st Para interviews, 61—71; "Paracommando Regt. Rept.: Dragon Rouge," 17; and "STAN-PAULIS," 19—21.
39. 1st Para interviews, 61—71; "Paracommando Regt. Rept.: Dragon Rouge," 17; and "STAN-PAULIS," 19—21.
40. 1st Para interviews, 41—45; "Paracommando Regt. Rept.: Dragon Rouge," 16; "STAN-PAULIS," 19—21, and Paracommando Regiment, 1st Battalion, 13th Company, "Objet: Operation STAN," CDH, hereafter cited as 13th Company, "STAN."

41. 1st Para interviews, 41–45; "Paracommando Regt. Rept.: Dragon Rouge," 16; "STAN-PAULIS," 21–22; and 13th Company, "STAN."
42. 1st Para interviews, 41–45; "Paracommando Regt. Rept.: Dragon Rouge," 16–17; "STAN-PAULIS," 21–22; and 13th Company, "STAN."
43. 1st Para interviews, 41–45; "Paracommando Regt. Rept.: Dragon Rouge," 16–17; "STAN-PAULIS," 21–22; and 13th Company, "STAN."
44. 1st Para interviews, 41–45; "Paracommando Regt. Rept.: Dragon Rouge," 16–17; "STAN-PAULIS," 21–22; and 13th Company, "STAN."
45. "Paracommando Regt. Rept.: Dragon Rouge," 14; and "STAN-PAULIS," 22–23.
46. "Paracommando Regt. Rept.: Dragon Rouge," 14; and "STAN-PAULIS," 22–23.
47. Gradwell interview, 140–45.
48. Ibid., 142–43.
49. Ibid.
50. Strobaugh, "Journal"; 1st Para interviews; and Centre d'Entrainement de Parachutage, "DRAGON ROUGE."
51. 1st Para interviews; Centre d'Entrainement de Parachutage, "DRAGON ROUGE"; Banning interview, 17; and Robinson interview, 17–19.
52. 1st Para interviews; Centre d'Entrainement de Parachutage, "DRAGON ROUGE"; and Banning interview, 12–61.
53. Banning interview, 12–61; 1st Para interviews; Gradwell interview, 145; and Strobaugh, "Journal."
54. Gradwell interview, 145; Strobaugh, "Journal"; and Banning interview, 32–34, 54–61.
55. Strobaugh, "Journal"; and Erdmann, "Journal–DRAGON ROUGE."
56. Huyberechts, "Stanleyville, Paulis."
57. Ibid.
58. 1st Para interviews.
59. Ibid., and Strobaugh, "Journal."
60. 1st Para interviews; Grinwis interview, 409–10; Strobaugh, "Journal"; Donald R. Strobaugh, Captain USAF, interview with *Reader's Digest, Reed Collection,* 11–12; Erdmann, "Journal–DRAGON ROUGE"; and DOD, *Congo Rescue,* 154.
61. Vandewalle records the junction as having occurred at 0930Z. Vandewalle, *L'Ommengang,* 354; "Paracommando Regt. Rept.: Dragon Rouge," 14; and Rattan, "Bukavu to Stanleyville," 66.
62. Rattan, "Bukavu to Stanleyville," 65–66. Vandewalle said first word of the drop came at 0520Z. Vandewalle, *L'Ommengang,* 354; and Message, COMISH Leopoldville 9494 to CINCMEAFSA, DTG 251630Z November 64, LBJ-NSF-CF: Congo, Container 84, Memos and Miscellaneous, vol. 9, 11/64.
63. Vandewalle, *L'Ommengang,* 362.
64. Ibid., 359–60; Vandewalle interview; and Laurent interview.
65. Rattan, "Bukavu to Stanleyville," 67–68; Rattan interview; Delbert Carper, interview with *Reader's Digest, Reed Collection,* 117–27; and Dowdy, *Jaws of the Lion,* 177–78.
66. Dowdy, *Jaws of the Lion,* 177–87.
67. As quoted in Ibid., 147–57, 187–88.
68. Rattan, "Bukavu to Stanleyville," 67–68; Carper interview, 117–27; and Dowdy, *Jaws of the Lion,* 188–89.
69. Vandewalle, *L'Ommengang,* 360; and Strobaugh, "Journal."

70. Gradwell interview, 146—47; and Strobaugh interview, 14—25.
71. Strobaugh, "Journal"; and Strobaugh interview, 14—25.
72. 1st Para interviews; "Paracommando Regt. Rept.: Dragon Rouge," 16; "STAN-PAULIS," 21—22; and 13th Company, "STAN."
73. 1st Para interviews; "Paracommando Regt. Rept.: Dragon Rouge," 16—17; "STAN-PAULIS," 21—22; and 13th Company, "STAN."
74. 1st Para interviews.
75. Strobaugh, "Journal"; and 1st Para interviews.
76. 1st Para interviews; 13th Company, "STAN"; and "Paracommando Regt. Rept.: Dragon Rouge," 17—18.
77. Huyberechts, "Stanleyville, Paulis"; Centre d'Entrainement de Parachutage, "DRAGON ROUGE"; and Regt. Para Commando, CM, "DRAGON ROUGE et NOIR."
78. Huyberechts, "Stanleyville, Paulis"; Centre d'Entrainement de Parachutage, "DRAGON ROUGE"; and Regt. Para Commando, CM, "DRAGON ROUGE et NOIR."
79. "Paracommando Regt. Rept.: Dragon Rouge," 18.
80. Vandewalle, *L'Ommengang*, 362; and Hoare, *Mercenary*, 135—37.
81. Laurent, "Journal"; Vandewalle interview; Laurent interview; Hoare, *Mercenary*, 132—33; Vandewalle, *L'Ommengang*, 369—70; and 1st Para interviews.

Chapter 6

1. The second Brussels conference centered on the towns of Bunia, Paulis, and Watsa. General Dougherty again headed the United States contingent, but this time, his team consisted of Lieutenant Colonel Gray, again representing USAFE, Lieutenant Colonel Dunn from the JCS, and to General Adams' satisfaction, Lieutenant Colonel James Sedberry, a planner from USSTRICOM. Again, Colonel Louvigny headed the Belgian team, but with Colonel Laurent and his staff down at Ascension Island, Lieutenant Colonel Janssens, the Paracommando Regiment's second in command, represented the unit.

   The planning parameters were the same as those of the earlier conference. The American team was not to mention American unilateral plans to intervene in the Congo. Indeed, the Low Beam operation, openly discussed with Belgians in the Congo, was to be considered "NOFORN" (not for foreign discussion) in the talks in Brussels. The guidance to General Dougherty from the JCS stressed this closed-mouth approach by flatly stating that no "indication will be given at any time that the US is planning to or would commit US ground forces to the Congo." The JCS emphasized this warning to Adams in a separate message concerning American and British consultations on the crisis. Every means of keeping the Belgians militarily up front was to be employed, a trend that would be matched on the diplomatic side. The assumption that the Belgians knew what was needed best was just fine, as it had been in the earlier conference. In fact, with the available American airlift supposedly already established, the Belgians would be firmly in control of the military planning for the follow-on operations.

   In beginning the second conference, the planners had several considerations to take into account. First, as in the original conference, was the question of available airlift. The Americans stated that to ensure an efficient airlift, it was essential—for maintenance and crew rest—to see that there was a minimum of forty-eight hours between the operation at Stanleyville and any subsequent missions. The second consideration was the question of Belgian ground strength, as the planners had to prepare for possible simultaneous missions, particularly if Vandewalle seized Stanleyville without the aid of Dragon Rouge. If Vandewalle singlehandedly took Stanleyville, the Belgian force to be used at Bunia, Paulis, and Watsa could mount two simultaneous missions, with a third mission following in forty-eight hours. Should Dragon Rouge occur before Vandewalle could seize Stanleyville, then the question of the Belgians maintaining control of the city till Vandewalle arrived would become an issue. Should Vandewalle arrive within forty-eight hours of the assault, then the Paracommandos could still mount simultaneous assaults on two targets. If control had to be maintained for more than forty-eight hours—pending the ANC's arrival in the city—then there would be fewer troops available for use in the proposed secondary missions.

The second planning conference in Brussels centered on three likely hostage locations in the northeastern Congo: Bunia, Paulis, and Watsa. In studying each city, the planners concentrated on the number of hostages, likely places of confinement, evolution of the operations of the ANC, ease of evacuation, and the availability of airfields for landing or airborne assault.

Bunia, thought to hold the greatest number of hostages after Stanleyville, had a 6,000-foot airfield suitable for C-130s. Additionally, the city was under pressure from Ops Kivu to the south, and its rebel population was growing increasingly nervous.

Paulis held the next smaller number of non-Congolese hostages, but its airfield was not as well built as that of Bunia. The strip was 4,200 feet in length, but it was made of compacted laterite (rock dust). In the past, Paulis had been utilized by C-47s, but the planners felt with the end of the rainy season approaching, it would be dry enough to handle C-130s. If not, then a purely airborne assault would be required with an overland evacuation via the railway to Bumba to link up with Ops Nord. Lieutenant Colonel Janssens did not support the idea of an overland evacuation with its constant risk of ambush.

Watsa presented the greatest difficulties to the planners, as its airfield, some 2,400 feet in length, could not accommodate the C-130s. Therefore, it would require an airborne assault that was reinforced overland from Bunia. Planners believed that the hostage population in Watsa was all male, and as its Simba garrison was not under ANC pressure, their risk, or perhaps their political importance, was perceived to be less than that of the hostages in Bunia or Paulis. With the above considerations in mind and the mission priorities established in planning Dragon Rouge, the combined staff arrived at a plan for each city.

Bunia, due to its number of hostages and its airfield, would be the first target after Stanleyville. To take the city, the Belgians would assault the airfield with one company, which would be dropped from three C-130s followed by an airland element of two C-130s carrying four armored and two radio jeeps. These two C-130s would be used for immediate refugee extraction, and the company would withdraw the next day. Paulis, assuming that its airfield was suitable for landing, would be assaulted in the same manner as Bunia in a simultaneous operation forty-eight hours after Dragon Rouge. During the conduct of these two assaults, one company would remain as a mobile reserve in Stanleyville. To mount these operations, the Paracommandos would need a resupply of 400 parachutes, 8 armored jeeps, and 4 radio jeeps, plus a second basic load of munitions. After the missions at Bunia and Paulis—dubbed Dragon Blanc and Dragon Noir—were completed, the paras would turn to Watsa.

Watsa, with its restricted airfield, posed a more complicated operational problem. Planners recognized that after operations at Stanleyville, Bunia, and Paulis, the Belgians and the Americans would require a rest of three to four days to recuperate and prepare for an airborne assault. They also recognized that during any such delay, the hostages would probably be massacred. A prolonged stay would also taint the character of the humanitarian operation. Furthermore, such an operation would necessitate equipping the Belgians with rigging suitable for use in the C-130s for dropping vehicles and ammunition into the airhead. Consequently, the planners turned to an alternative solution.

Immediately after the assault on Bunia, a reinforced platoon drawn from the reserve at Stanleyville would push overland from Bunia to Watsa. At the same time, an airborne operation—again from the reserve—would drop on the airfield and seek out the hostages. The overland column, mounted in three-ton trucks would link up with the airborne assault element and then return overland to Bunia. The plan, more flamboyant than those previously discussed, held recognized risks. The greatest danger, and the most obvious, was the risk to the airborne element and the hostages. If the ground column did not arrive on time or did not get through, the refugees and their rescuers stood every chance of being slaughtered. The other risks, diplomatic in nature, were no less serious; and in fact, they ultimately asserted their primacy. As Watsa was close to the eastern border of the Congo, the planners recognized that the Belgian assault could draw rebel reinforcements from across the border. At a minimum, Watsa's proximity to the Sudanese and Ugandan border invited denunciations from the OAU and the UN, a situation which the planners recognized as being extremely sensitive to Belgium after her 1960 experience in the Congo. In addition to the tactical and diplomatic risks, the operation at Watsa (Dragon Vert) also would entail several logistic problems. To conduct the overland movement, the Belgians estimated that eighteen 3-ton trucks would be needed, trucks that would have to be flown in from Belgium. The United States airlift force was not large enough to support this requirement and would have to be reinforced. Dragon Vert, then, was a thorny problem for the Brussels planning group, one that had to be considered with respect to other requirements.

After establishing the guidelines for each mission, the planners placed them in priority according to their logistical support requirements. The first priority before any follow-on missions could be mounted was the replenishment of the Paracommandos' basic load of ammunition, a mission that would be handled via a Sabena Airlines Boeing 707. The second priority was the transport of the required parachutes and vehicles for Dragon Blanc and Dragon Vert. Four aircraft, either C-130s or C-124s, were necessary for this mission because of the lift requirement of 8 armored and 4 radio jeeps, 400 parachutes, and 5,200 pounds of munitions and rations. To mount both operations simultaneously, a total of eleven C-130s would be necessary. The third priority was to be the support necessary for Dragon Vert, which required four C-130s or C-124s to transport eight 3-ton trucks from Belgium to Leopoldville. From there, they would be flown by C-130s into Bunia. Only one C-130 was required for this airborne operation since only a platoon would jump on Watsa. The fourth priority was to be another supply lift, again by Sabena Airlines, on D plus three consisting of uniforms, ammunition, and rations. Lastly, the combined staff planned to bring in ten additional trucks to reinforce the rescue effort at Watsa using another five C-130s or C-124s. All told, it was a fairly substantial logistical effort to support a light infantry battalion inside central Africa.

By 20 November, the draft plans were ready. With Dragon Rouge as D-day, the follow-on operations were to be completed as follows:

Dragon Blanc—Bunia	D plus two
Dragon Noir—Paulis	D plus two
Dragon Vert—Watsa	As soon as possible after Bunia

Other issues were also resolved or addressed by the planners. In the supplemental plan to OPLAN 319/64, the planners did not work out a definite redeployment schedule for the Belgians. Their concept was simply to regroup the force at Kamina as quickly as possible to minimize their visibility. From Kamina, they expected Sabena charter flights to return the Paracommandos to their base in Belgium while the American airlift assets recovered the regiment's equipment. Command and control of the operation, once national-level approval had been reached in Brussels and Washington, would be on the same basis as Dragon Rouge. These details addressed, the planners published the supplement to OPLAN 319/64, which went to the JCS as USCINCEUR Message ECJC-A 00340 on 21 November. Meanwhile, additional discussions were going on concerning Dragon Rouge.

DOD, *Congo Rescue*, 50, 52—53; Letter, James Sedberry, Colonel USAF Ret., to Dr. John Partin, Command Historian, U.S. Readiness Command, 17 June 1986; "Rapport JS-3"; Message, AMEMBASSY 1895 to STATE, received 8:42 p.m., 14 November 1964; and Message, JCS 001984 to AMEMBASSY Brussels, DTG 172359Z November 1964, State HF, POL 23-9 THE CONGO. Message, JCS 001944 to CINCSTRIKE/USCINCMEAFSA, DTG 171536Z November 1964; and Message, JCS 001967 to CINCSTRIKE/USCINCMEAFSA, DTG 172055Z November 1964; both in LBJ-NSF-CF: Congo, Container 83, Memos and

Miscellaneous, vol. 7, 11/64. Message, USCINCEUR ECJC-AO 0340 to JCS, DTG 211030Z November 1964, LBJ-NSF-CF: Congo, Container 84, Memos and Miscellaneous, vol. 8, 11/64.

2. Ironically, the State Department's intelligence analysts had a difficult time in deciding if or how the Simbas would react to the news from Stanleyville. U.S. Department of State, Director of Intelligence and Research, "Intelligence Note to the Secretary, Subject: Dragon Rouge—Initial Observations and Projections," dated 24 November 1964, LBJ-NSF-CF: Congo, Container 84, Memos and Miscellaneous, vol. 8, 11/64.

3. In Washington, members of the CWG assembled to await the results of Dragon Rouge. Harriman came in wearing formal dress and then retired for the evening; events were clearly out of his hands. Wagoner, *DRAGON ROUGE*, 169; and Reed, *111 Days*, 243. In Texas, LBJ retired for the evening only to be awakened by early-hour phone calls. The White House, "President Lyndon B. Johnson Daily Diary," 23—24 November 1964, Erdmann Papers. In Brussels, Spaak, Segers, and Ambassador MacArthur met secretly on the second floor of the U.S. Embassy to use a secure phone line to the U.S. European Command. Ambassador Douglas MacArthur II, interview with Dr. James Erdmann, 25 July 1976, Erdmann Papers.

4. After his low-level pass over the airfield, Isaacson had experienced radio difficulty and was out of contact until he arrived at Leopoldville. Isaacson interview, 19—20; Message, COMDR JTF LEO 0544 to STATE, DTG 240710Z November 1964, LBJ-NSF-CF: Congo, Container 84, Memos and Miscellaneous, vol. 8, 11/64; and DOD, *Congo Rescue*, 154.

5. Godley's cable, based on Isaacson's report, described the operation in glowing terms. Godley reported that Isaacson "never saw [a] better coordinated operation and perfect drop." The tag on the end must have come as a shock to its readers in Washington and Brussels. Message, AMEMBASSY Leopoldville 2091 to STATE, DTG 240735Z November 1964, LBJ-NSF-CF: Congo, Container 84, Congo Cables, vol. 8, 11/64; and DOD, *Congo Rescue*, 154.

6. Message, JCS 002230 to CINCAL, DTG 241348Z November 1964; Congo Special Situation Report no. 9, 6:00 a.m., 24 November 1964, LBJ-NSF-CF: Congo, Container 84, Memos and Miscellaneous, vol. 8, 11/64; and DOD, *Congo Rescue*, 154—55.

7. DOD, *Congo Rescue*, 139—63.

8. Message, AMEMBASSY Leopoldville 2141 to STATE, DTG 251525Z November 1964, State HF, POL 23-9 THE CONGO; and Message, AMEMBASSY Leopoldville 2105 to STATE, DTG 241333Z November 1964, LBJ-NSF-CF: Congo, Container 84, Congo Cables, vol. 8, 11/64. The success of the rescue at Aketi gave rise to false hopes in Washington. Analysts pointed to this operation as proof that the ground columns could rescue the hostages unharmed. U.S. Department of State, Director of Intelligence and Research, Research Memorandum RAF—58, Subject: Considerations Affecting a Possible Paradrop on Paulis, Bunia, and Watsa, 24 November 1964, LBJ-NSF-CF: Congo, Container 84, Memos and Miscellaneous, vol. 8, 11/64. While the argument was legitimate before Dragon Rouge, it failed to account for the time required for the ground columns to reach the outlying areas or the predictable Simba desire for revenge after the news of Stanleyville spread to those areas. General Adams directed Colonel Isaacson to assess the likelihood of a rapid ground column assault on Paulis, Watsa, and Bunia. Isaacson reported that, at best, it would require four to five days for the ANC to reach these areas, assuming, of course, that everything went as planned. Message, CINCSTRIKE/USCINCMEAFSA 12670 to COMUSJTFLEO, DTG 251534Z November 1964; and Message, COMUSJTFLEO 0563 to CINCSTRIKE/USCINCMEAFSA, DTG 252110Z November 1964; both in State HF, POL 23-9 THE CONGO. Actually, the Third World reaction to Dragon Rouge began in a fairly subdued manner. However, by the end of the 25th in Washington, its intensity had exceeded all expectations. Congo Special Situation Report no. 9, 6:00 a.m., 24 November 1964; and Congo Special Situation Report no. 10, 5:00 p.m., 24 November 1964; both in LBJ-NSF-CF: Congo, Container 84, Memos and Miscellaneous, vol. 8, 11/64. Congo Special Situation Report no. 11, 6:00 a.m., 25 November 1964; and Congo Special Situation Report

no. 12, 5:00 p.m., 25 November 1964; both in LBJ-NSF-CF: Congo, Container 84, Memos and Miscellaneous, vol. 9, 11/64.

9. Message, AMEMBASSY Leopoldville 2111 to STATE, DTG 241800Z November 1964, State HF, POL 23-9 THE CONGO. Spaak echoed Godley's idea; he, too, wished to withdraw the paras to Kamina. Message, AMEMBASSY Brussels 1072 to STATE, DTG 251220Z November 1964, released by STATE, 30 April 1986, LBJ-NSF-CF: Congo, Container 84, Congo Cables, vol. 9, 11/64.

10. DOD, *Congo Rescue*, 100.

11. Ibid., 100—101; and Message, STATE 1179 to AMEMBASSY Brussels, transmitted 7:59 p.m., 24 November 1964, State HF, POL 23-9 THE CONGO.

12. DOD, *Congo Rescue*, 101.

13. Message, CINCSTRIKE/USCINCMEAFSA 12594 to JCS, DTG 250555Z November 1964, State HF, POL 23-9 THE CONGO; and Congo Special Situation Report no. 11.

14. "Paracommando Regt. Rept.: Dragon Rouge," 17; "STAN-PAULIS," 28; Message, STATE 3516 to AMEMBASSY London, transmitted 9:21 p.m., 25 November 1964, LBJ-NSF-CF: Congo, Container 84, Memos and Miscellaneous, vol. 9, 11/64; Message, STATE 1034 to all African Posts, transmitted 12:23 a.m., 25 November 1964, State HF, POL 23-9 THE CONGO; Laurent, "Journal"; and Laurent and Ledant interview.

15. "Paracommando Regt. Rept.: Dragon Rouge," 18. The Ministry of Defense in Brussels turned down the request for helicopters. Laurent interview.

16. Strobaugh, "Journal"; and "Paracommando Regt. Rept.: Dragon Rouge," 18—19.

17. Isaacson interview, 21—22; and "Paracommando Regt. Rept.: Dragon Rouge," 19.

18. 13th Company, "STAN"; and "Paracommando Regt. Rept.: Dragon Rouge," 20. Vandewalle states that Wauters was killed by a stray Belgian bullet. Vandewalle, *L'Ommengang*, 361. Message, AMEMBASSY Leopoldville 2136 to STATE, DTG 251120Z November 1964, State HF, POL 23-9 THE CONGO; Laurent and Ledant interview; and Mine, Rousseaux, and Raes interview.

19. "STAN-PAULIS," 28—29.

20. Message, AMEMBASSY Leopoldville 2136 to STATE, DTG 251120Z November 1964.

21. DOD, *Congo Rescue*, 101—2; George W. Ball, *The Past Has Another Pattern: Memoirs* (New York: W.W. Norton & Co., 1982), 324; and Wagoner, *DRAGON ROUGE*, 186.

22. "STAN-PAULIS," 28, 55; and Congo Special Situation Report no. 12.

23. Message, STATE 3516 to AMEMBASSY London, transmitted 9:21 p.m., 25 November 1964; Message, STATE 1034 to all African posts, transmitted 12:23 a.m., 25 November 1964; Message, COMUSJTFLEO 0563 to CINCSTRIKE/USCINCMEAFSA, 252110Z November 1964; Message, AMEMBASSY Leopoldville 2105 to STATE, DTG 241333Z November 1964; U.S. Department of State, Director of Intelligence and Research, Research Memorandum RAF—58, Subject: Considerations Affecting a Possible Paradrop on Paulis, Bunia, and Watsa, 24 November 1964; and Message, CINCSTRIKE/USCINCMEAFSA 12670 to COMUSJTFLEO, DTG 251534Z November 1964.

24. Lieutenant Colonel Lindsey and Major Poore felt that the B-26 runs had only served to awaken the sleeping Simba gunners around the field. Erdmann, "Journal—DRAGON ROUGE"; Poore interview; Laurent and Ledant interview; and Mine, Rousseaux, and Raes interview.

25. Message, COMUSJTFLEO 0549 to CINCSTRIKE/USCINCMEAFSA, DTG 241519Z November 1964, State HF, POL 23-9 THE CONGO.

26. Message, CINCSTRIKE/USCINCMEAFSA 12670 to COMUSJTFLEO, DTG 251534Z November 1964; "STAN-PAULIS, 24—27 Novembre, 64," 29; "Paracommando Regt. Rept.: Dragon Rouge," 20—21; and Letter, Major André Anne de Molina to Lieutenant Colonel

James M. Erdmann, 19 January 1965, and enclosure to letter: translation into French of Flemish article in *Ons Zondags-blad*, 6 December 1964, Erdmann Papers.

27. Team Rav Air, Centre d'Entrainement de Parachutage, "Objet: Operations DRAGON ROUGE et NOIR," CDH.
28. "STAN-PAULIS," 68.
29. Ibid.
30. Gradwell interview, 146—47; and Strobaugh interview, 14—25.
31. Congo Special Situation Report no. 11; Gradwell interview, 146—49; Strobaugh interview, 14—25; and Isaacson interview, 21—22.
32. Erdmann interviews.
33. Gradwell interview, 151, 161—62; Isaacson interview, 21—22; and Poore interview.
34. Gradwell interview, 156—57; Strobaugh, "Journal"; and Poore interview.
35. Gradwell interview, 160—61.
36. Strobaugh, "Journal"; and Poore interview.
37. Poore interview.
38. DOD, *Congo Rescue*, 102; and Gradwell interview, 153—55.
39. Strobaugh, "Journal"; and Gradwell interview, 156—58.
40. "STAN-PAULIS," 30; and Poore interview.
41. Strobaugh, "Journal"; and Gradwell interview, 159—60.
42. Gradwell interview, 161—62.
43. Ibid., 166—67; and "Paracommando Regt. Rept.: Dragon Rouge," 23.
44. Gradwell interview, 170—71.
45. Ibid., 162—63.
46. Laurent interview.
47. The Simbas had reinforced Paulis prior to Dragon Noir. "Paracommando Regt. Rept.: Dragon Rouge," 23; Message, COMUSJTFLEO 0580 to CINCSTRIKE/USCINCMEAFSA, DTG 270030Z November 1964, LBJ-NSF-CF: Congo, Container 84, Memos and Miscellaneous, vol. 9, 11/64.
48. Centre d'Entrainement de Parachutage, "DRAGON NOIR manifests," CDH; Gradwell interview, 164; and "Paracommando Regt. Rept.: Dragon Rouge," 23—24.
49. Gradwell interview, 164; and "Paracommando Regt. Rept.: Dragon Rouge," 23—24.
50. Gradwell interview, 164; Huyberechts, "Stanleyville, Paulis"; and 1st Para interviews.
51. 1st Para interviews; and "STAN-PAULIS," 31—33.
52. Message, AMEMBASSY Leopoldville 2158 to STATE, DTG 261155Z November 1964; and Message, AMEMBASSY Leopoldville 2182 to STATE, DTG 262130Z November 1964; both in LBJ-NSF-CF: Congo, Container 84, Congo Cables, vol. 9, 11/64. Message, COMUSJTFLEO 0580 to CINCSTRIKE/USCINCMEAFSA, DTG 270030Z November 1964.
53. "STAN-PAULIS," 31—33; "Paracommando Regt. Rept.: Dragon Rouge," 24; and 1st Para interviews.
54. "STAN-PAULIS," 31—33; "Paracommando Regt. Rept.: Dragon Rouge," 24; and 1st Para interviews.
55. "STAN-PAULIS," 31—33; "Paracommando Regt. Rept.: Dragon Rouge," 24; and 1st Para interviews.
56. "STAN-PAULIS," 31—33; "Paracommando Regt. Rept.: Dragon Rouge," 24; and 1st Para interviews.

57. "STAN-PAULIS," 31—33; "Paracommando Regt. Rept.: Dragon Rouge," 24; and 1st Para interviews.

58. Captain Vanderperre, "Rapport Du Cpn Vanderperre," CDH; and 13th Company, "STAN."

59. Message, COMUSJTFLEO 0580 to CINCSTRIKE/USCINCMEAFSA, DTG 270030Z November 1964; Gradwell interview, 167—68.

60. "Paracommando Regt. Rept.: Dragon Rouge," 25.

61. Ibid., 25—27; "STAN-PAULIS," 33—36; Huyberechts, "Stanleyville, Paulis"; and 1st Para interviews.

62. "Paracommando Regt. Rept.: Dragon Rouge," 25—27; "STAN-PAULIS," 33—36; Huyberechts, "Stanleyville, Paulis"; and 1st Para interviews.

63. "Paracommando Regt. Rept.: Dragon Rouge," 25—27; "STAN-PAULIS," 33—36; Huyberechts, "Stanleyville, Paulis"; and 1st Para interviews.

64. "Paracommando Regt. Rept.: Dragon Rouge," 25—27; "STAN-PAULIS," 33—36; Huyberechts, "Stanleyville, Paulis"; and 1st Para interviews.

65. "Paracommando Regt. Rept.: Dragon Rouge," 25—27; "STAN-PAULIS," 33—36; Huyberechts, "Stanleyville, Paulis"; and 1st Para interviews.

66. "Paracommando Regt. Rept: Dragon Rouge," 25—27; "STAN-PAULIS," 33—36; Huyberechts, "Stanleyville, Paulis"; and 1st Para interviews.

67. "Paracommando Regt. Rept.: Dragon Rouge," 25—27; "STAN-PAULIS," 33—36; Huyberechts, "Stanleyville, Paulis"; 1st Para interviews; and Vanderperre, "Rapport."

68. "STAN-PAULIS," 36; and Laurent interview.

69. "STAN-PAULIS," 36; Laurent interview; Mine, Rousseaux, and Raes interview; and 13th Company, "STAN."

70. "STAN-PAULIS," 36; 1st Para interviews; and Laurent interview.

71. Gradwell interview, 180—83; Letter, Lieutenant Colonel John R. Ewing to Dr. James M. Erdmann, 27 February 1976, Erdmann Papers; and Laurent interview.

72. "STAN-PAULIS," 36—37; and USAF film.

73. Gradwell interview, 183; and "STAN-PAULIS," 37.

74. DOD, *Congo Rescue*, 103—4. Message, STATE 1436 to AMEMBASSY Leopoldville, transmitted 9:16 p.m., 6 November 1964; Message AMEMBASSY Brussels 1082 to STATE, DTG 261211Z November 1964; and Message, STATE 1050 Circular, transmitted 5:00 p.m., 28 November 1964; all in State HF, POL 23-9 THE CONGO. Message, AMEMBASSY Brussels 1075 to STATE, DTG 260125Z November 1964, released by STATE, 30 April 1986; and Message, AMEMBASSY Leopoldville 2174 to STATE, DTG 261825Z November 1964, released by STATE, 30 April 1986; both in LBJ-NSF-CF: Congo, Container 84, Congo Cables, vol. 9, 11/64.

75. Message, AMEMBASSY Leopoldville 2160 to STATE, DTG 261225Z November 1964, State HF, POL 23-9 THE CONGO. Ambassador De Kerchove visited Godley on the 26th to pass on Spaak's desire to get the paras out of Paulis that evening. Message, AMEMBASSY Leopoldville 2174 to STATE, DTG 261825Z November 1964.

76. Congo Special Situation Report no. 12; President Johnson, as quoted by Ball, *The Past*, 324; and Wagoner, *DRAGON ROUGE*, 192.

77. Message, STATE 1443 to AMEMBASSY Leopoldville, transmitted 3:06 p.m., 26 November 1964, State HF, POL 23-9 THE CONGO.

78. Still concerned with the hostages in the northeast, Godley tried to come up with alternatives. He took Spaak's decision to leave the armored jeeps behind and suggested leaving some of Laurent's men with them. Ultimately, Laurent did leave behind his armored jeeps—and perhaps some of his men. Next, he recommended that Kanza be approached to mediate a release of the remaining hostages. Message, AMEMBASSY Leopoldville 2212

to STATE, DTG 272256Z November 1964; and Message, AMEMBASSY Leopoldville 2215 to STATE, DTG 281145Z November 1964; both in LBJ-NSF-CF: Congo, Container 84, Congo Cables, vol. 9, 11/64. Laurent interview and Vandewalle interviews.

79. Strobaugh, "Journal"; and Erdmann, "Journal—DRAGON ROUGE."
80. Vandewalle interviews.
81. Strobaugh, "Journal"; Rattan interview; and Message (C), ARMA Leopoldville INFO STATE, DTG 273000Z November 1964 (U), LBJ-NSF-CF: Congo, Classified Holdings, information declassified 5 March 1986.
82. Rattan interview; Strobaugh, "Journal"; and Laurent interview.
83. Strobaugh, "Journal."
84. Strobaugh, "Journal"; Vandewalle, *L'Ommengang*, 369—88.
85. Strobaugh, "Journal."
86. Wagoner, *DRAGON ROUGE*, 205; and U.S. Department of State, Director of Intelligence and Research, Research Memorandum RAF-58, Subject: Considerations Affecting a Possible Paradrop on Paulis, Bunia, and Watsa, 24 November 1964.
87. Vandewalle, *L'Ommengang*, 421, 434.
88. Lemercier, *"Journal,"* 43.
89. Vandewalle, *L'Ommengang*, 424; and Vandewalle interview.
90. "JTF Leo Historical Report," 11; and Hoare, *Mercenary*, 332.

Chapter 7

1. LBJ-NSF-CF: Congo, Container 81, Memos and Miscellaneous, vol. 1, 11/63—6/64.
2. Laurent interview.
3. Erdmann, "Journal—DRAGON ROUGE."
4. State, Dragon Rouge: African Reactions and Other Estimates, 18 November 1964.

Note: This manuscript was reviewed and cleared by government agencies, which required the deletion of some material references in the notes in order for this document to be UNCLASSIFIED.

Bibliography

Papers and Special Collections: (Primary Sources)

Adams, Paul DeWitt. Oral History. U.S. Army Military History Institute, Carlisle Barracks, PA, 5—8 May 1975.

———. Papers. U.S. Army Military History Institute, Carlisle Barracks, PA.

Collection on Dragon Rouge. Boxes 211—15. Centre de Documentation Historique (CDH) des Forces Armées Belge. Brussels, Belgium.

Confidential File 29. Container 7. Lyndon Baines Johnson Library, Austin, TX.

Confidential File 52. Container 24. Lyndon Baines Johnson Library, Austin, TX.

Country Files: Congo. Containers 81—87. National Security Files. Lyndon Baines Johnson Library, Austin, TX.

Erdmann, James M. Papers. Department of History, University of Denver, Denver, CO.

Rattan, Donald V. Papers. San Antonio, TX.

The Reed Collection

Oral histories on Dragon Rouge in the collection compiled by David Reed. Microfilm ed. Library, Hoover Institution on War, Revolution, and Peace, Stanford, CA.

U.S. Department of State. "Administration History." Vol. 1. Austin, TX: Lyndon Baines Johnson Library, n.d.

———. Historical Records, File POL 23-9 THE CONGO. Washington, DC.

Vandewalle, Frédéric J. L. A. Papers. Brussels, Belgium.

Wagoner, Fred E. Papers. Columbia, SC.

Interviews and Letters

Brashears, Bobby F., Brigadier General USA. Interview with the author. Fort Leavenworth, KS, 12 July 1985.

Erdmann, James M., Lieutenant Colonel USAF Ret. Interviews with the author. Denver, CO, 6 October 1985.

Hamilton, Richard, Colonel USAF Ret. Telephonic interview with the author. 21 August 1986.

Janssens, Emile, Lieutenant General e.r. Belgian Army. Interview with the author. Brussels, Belgium, 8 January 1986.

Larned, Dan, Lieutenant Colonel USA. Interview with the author. Fort Leavenworth, KS, 20 September 1985.

Laurent, Charles, Major General e.r. Belgian Army. Interview with the author. Ville Franche,.France, 9 January 1986.

Laurent, Charles, Major General e.r. Belgian Army, and Georges Ledant, Colonel e.r. Belgian Army. Interviews with the author. Ville Franche, France, 9 January 1986.

Mine, Jean, Jacques Rousseaux, and Luc Raes, Colonels e.r. Belgian Army. Interview with the author. Bouge, Belgium, 13 January 1986.

Poore, James E., Colonel USAF Ret. Interview with the author. Charleston, SC, 10 April 1986.

Rattan, Donald V., Major General USA Ret. Interview with the author. San Antonio, TX, 14 October 1985.

Sedberry, James, Colonel USAF Ret. Letter to Dr. John Partin, Command Historian, United States Readiness Command, 17 June 1986.

Vandewalle, Frédéric J. L. A., Colonel e.r. Belgian Army. Interviews with the author. Brussels, Belgium, 11 and 14 January 1986.

Government Documents

Burkard, Dick J. *Military Airlift Command: Historical Handbook, 1941– 1984.* Scott Air Force Base, IL: Military Airlift Command, December 1984.

U.S. Agency for International Development. *Police Survey Mission to the Congo.* With annexes. Washington, DC: U.S. Government Printing Office, June 1963.

U.S. Air Force. 322d Air Division. "History of the 322d Air Division (MATS) Eastern Transport Air Force, 1 July 1964–31 December 1964." Evreux, France, 1965.

U.S. Air Force. 839th Air Division. "History of the 464th Troop Carrier Wing (Medium) and Pope Air Force Base, North Carolina, 1 July–31 December 1964." Pope Air Force Base, NC, 1965.

U.S. Air Forces Europe. Office of Information. Historical Division. *The Congo Airlift—1960.* By Royce E. Eckuright, Gerald T. Cartwell, and William Sluis. Frankfurt, Germany, 1 March 1961.

U.S. Army Europe. Operations Division. Historical Section. *Operations Dragon Rouge and Dragon Noir.* By Lieutenant Colonel W. M. Glasgow. 1965.

U.S. Commander in Chief Middle East, Africa, South Asia. *Military Assistance Planning Reference Book: Congo.* MacDill Air Force Base, FL, 1 August 1964.

U.S. Department of Defense. Director of Defense Research and Engineering. Weapons Systems Evaluation Group. "The Congo Rescue Mission of November 1964." Washington, DC, 8 April 1965.

U.S. Department of State. Foreign Area Research Documentation Center. External Research Staff. "The Congolese Rebellion of 1964." With subarticles: "The Rise and Fall of the Rebel Movement" by Keith Wheelock and "Political Dynamics of the Rebellion" by M. Crawford Young. Washington, DC, June 1965.

U.S. Joint Chiefs of Staff. Joint Secretariat. Historical Division. *History of the Unified Command Plan.* Washington, DC, 20 December 1977.

U.S. Strike Command. "JTF Leo Historical Report." MacDill Air Force Base, FL, 30 December 1965.

Books and Articles: (Primary Sources)

Attwood, William. *The Reds and the Blacks: A Personal Adventure.* New York: Harper & Row, 1967.

Ball, George W. *The Past Has Another Pattern: Memoirs.* New York: W.W. Norton & Co., 1982.

Carlson, Lois. *Monganga Paul.* New York: Harper & Row, 1966.

Centre de Recherche et d'Information Socio-Politiques (CRISP). *Congo 1964: Political Documents of a Developing Nation.* Princeton, NJ: Princeton University Press, 1966.

Ewing, John R., Captain USAF. "Congo Rescue," *The Airman* 9 (November 1965):10—13.

Hoare, Mike. *Mercenary.* New York: Bantam Books, 1979.

Hoyt, Jo Wasson. *For the Love of Mike.* New York: Random House, 1966.

Laurent, Charles, Colonel. "Mission Accomplie," *Pourquoi Pas?*, No. 2401—4 December 1964:3—15.

Mueller, Siegfried. *Les Nouveaux Mercenaires.* Translated from the German by A. Saint-Germain. Paris: France-Empire, 1965.

O'Brien, Conor Cruise. *To Katanga and Back: A UN Case History.* New York: Simon and Schuster, 1962.

Spaak, Paul-Henri. *The Continuing Battle: Memoirs of a European, 1939—1966.* Translated from the French by Henry Fox. London: Weidenfeld, 1971. Originally published in French as *Combats Inacheves.*

T. T. U. [Vandewalle, Frédéric J. L. A.] "USEUCOM OPLAN 319-64: DRAGON ROUGE III." *Tam Tam Ommengang*, No. 48—December 1985:27—39.

Vandergoten, Pierre. "Stan-Paulis Nov 1964." *Centurio*, January—February 1965:7—15.

Vandewalle, Frédéric J. L. A. *L'Ommengang: Odyssée et Reconquête de Stanleyville, 1964*. Brussels, Belgium: Le Livre Africain, Collection Temoinage Africain, 1970.

Unpublished: (Primary Sources)

Erdmann, James M., Lieutenant Colonel USAF. "Journal—DRAGON ROUGE." Erdmann Papers.

Hoyt, Michael P. E., and David K. Grinwis. "A Journal of the Experiences of the Staff of the American Consulate in Stanleyville from 1 August through 29 November 1964." May 1966. Unpublished manuscript. Copies exist in the Erdmann Papers and *The Reed Collection*, cited elsewhere in this bibliography.

Laurent, Charles, Colonel. "Journal de Campagne," [17—27 November 1964]. Unpublished diary. Archives Laurent, Centre de Documentation Historique des Forces Armées Belge, Brussels, Belgium.

Rattan, Donald V., Major General USA Ret. "The Congo, 9 August—9 December, Bukavu to Stanleyville." Unpublished and undated manuscript. Rattan Papers.

Strobaugh, Donald R., Captain USAF. "Journal: Operation Dragon Rouge, Stanleyville, Republic of the Congo, 24—27 November 1964." Wiesbaden, Germany: Det. 1, 5th Aerial Port Squadron, 322d Air Division, 3 December 1964. Erdmann Papers.

Books and Articles: (Secondary Sources)

American University, Washington, DC. Foreign Area Studies. *Zaire: A Country Study*. DA Pam 550—67. Washington, DC: U.S. Government Printing Office, 1979.

"L'Assistance Technique de la Force Aerienne au Congo: Un An de Presence." *Nos Forces*, No. 130—15 July 1965: no page numbers.

Christian Science Monitor for 25, 27, and 28 November 1964.

Clas, Max. "The Chinese Role in the Congo: Fact or Fiction?," *Africa Report*, January 1965:18—19.

"The Congo: Arrows to Heaven." *Time*, 11 June 1965:40—41.

"The Congo: La Nuit Infernal." *Time*, 11 December 1965:45—46.

"The Congo: Lumumba Jumbo." *Time*, 25 December 1964:21.

"The Congo Massacre." *Time*, 4 December 1964:28—32.

"The Congo: Needed—A Divine Force." *Time*, 18 December 1964:30.

"The Congo: The Hostages." *Time*, 27 November 1964:36.

Conrad, Joseph. *Heart of Darkness* and *The Secret Sharer*. New York: New American Library, 1983.

Davidson, Basil. *The Story of Africa*. London: Mitchell Beasley Publishers and Mitchell Beasley Television, 1984.

Dessart, Charles, ed. *Le Pari Congolais*. Brussels: Charles Dessart, n.d.

Dowdy, Homer E. *Out of the Jaws of the Lion*. New York: Harper and Row, 1965.

Franck, Thomas M., and John Carey. *The Legal Aspects of the United Nations Action in the Congo*. New York: Oceana Publications, 1963.

Francois, Frédéric. "Stan." *Moustique, TV, Radio*, No. 2027—3 December 1964:31—36.

Hymof, Edward. *Stig Von Bayer: International Troubleshooter for Peace*. New York: James H. Heineman, 1965.

Kalb, Madeleine G. *The Congo Cables: The Cold War in Africa—From Eisenhower to Kennedy*. New York: Macmillan Publishing Co., 1982.

LeFever, Ernest W. *Crisis in the Congo: A United Nations Force in Action*. Washington, DC: Brookings Institution, 1965.

LeFever, Ernest W., and Wynfred Joshua. *United Nations Peacekeeping in the Congo, 1960—1964: An Analysis of Political, Executive, and Military Control*. 4 vols. Washington, DC: Brookings Institution, 1966.

Legum, Colin."Peking's Strategic Priorities." *Africa Report*, January 1965:19—25.

Marchetti, Victor, and John D. Marks. *The CIA and the Cult of Intelligence*. New York: Alfred A. Knopf, 1974.

"Merci, les gars!" *Nos Forces*, No. 118—15 December 1964:1—22.

Mezerik, A. G., ed. *Congo and the United Nations*. 3 vols. New York: United Nations International Review Service, 1960.

New York Times for 4, 13, 18, 20, and 22 August; 4 and 6 September; 29 October; and 8 and 25—30 November 1964. New York Times Index for 1964, Subject: "Congo."

"Operations Humanitaire au Congo (Zaire) en 1964 et en 1965." *Forum*, October 1965:4—11.

Powers, Thomas. *The Man Who Kept the Secrets*. New York: Alfred A. Knopf, 1979.

Ray, Ellen, et al., *Dirty Work 2: The CIA in Africa*. Secausus, NJ: Lyle Stuart, 1980.

Reed, David. *111 Days in Stanleyville*. New York: Harper & Row, 1965.

Rochefort, David A. "A Bipolar Foreign Policy in the Third World: America's Congo Policy in 1964." In *Monograph on National Security Affairs*. Providence, RI: Brown University, April 1979.

Thomas, Gerry S. *Mercenary Troops in Modern Africa*. Boulder, CO: Westview Press, 1984.

Vandevoorde, Pierre. *Paras du Monde Entier*. Namur, Belgium: Wesmael-Charlier, 1981.

Wagoner, Fred E. *DRAGON ROUGE: The Rescue of Hostages in the Congo*. Washington, DC: National Defense University, 1980.

Weissman, Stephen R. *American Foreign Policy in the Congo, 1960—1964*. Ithaca, NY: Cornell University, 1974.

Wilson, Barbara A. "The Congo (Republic of the Congo—Leopoldville) Since January 1964." In *Research Notes on Insurgency Potential in Africa South of the Sahara*. Washington, DC: American University, August 1965.

Young, M. Crawford. "The Congo Rebellion." *Africa Report*, April 1965:6—11.

———. *Politics in the Congo: Decolonization and Independence*. Princeton, NJ: Princeton University Press, 1965.

Young, M. Crawford, and Thomas Turner. *The Rise and Decline of the Zairian State*. Madison: University of Wisconsin Press, 1985.

Unpublished: (Secondary Sources)

Ferraro, Freddy, Captain, Belgian Army. "Stanleyville, 1964." Unpublished student paper, Belgium, 1971.

Genot, E., Major, Belgian Army. "Dragon Rouge et Dragon Noir." Chapter 3, pages 190—214, from the manuscript of an untitled work on the Belgian Paracommando Regiment. To be published.

LEAVENWORTH PAPERS

1. *The Evolution of U.S. Army Tactical Doctrine, 1946—76*, by Major Robert A. Doughty
2. *Nomonhan: Japanese-Soviet Tactical Combat, 1939*, by Dr. Edward J. Drea
3. *"Not War But Like War": The American Intervention in Lebanon*, by Dr. Roger J. Spiller
4. *The Dynamics of Doctrine: The Changes in German Tactical Doctrine During the First World War*, by Captain Timothy T. Lupfer
5. *Fighting the Russians in Winter: Three Case Studies*, by Dr. Allen F. Chew
6. *Soviet Night Operations in World War II*, by Major Claude R. Sasso
7. *August Storm: The Soviet 1945 Strategic Offensive in Manchuria*, by Lieutenant Colonel David M. Glantz
8. *August Storm: Soviet Tactical and Operational Combat in Manchuria, 1945*, by Lieutenant Colonel David M. Glantz
9. *Defending the Driniumor: Covering Force Operations in New Guinea, 1944*, by Dr. Edward J. Drea
10. *Chemical Warfare in World War I: The American Experience, 1917—1918*, by Major Charles E. Heller, USAR
11. *Rangers: Selected Combat Operations in World War II*, by Dr. Michael J. King
12. *Seek, Strike, and Destroy: U.S. Army Tank Destroyer Doctrine in World War II*, by Dr. Christopher R. Gabel
13. *Counterattack on the Naktong, 1950*, by Dr. William Glenn Robertson

RESEARCH SURVEYS

1. *Amicicide: The Problem of Friendly Fire in Modern War*, by Lieutenant Colonel Charles R. Shrader
2. *Toward Combined Arms Warfare: A Survey of 20th-Century Tactics, Doctrine, and Organization*, by Captain Jonathan M. House
3. *Rapid Deployment Logistics: Lebanon, 1958*, by Lieutenant Colonel Gary H. Wade
4. *The Soviet Airborne Experience*, by Lieutenant Colonel David M. Glantz
5. *Standing Fast: German Defensive Doctrine on the Russian Front During World War II*, by Major Timothy A. Wray
6. *A Historical Perspective on Light Infantry*, by Major Scott R. McMichael

STUDIES IN PROGRESS

Deciding What Has to Be Done: General William E. DePuy and the 1976 Edition of FM 100-5

•

Power Pack: U.S. Intervention in the Dominican Republic, 1965—66

•

Petsamo-Kirkenes Operation, October 1944

•

Huai Hai Campaign: Chinese People's Liberation Army Performance at the Operational Level of War

•

Busting the Bocage

•

Japan's Okinawa, April—June 1945

•

The Struggle for Decisive Terrain in the Sinai: The Battles of Abu Ageila in 1957 and 1967

•

The Russian/Soviet Experiences in Unconventional Warfare in Asia Since 1801

•

Brazilian Internal Security and Defense Measures, 1964—1984

•

U.S. Army World War II Corps Commander's Profile

•

Lam Son 719

•

Battles in the Support Area (Rear Area Operations During the Korean War)

•

Operations of Third U.S. Army Against the German First Army, France, August 1944

•

An Assessment of Soviet Military Historiography

☆ U.S. GOVERNMENT PRINTING OFFICE: 1991 554-001/42031

www.ingramcontent.com/pod-product-compliance
Lightning Source LLC
Chambersburg PA
CBHW080538170426
43195CB00016B/2597